Island Voices

Island Voices

Air Bilibh an t-Sluaigh

Traditions of North Mull

Edited by Ann MacKenzie

Foreword by Donald W. MacKenzie

ORIGIN

This edition published in 2018 by
Birlinn Origin, an imprint of
Birlinn Limited
West Newington House
10 Newington Road
Edinburgh
EH9 1QS

www.birlinn.co.uk

First published by Birlinn Limited in 2002
Copyright © Ann MacKenzie, 2002

ISBN: 978 1 91247 611 4
eBook ISBN: 978 0 85790 962 6

British Library Cataloguing-in-Publication Data
A catalogue record for this book is available
from the British Library

Typeset by Edderston Book Design, Peebles
Printed and bound by Clays Ltd, St Ives, plc

Dedicated to my family with love,
and also to the memory of
Ann Crozier and Tard McIntyre

CONTENTS

My wish has been simply to gather some specimens of the wreck so plentifully strewn on the coasts of old Scotland, and to carry it where others may examine it; rather to point out where curious objects worth some attention may be found, than to gather a great heap. I have not sought for stranded forests. I have not polished the rough sticks which I found; I have but cut off a very few offending splinters, and I trust that some may be found who will not utterly despise such rubbish, or scorn the magic which peasants attribute to a fairy egg.

John Francis Campbell, *Popular Tales of the West Highlands*, vol.1, 2nd edn, 1890

There were many many things he (Hugh MacNeilage) would say in Gaelic that he would never think to say in English. It was as though he had a secret knowledge that only existed in Gaelic and which he could only reveal to those whom he trusted and knew the language. The language was the key to something beyond the language.

Lachie MacLean, Knock, in Timothy Neat, *When I was Young*, 2000

Everything depends on who you are, what you think, what you feel, what you see, where you stand and what stands around you, where you come from, where you will go. And there *is* a difference between the lives of half a dozen children brought up on Eilean nan Roan off the Sutherland coast amidst Presbyterian rigour and the thousands of children being brought up in Shakespeare's now suburban, multicultural West Midlands. Both experiences are vivid but one is relatively common, the other very rare. These books [*When I was Young*, etc.] are proud to present that which was always rare, and will not be again.

Timothy Neat, *When I was Young*, 2000

He who loses his language loses his world.

Iain Crichton Smith

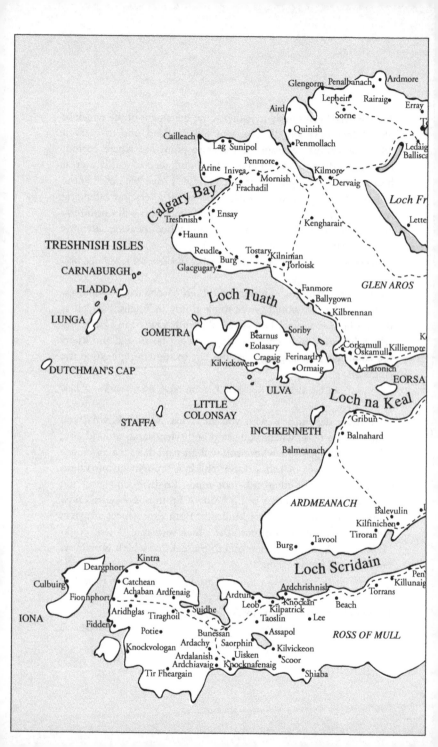

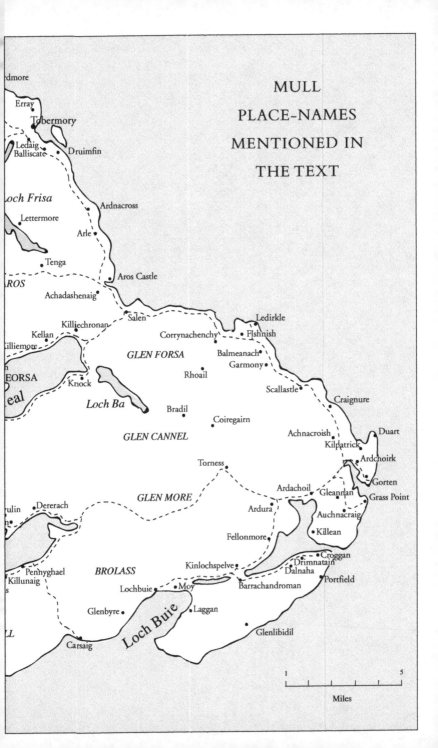

MULL
PLACE-NAMES
MENTIONED IN
THE TEXT

ACKNOWLEDGEMENTS

Island Voices would not have been possible without the kindness and willingness of the following people to share and make available the information contained in it.

Firstly, to my family, with their connections to Mull (Ulva), Argyll (Inveraray) and the Isle of Lewis, for creating an interest in this material from stories told about the people of these places in the past, especially to my father, Donald W. MacKenzie, for his endless enthusiasm and apparently limitless knowledge on a wide range of subjects. I appreciate immensely his help with this book – in translating and transcribing recordings, in sourcing material, and for his own contributions and foreword. The continued support of my family while living in Mull is beyond expressing adequately in words, as is the friendship and assistance given by Donnie Campbell and Anne Walker, Salen. I am also indebted to those who have given me employment while continuing to collect material for the book.

The importance of the Muile air Mheamhair Oral History Project, which was formed by Myles Campbell and Duncan Ferguson with the Mull Gaelic Partnership in 1992, is the core of this book, and without the project much valuable information would have been lost for ever.

I would like to pay tribute to all the informants: the late Alan Beaton, Donnie Campbell, the late Colin Fletcher, the late Ishbel Lloyd, Willie MacAllister, Effie MacCuaig, Archie MacCuish, Calum and Margaret MacDonald, Morag MacDonald, Chrissie MacDonald, Jane Ann MacFarlane, Kirsty MacGillivray, the Mac-Gillivrays of Gribun, Donald W. MacKenzie, Janet MacKeracher, Betty MacLean, Iain MacLean, Lachie MacLean, the late Peter MacLean, Lachie MacNeill, the late Roddy MacNeill, the late Duncan MacNeillage, Iain Robertson, Mary Morrison, the late Donald Morrison and the late Johnnie Simpson. Their keenness to impart their stories, and help with locating further information, is greatly appreciated, and this book is also dedicated to them with my gratitude and affection.

A special mention is made for Peter MacLean and Calum MacDonald, as I have spent more time with them and they have sourced material I had thought no longer in existence. Calum's extensive research and memory for historical detail and anecdote, combined with Peter's tales (I am especially grateful for the Shark and the Oranges story), and his unique way of recounting these, have made this a much richer collection.

I have also had invaluable support from the Isle of Mull Museum; from its excellent library, archive and photographic collection, but mostly from the people involved in the work of the museum. I am very appreciative of the locating of prints by Pat James; the copying and fine printing of the photographs by Ted Brockie; help with information and sources from Hilary and Alistair Garvie and Jean Whittaker (who also supplied invaluable indices, the location of the 'Rats' Satire' and for reading and making helpful suggestions on the text); and Dr Bill Clegg who kindly loaned his own photographs and recalled some stories from Dr MacIntyre. Again, material was brought to my notice, for which I am grateful.

I would also like to thank Effie MacCuaig, the Howards of Ulva, Calum and Margaret MacDonald, Janet MacDonald, Morag MacDonald, Betty MacLean, Chrissie MacLennan, Roc Sandford, the Isle of Mull Museum, the Scottish Life Archive (and Dorothy Kidd) and the Museum of Antiquities for their kind permission to reproduce photographs.

I am indebted to the following for the loan of books – Mrs Mary Campbell, Vikki Headspeath, Calum MacDonald and Anne Walker, and to all the authors and publishers who have granted permission to include their material, and to Hugh Andrew of Birlinn for the opportunity to write *Island Voices*. I am very grateful for the time and patience of Dorothy Aitken in typing and organising the text onto disk, and the final preparation of the manuscript by Jim Spence. I would also like to acknowledge the assistance of Ronald Black in proof-reading (Gaelic and English) and giving advice and additional information.

Finally, I would like to thank Mrs Donald MacLean; the School of Scottish Studies, Edinburgh University; and An Tobar, Tobermory, for the use of their recordings and archives.

Although this material is based on the parishes of Kilninian and Kilmore, there are stories included in the overlapping areas of Salen and Glenforsa. As this is not a definitive description of North Mull and its people, but a collection of what was available in a limited time of writing, I would be interested in any further information from Mull or the surrounding islands on similar subjects.

Dervaig, 2001   *Ann MacKenzie*

FOREWORD

The three-hundred-mile-long shoreline of Mull is deeply indented by sea-lochs, and from early times population centres were to be found on or near the coastal plains, known in Gaelic as *An Lethir Mhuileach* collectively and, in some instances more specifically, as, for example, *Lethir Thorloisg,* the Torloisk coastal plain. Remains of Viking settlements are still to be seen near the shore.

The interior of Mull is opened up by long glens between the hills and there, too, are to be seen the remains of inland settlements of the past.

The Island of Mull is 'cut into two nearly equal parts by a deep bay from the Atlantic called Lochnakell or Lochnangaul which penetrates into the country so far as to be scarce three miles distant from the coast of the Island at Aros Bay on the Sound of Mull' (O.S.A.).

The two 'halves' of Mull joined by this 'three-mile-long' isthmus were traditionally known in Gaelic as *An Leth Iochdrach* and *An Leth Uachdrach*, the low-lying half and the high-ground half, and referred to in English as North Mull and South Mull respectively. An imprecisely defined area in south Mull, inland among the hills, is known as *Braigh Mhuile*, the upland country of Mull. South Mull itself consists of two parts – the South West and the South East.

The Revd Dr John Walker, *Report on the Hebrides 1764 and 1771,* describes the extent of the three ecclesiastical parishes of Mull:

Mull contains three very extensive Parishes.
1. *The Parish of Ross*, all the South West part of the island, on both sides of Loch Screedan, consists of the two united Parishes of Kilfinichen and Kilvickewin (24 miles long, 12 broad, 1,676 inhabitants). The island of Icolumbkil is in this Parish. Four places of worship: Kilfinichen, Bunnessan, Torvia and Icolumbkil. No church or manse in any.
2. *The Parish of Torasay*, comprehending the united Parish of Pennigown, lies on the South East part of the island (19 miles long and 15 broad, inhabitants: 1,200). Three places of worship: Torasay, Pennigown and Kinlochspelven. No church, manse or glebe.

3. *The united Parishes of Kilninian and Kilmore*, all the North parts of the Island (27 miles long & 18 broad) 2,449 inhabitants. The Island of Ulva is in this parish. Places of worship: Kilninian, Kilmore, Aros and Ulva. No Manse or glebe. At Aros there is kept one of the 4 Latin Schools which are supported in the Highlands upon the Royal Bounty. Teacher, £25 yearly, 30 Scholars. English, writing, Latin, Greek, Elements of Mathematics and Book-keeping.

The total population of Mull 2,325.

Island Voices is focused on North Mull, an area coterminous with the United Parish of Kilninian and Kilmore as described by Walker, known by local Gaelic-speakers as *An Leth Iochdrach*. It is an area of great historical interest, with sites and placenames and tradition that link it with events and movements of Scotland's past. There are reminders here of the old Dalriadic Kingdom, of the Norse settlers, of the Lordship of the Isles, of the Clan system with its feuds and intrigues, of Jacobitism and the break-up of the Clan system with the subsequent changes in land-holding. Here, too, we have the familiar records of the kelp industry and its collapse, of potato cultivation and the potato famine, the introduction of Lowland sheep and the resultant clearances, evictions and emigrations.

World events had also reverberations upon the lives of the people of North Mull: the expansion of the British Empire and the wars in Europe, India and North America and elsewhere, the two World Wars in the 20th century, all had a profound effect on the local communities and their way of life.

A great deal of the history of Mull has been written, not by the Gaelic-speaking islanders but by visitors reporting on them in English. Fortunately, however, there were local genealogists, historians and scholars who preserved in manuscripts, written in Gaelic, the oral traditions, songs and family history that had been passed down orally through the generations. An outstanding family in North Mull who rendered this invaluable service to the people of Mull were the Morisons of Kengharair, descendants of the ancient clan known as Clann Duiligh or Clann Mhic Fhraing.

With the growing literacy in both Gaelic and English and the proliferation of periodicals dealing with Celtic and particularly

Gaelic matters, much of the folklore of the Gaelic speakers was preserved and translated into English for the benefit of those who had no Gaelic. *Island Voices* takes account of these written sources because they are derived from the spoken word of the local people, but adds to them material collected directly from local people over the past ten years. All of them were articulate in both Gaelic and English and recorded in both languages, but it was in Gaelic that these traditions and tales were handed down. Some of them are from the distant past while others are vivid recollections of the teller's own lifetime and experiences. Some have never been recorded previously.

Gathered together, these recollections provide a colourful and many-faceted picture of life in this part of Mull and fill in details that are absent from the more formal accounts, written mainly in English, by outsiders 'looking in from the outside'. The official Reports, Statistical Accounts, Estate papers etc. give details of population statistics, lists of trades and occupations, of buildings, schools and churches, of exports and imports, of health and medicine, fishing and agriculture, whisky-making and excise. In the oral tradition we hear about individuals, boat-builders, millers, blacksmiths, fishermen and farmers, doctors, ministers, teachers, lairds, the men who made whisky and evaded the excise cutters: about cures, beliefs, customs and superstitions, songs and stories about contemporary happenings and neighbours. The statistics of the official reports and accounts are fleshed out and personalised. Taken together, the written and oral tradition gives a rounded picture of North Mull and its people.

In his introduction to *A Very Civil People*, Hugh Cheape (ed.) quotes the author, John Lorne Campbell, as saying, 'I have been glad to give Gaelic-speaking Hebrideans a chance to have their own say in translations of some of their memories recorded in their own language.'

The author of *Island Voices* could well echo this sentiment: in it, the Gaelic speaking people of North Mull have been given 'a chance to have their own say'.

Perth, 2001 *Donald W. MacKenzie*

Chapter 1

CHILDHOOD AND SCHOOLING

Both Dr. Samuel Johnson and James Boswell, who passed through Mull in 1773, speak of the inhabitants. The former makes mention of fosterage, marriage, roads, and a great frost. Fosterage consists in a laird sending his child to a tacksman, or tenant to be cared for and brought up.

'In Mull the father sends with his child a certain number of cows, to which the same number is added by the fosterer. The father appropriates a proportionable extent of ground, without rent, for their pasturage. If every cow brings a calf, half belongs to the fosterer, and half to the child; but if there be only one calf between two cows, it is the child's, and when the child returns to the parents, it is accompanied by all the cows given both by the father and by the fosterer, with half of the increase of the stock by propagation.'

In some instances this custom was so exacting as to bring the fosterer to the brink of financial ruin.

J. P. MacLean, *History of the Island of Mull*, vol. 2, 1925

EDUCATION AND RELIGIOUS INSTRUCTION IN THE 18TH CENTURY

The affairs of the Society for Propagating Christian Knowledge were directed by Lowlanders, who had the same liking for the Gaelic language as they harbored for papacy. Hence Gaelic in the schools was suppressed, and any caught using it was summarily punished. The majority of the children knew none other, and hence they learned only mechanically to read the Proverbs, Confession of Faith, Shorter Catechism, Vincent's Catechism, Protestant Resolutions, Pools' Dialogue and Guthrie's Trials, which with their very poor completed school books, they utterly failed to comprehend. As a result when they left their books their learning was also lost.

The absurdity of the situation finally dawned upon the Society; so in 1767 the directors caused the New Testament to be printed in Gaelic, followed by translations of other works, which were introduced into the schools.

The teacher instructed all the children in the principles of the reformed religion, and catechised them twice a week, and prayed with them twice a day publicly. He was also catechist for the district.

The teacher now worked on a more rational system. In 1811 Gaelic spelling books were introduced. The Act of 1872 introduced better buildings and improved teachings.

J. P. MacLean, *History of the Island of Mull*, vol. 2, 1925

SOCIAL CHANGES WITHIN THE EDUCATION OF THE LAIRDS' FAMILIES

The loss to the islands of the young men who settled in America [after the Seven Years' War (1756-63)] had its effect on those who stayed at home. It was, however, those who returned home from the war who had the greater influence. Larger numbers had been exposed to southern influence than ever before, and those who came home had money in their pockets with which to copy the new fashions . . .

The traditional method of educating a laird's son was to have him brought up in a tacksman's or a tenant's family. This method had meant that the laird and his people shared a cultural heritage, and an easy familiarity existed between them. It did not help prepare gentlemen's sons for success in the wider world that was now open . . .

The marriage pattern of the lairds was to be affected by the new fashions. At the start of our decade all those in Mull, Coll and Tiree were married to the daughters of neighbouring proprietors. Five years later a change is perceptible. Ardgour had married the daughter of a wealthy non-Highland Glasgow merchant. Lauchlan, the new laird of Torloisk, had also married outside the area . . .

The most outward change was in housing. In the past only the heads of ancient families such as Duart, Lochbuie, Coll and Mackinnon, who had risen to prominence under the Lords of the Isles, lived in castles. Other lairds had lived in one-storey huts little different from those of the people . . .

Johnson noted that the lairds had discovered 'the art of spending more than they received', and the fact that the new, fashionable way of life was expensive was constantly commented upon . . .

A commercial age increasingly required men in business, or at least familiar with business methods, if they were to retain their estates.

Nicholas Maclean Bristol, *Hebridean Decade*, 1982

EDUCATION IN THE NINETEENTH CENTURY

The common language of Mull is the Gaelic, though several can speak English: and were the schools properly encouraged, this language would gain ground fast, but they are for the most part ill managed and ill attended; indeed, the encouragement given to school-masters, not only here, but in the greater part of the highlands, is insufficient to induce persons properly qualified to undertake this useful office. In general, the common labourers are better paid, and better able to support a family, than the school-masters.

There are two stated ferries in the island, one to Morven, and the other from Achnacraig to Kerrera, and thence to the main land near Oban.

Thomas Garnett, *Tour through the Highlands and Part of the Western Isles*, 1811

EIGHTEENTH-CENTURY PROPOSAL TO ESTABLISH A COLLEGE AT AROS CASTLE

It should be noted that there was a gathering of Highland chiefs at the old castle of Aros to consider the possibility of establishing a college where Highland youths could be as well educated as in the south, and the seat of the institution should be at Aros. What steps were taken to realize this enterprise may not be known; but the unfortunate battle at Culloden was destructive to its realization.

J. P. MacLean, *History of the Island of Mull*, vol. 2, 1925

THE LATIN SCHOOL AT AROS

The most important improvement instigated by the church was the provision of schools. In 1761 the Assembly's first commissioners recommended that there should be one of the 'higher kind' at Aros for teaching Latin and Greek 'together with arithmetic, writing and other branches of literature', and in 1764 Dr Walker noted that it had thirty scholars. The Maclean lairds and their allies were not to control it. In 1771 Kingerloch wrote to Airds in favour of one Alexander Campbell, 'who is married to our friend Big Chrissy Roy Maclean my uncle's daughter', but he was not appointed.

Nicholas Maclean Bristol, *Hebridean Decade*, 1982

LATIN SCHOOL

At Aros there is kept one of the 4 Latin Schools which are supported in the Highlands upon the royal Bounty. The School-master has a salary of £25 a year and has usually about 30 Scholars. Besides English and writing, he teaches Latin and Greek and the Elements of Mathematicks and Book-keeping.

The Revd Dr John Walker, *Report on the Hebrides of 1764 and 1771*

COCK-FIGHTING IN SCHOOLS

In the olden days school life was varied by games of shinty and cock-fighting. The latter was observed once a year, and the fighting took place in the school room. The fighting took place before the school and parents, – the minister usually present. Every boy was compelled to bring a bird. The victorious bird was returned to its owner. The defeated ones and those escaping became the property of the schoolmaster.

J. P. MacLean, *History of the Island of Mull*, vol. 2, 1925

EDUCATION IN THE TWENTIETH CENTURY

When the population was larger than it is now, more school accommodation was necessary; at the time of the *New Statistical Account* there were eight schools in the parish, but their exact location is not easy to establish. On the hill between Reudle and Ensay are the ruins of a school believed to have been built between 1860 and 1862 and to have been closed after the erection of the present Fanmore School near Kilninian about 1877. An old school at Killiemore, three or four miles east of Ulva Ferry, belonged to the class of schools known as 'parliamentary'.[1] There was also in existence as late as 1865 another school known as the 'parish' school. One or other of the foregoing schools may have been the third Ulva school mentioned in the *New Statistical Account*. Killiemore school was in use within living memory and may have been closed when the present Ulva Ferry school, situated on the mainland as being more convenient, was opened. All that remains of the two old schools of the island of Ulva comprises overgrown mounds.

In more recent times there were schools at Sorn, Ensay, Tenga and Gometra, all except the first being classed as 'side' schools, which were not required to be kept open for as many days annually as was necessary in the 'public' schools. When the education authority took over responsibility for education in 1919, it tried to improve the side schools by requiring the same annual number of attendances as were made in public schools and by replacing, as opportunity occurred through vacancies, their unqualified instructors by certificated teachers. All these schools were closed during the years from 1923 to 1941, because the pupils dwindled to one or two or vanished altogether. If any reasonable number of young children returned to these areas, local schools would doubtless be again set up.

There are at present four schools in the parish, one each at Dervaig, Mornish, Fanmore and Ulva Ferry, and in no case does the roll exceed twelve pupils.[2] The regrettable fall of the school population in a short time may be judged from the fact that, in 1900, the school children were more than four times greater, being actually 145. All these schools give instruction in primary subjects only. For their secondary education the local pupils must go to a junior secondary school such as Tobermory or a senior secondary school such as Oban High, but in either case the pupils must leave home and live in hostels or in lodgings.

Mrs E. MacKenzie
The Third Statistical Account of Scotland: The County of Argyll, 1961

1. In 1838 it became compulsory for every *quoad sacra* parish to have a school.
2. In 1958 the roll at Dervaig had risen to 16.

TRESHNISH SCHOOL, 1910–1920s

Peter walked to school from Haunn. He was the only pupil from Haunn (only two families left at Haunn then), and the other 10-12 came from other areas in Treshnish, Ensay and Calgary. The teacher at that time was a Miss Frazer from Tobermory, and, at first, when he was five years old, there was a Miss Shanks.

Peter stayed at school until he was fourteen and apart from school holidays, time was not given off to help at home.

The generation before, when there was ten in the family, they walked the four miles to Mornish School and went barefoot in the summer. Some children went to Kilninian School further back, but in Peter's time Rheudle School was closed, as Crackaig and Glac Gugairidh were no longer occupied.

The teacher at Treshnish did not speak Gaelic and it was discouraged even in the playground. Gaelic was taught at Dervaig by Mr MacMillan. There was little music or singing taught.

Peter MacLean, Dervaig. Recorded for An Tobar, 1996

SCHOOLING IN ULVA, 1920s

Well, I never went to school until I was twelve years old when I went to Oban High School. There was no school in Ulva when we were there. The school was across the ferry. But my father got permission to teach us at home, and that was easy enough for him to do because he had been a teacher before he went in for the ministry. He taught in many schools in the Islands and Highlands. He was with the Ladies' Schools, and he got permission, therefore, to educate us at home.

It was in our own home we were learning reading and writing and the like. And the education we got was somewhat different from that of the others, for my father was teaching Latin to us, and I could read 'Caesar's Gallic Wars' when I was about ten years old. And he was also teaching us something he himself called Euclid, and that was Geometry when we were pretty young and that's how we were educated until we were the age to go to high school. We had to sit the qualifying examination but we got that without any trouble. But it was at home that we got our first education.

Donald W. MacKenzie. Recorded by Ann MacKenzie, 1992

MORNISH SCHOOL, 1930S AND 1940S

This was my first teaching post and the numbers of pupils varied; a dozen, fifteen and once down to five. There was no other teacher, but at one time there were sixty pupils. All the subjects here taught – English, Gaelic, arithmetic, reading, drawing but they were not taught in Gaelic. None of the children had Gaelic naturally and Gaelic was just a 'lesson' to them. They learned rhymes and songs and a singing teacher came round once a week. Gaelic was not spoken in the homes of the children and their parents did not encourage them to speak Gaelic; English was important. Incomers were getting land and houses, and bringing in non-Gaelic workers so they thought that Gaelic would not help them. Playgroups (*cròileagain*) are the only hope for Gaelic as learning in primary and secondary schools is too late. Children must learn young otherwise they will never get the correct sound.

Mary Morrison, Penmore. Recorded by Ann MacKenzie, 1992

CHILDREN'S GAMES

Gaelic conundrums, tongue-twisters and guessing games formed part of the fireside entertainments. One guessing game was accompanied by a Gaelic rhyme:

H-aon a mhicean, han a bhuicean
Maide-sùirn, cùl an dùirn
Seall romhad 's as do dhéidh
Cia meud adhairc th' air a' bhoc?

Little son, little buck
Kiln-flue, back of fist
Look before you, look behind
How many horns has the buck?

This was recited as you submitted the top of your head to the knuckles of another player's fist. At the end of the last line the knuckle wielder would raise a number of fingers or none at all and you had to guess how many. If you guessed wrongly all the participants would join in the skull-knuckling.

Donald W. MacKenzie, *As it Was*, 2000

CHILDHOOD GAMES – PLOLLY/POLOLLY

This game has been played in Tobermory (and possibly other Mull schools?) until recent times (1950s–60s), and is described as being mainly a summertime amusement. A box is marked out, sometimes using an old ornament (plaster) of their mothers to draw a rectangle divided into six squares. Each person throws a ball or stone into the box and if successful, hops around from square to square until the last is reached and then they return in reverse order to the first box.

Iain MacLean, Morag MacDonald and Willie MacAllister, Tobermory.
Recorded for An Tobar, 1996, and from further notes from Willie MacAllister

POTATO YO-YOS

A hand-made toy can be seen in the Isle of Mull Museum, Tobermory, which was made of a stick about eight inches long with a potato on the end, which was prevented from moving by a hazel nut shell above it. By attaching a string to the top of the stick a yo-yo was created. It was donated by Roddie MacNeill, Salen.

PLANT GAMES

Plant games played at Tobermory at school and in the holidays:

1. Making whistles by blowing across the edge of grass or reeds held between the thumbs.
2. Boats made with *seilisdeir* [wild iris], the Gaelic name used even when speaking in English to describe the game.
3. Making 'peewits nests' by 'thumping out a hollow with a stone and placing four stones in it'. [There was no real purpose to this game apart from making several of these].
4. Using plantain stalks in a game sometimes known as Mary Queen of Scots. The stalk was held out to the opponent and each took turns to knock the head off, with their own plantain.
5. A leaf [the plant was not known but it was suggested that it was a sourock = sorrel] was picked apart by two people so

that the veins of the plant were left. The amount of veins would show how many lies were told and if they were big or small.

Iain MacLean, Morag MacDonald and Willie MacAllister.
Recorded for An Tobar, 1996

Note: These games, although mentioned in a recording of school-days in the 1950s, are of a much earlier date and were also spoken of by Donald W. MacKenzie.

RANN CLOINNE: CHILDREN'S RHYME

An Cat glas agus an Luchag:

Thuirt an cat glas ris an luchag:
'Luchag, luchag anns an toll,
Càirdeas is coibhneas ma thig thu mach.'

Thuirt an luchag ris a' chat ghlas:
''S eòlach mis' air an dubhan crom
Th' agad ann am bonn do chas;
Mharbh thu mo phiuthair an dé
Is thar mi fhéin air éigin as.'

The grey cat said to the little mouse:
'Mousey, mousey in the hole,
Friendship and kindness if you come out!'

The little mouse said to the grey cat:
'Well I know of the bent hook
You have in the sole of your feet;
You killed my sister yesterday
And I myself barely escaped.'

Peter learned this rhyme from his grandfather's brother who died when Peter was six or seven.

Peter MacLean, Dervaig, 2000

A Puzzle for Mull People

Tha achadh 'am Muile 's shuaicheanta 'chumadh, cha'n'eil glac ann, no tulaich, no stubag, no reidhleach; seachd croinn ann le'n gearrain treobhaidh comhla 'san Earrach, gun aon diubh bhi'n sealladh a chéile.

There is a field in Mull of very strange shape, without valley, or hillock, waterhole or plain; seven ploughs can work there together, all out of sight of each other.

This is a conundrum (Gaelic *tòimhseachan*) typical of its kind, for children. There is no such field in Mull or anywhere else! The catch is in the third line: 'Seven ploughs with their horses ploughing together in spring'.

The seven ploughs with their horses are seven moles tunnelling under the surface of a field.

Anon., *The Celtic Monthly*, vol. 15, 1906–07
Translation and notes by Donald W. MacKenzie

A Curious Old Gaelic Play

The following curious play has been sent us by Mr Donald Beaton, Queensland, who says he heard it last at a *Ceilidh* in Dervaig, Isle of Mull, fifty-two years ago, and saw it acted at Arisaig, fifty-seven years ago. It is after the style of 'Murachan is Mearachan' or the English rhyme, 'The House that Jack Built'.

CLEAS-CHLUICHE

Dh'fhalbh Dubhag-tòn-ri-teallaich do'n tràighe a dh'iarraidh maoraich; cha'n fhac i tràigh no lìonadh riamh roimhe, 's 'nuair thàinig an lìonadh mu'n cuairt di shaoil i gu'n robh am bràth (deireadh an t-saoghail) air tighinn.

Dh'fhalbh Dubhag-tòn-ri-teallaich agus ràinig i Pocan-a'-bhaile-fhàsaich. "A bheil thu stigh a Phocain-a'-bhaile-fhàsaich, so am bràth air tighinn." "Cò chuala na chunnaic e?" arsa Pocan-a'-

bhaile-fhàsaich. "Mise chuala 's a chunnaic e," arsa Dubhag-ton-ri-teallaich, "fo m' bhonnaibh a thàinig e."

An sin dh'fhalbh Dubhag-tòn-ri-teallaich agus Pocan-a'-bhaile-fhàsaich agus ràinig iad Fàsach-a'-bhaile-fhionnaich. "A bheil thu stigh Fhàsaich-a-bhaile-fhionnaich, so am bràth air tighinn." "Có chuala na chunnaic e?" arsa Fàsach-a'-bhaile-fhionnaich. "Mise chuala 'sa chunnaic e," arsa Dubhag-tòn-ri-teallaich, "fo'm bhonnaibh a thàinig e."

Dh'fhalbh Dubhag-tòn-ri-teallaich agus Pocan-a'-bhaile-fhàsaich agus Fàsach a'-bhaile-fhionnaich agus ràinig iad Tierna Loch-odha. "Bheil thu stigh a Thierna Loch-odha, so am bràth air tighinn." "Có chuala no chunnaic e?" arsa Tierna-Loch-odha. "Mise chuala 'sa chunnaic e," arsa Dubhag-tòn-ri-teallaich, fo 'm bhonnaibh a thàinig e."

Dh'fhalbh Dubhag-tòn-ri-teallaich agus Pocan-a'-bhaile-fhàsaich, agus Fàsach-a'-bhaile-fhionnaich, agus Tierna Loch-odha agus rainig iad Gobha-'bhaile-bhric. "Bheil thu stigh a Ghobha-'bhaile-bhric, so am bràth air tighinn." "Có chuala no chunnaic e?" arsa Gobha-'bhaile-bhric. "Mise chuala 'sa chunnaic e," arsa Dubhag-tòn-ri-teallaich, "fo m' bhonnaibh a thàinig e."

Dh'fhalbh Dubhag-tòn-ri-teallaich agus Pocan-a'-bhaile-fhàsaich agus Fàsach-a'-bhaile-fhionnaich agus Tierna Loch-odha agus Gobha-bhaile-bhric agus ràinig iad Minidh agus Ceap. "Bheil thu stigh a Mhinidh agus a Cheip, so am brath air tighinn?" "Có chuala 'sa chunnaic e?" arsa Minidh agus Ceap. "Mise chuala 'sa chunnaic e," arsa Dubhag-tòn-ri-teallich, "fo m' bhonnaibh a thàinig e."

Dh'fhalbh Dubhag-tòn-ri-teallaich agus Pocan-a'-bhaile-fhàsaich agus Fàsach-a-bhaile-fhionnaich, Tierna Loch-odha, Gobha-bhaile-bhric, Minidh agus Ceap agus ràinig iad Daorad-am-sgailc. "Bheil thu stigh a Dhaorad-am-sgailc, so am bràth air tighinn?" "Có chuala 's a chunnaic e?" arsa Daorad-am-sgailc. "Mise chuala 's a chunnaic e," arsa Dubhag-tòn-ri-teallaich, "fo m' bhonnaibh a thàinig e."

Dh'fhalbh-Dubhag-ton-ri-teallaich agus Pocan-a'-bhaile-fhàsaich, Fàsach-a'-bhaile-fhionnaich, Tierna Loch-odha, Gobha-bhaile-bhric, Minidh agus Ceap 's Daorad-am-sgailc agus ràinig iad am Fear-a-bha-'san-t-sloc. "Bheil thu stigh Fhir-a-bha-'san-t-sloc, so am bràth air tighinn?" "Có chuala no chunnaic e?" ars' am Fear-a-bha-'san-t-sloc. "Mise chuala 'sa chunnaic e," arsa Dubhag-tòn-ri-teallaich, "fo m' bhonnaibh a thàinig e."

Dh'fhalbh Dubhag-tòn-ri-teallaich, Pocan-a'-bhaile-fhàsaich, Fàsach-a'-bhaile-fhionnaich, Tierna Loch-odha, Gobha-'bhaile-bhric, Minidh agus Ceap, Daorad-am-sgailc, am Fear-a-bha-'san-t-sloc agus ràinig iad Tuthadair-na-h-atha. "Bheil thu stigh a Thuthadair-na-h-àtha, so am bràth air tighinn?" "Có chuala na chunnaic e?" arsa Tuthadair-na-h-àtha. "Mise chuala 's a chunnaic e," arsa Dubhag-tòn-ri-teallaich, "fo m' bhonnaibh a thàinig e."

Dh'fhalbh Dubhag-tòn-ri-teallaich agus Pocan-a'-bhaile-'fhàsaich, Fàsach-a'-bhaile-fhionnaich, Tierna Loch-odha, Gobha-bhaile-bhric, Minidh agus Ceap, Daorad-am-sgailc, am Fear-a-bha-'san-t-sloc, agus Tuthadair-na-h-atha agus ràinig iad Tuthadair-a'-mhuilinn. "Bheil thu stigh a Thuthadair-a'-mhuilinn, so am bràth air tighinn." "Có chuala no chunnaic e?" arsa Tuthadair-a'-mhuilinn. "Mise chuala 's a chunnaic e," arsa Dubhag-tòn-ri-teallaich, "fo m' bhonnaibh a thàinig e."

Dh'fhalbh Dubhag-tòn-ri-teallaich agus Pocan-a'-bhaile-fhàsaich, Fàsach-a'-bhaile-fhionnaich, Tierna Loch-odha, Gobha-bhaile-bhric, Minidh agus Ceap, Daorad-am-sgailc, am Fear-a-bha-'san-t-sloc, Tuthadair-na-h-atha agus Tuthadair-a'-mhuilinn agus ràinig iad an Gearan-bacach-bàn. "Bheil thu stigh a Ghearain bhacaich, bhàin, so am bràth air tighinn." "Có chuala no chunnaic e?" ars' an Gearan bacach bàn. "Mise chuala 'sa chunnaic e," arsa Dubhag-tòn-ri-teallaich, "fo m' bhonnaibh a thàinig e."

Dh'fhalbh Dubhag-tòn-ri-teallaich agus Pocan-a-bhaile-fhàsaich, Fàsach-a'-bhaile-fhionnaich, Tierna Loch-odha, Gobha-'bhaile-bhric, Minidh agus Ceap, Daorad-am-sgailc, am-Fear-a-bha-'san-t-sloc, Tuthadair-na-h-atha, Tuthadair-a'-mhuilinn agus an Gearan bacach bàn, 's chaidh iad uile gu léir a bhàthadh anns a' Bhràth.

C. Beaton, *The Celtic Monthly*, vol. 14, 1905–06

This belongs to a genre of tales, rhymes, games, recited by or to children for amusement and, I suspect, for developing their verbal skills and could be accompanied by mime. (Donald Beaton saw this one 'acted out' in Arisaig.) Such stories or rhymes begin with a simple statement which recurs again and again, with each repetition having accretions added till the final repetition is very long like the carol 'The Twelve Days of Christmas'. By the time you come to the twelfth day think of all the gifts that have been added to the gift given on the first day, 'a partridge in a pear-tree'! Similarly, 'This is the House that Jack Built' ends up with a whole menagerie of animals and an assortment of people.

In the Gaelic examples of these kind of stories/rhymes the names of people are fanciful and made-up-nonsense or rhyming names e.g. Muireachan and Mearachan.

The names of the people in the story in the *Celtic Monthly* are fantastic:

Dubhag-tòn-ri-teallaich: Little black-one-backside-to-hearth
Pocan-a'-Bhaile-fhàsaich: Little-squat-one-of the deserted village
Fàsach-a'-Bhaile-fhionnaich: Wilderness of the rough village
Tierna-Loch-odha: Lord of Loch Awe
Gobha-'bhaile-bhric: Smith of the dappled village
Minidh agus Ceap: Minnie and Ceap
Daorad-am-sgailc: Dearness-the-bald?
Fear-a-bha-'san-t-sloc: The man who was in the pit
Tuthadair-na-h-àtha: Thatcher of the kiln
Tuthadair-a-mhuilinn: Thatcher of the mill
Gearan-bacach-bàn: The lame white gelding. (See p. 195 below.)

Synopsis of the story: Little-black-one . . . goes to the shore to gather shellfish. She had never seen ebb and flow before and when the tide came in around her she thought the end of the world (*Bràth*) had come. She goes to Pocan . . . 'Are you in, Pocan?' she says. 'The end of the world has come.' 'Who heard it or saw it?' said Pocan. 'I heard it and saw it,' said Dubhag, 'coming in under the soles of my feet.' The two of them go to the next person and the same conversation takes place and the three go to the fourth person and this continues until all twelve arrive together at the shore and they are all drowned.

Note: The word used for 'the end of the world' (*bràth* = doomsday, judgement) is now used only in the phrase *gu bràth* meaning 'forever', e.g. *Alba gu bràth* (pronounced *bràch*) = Scotland for ever.

Under *bràth* Dwelly gives:

> Seachd bliadhna roimh 'n bhràth
> Thig a' mhuir air Eirinn ré aon thràth.
> (Seven years before the day of judgement
> The sea at one tide shall cover Ireland.)

Perhaps the story originated in Ireland.

Translation and notes by Donald W. MacKenzie, 2001

Chapter 2

PAST EVENTS

New-Year's night, or Hogmanay, was variously known as 'the night of the candle' (*oidhche Choinnle*) and 'the night of the blows or pelting' (*oidhche nan Calluinnean, a Challuinn*). The former name may have been derived from some religious ceremonies being performed by candle-light, as is suggested to be the origin of the English name Candlemas (2nd February), or from a candle being kept lighted till the New Year came in. The other name is said to be from the showers of rattling blows given to a dry cow's hide used in the ceremonies of the evening, *colluinn* being also used to denote a thundering blow, or what is called in the Lowlands 'a loundering lick' (*stràic mhòr*). Thus, *thug e aon cholluinn air* (he gave him one resounding blow); *bi tu air do dheagh cholluinneachadh* (you will be severely beaten). The word, however, as was long ago pointed out by Lhuyd (*Archaeologia Britannica*, 1707) is from *Calendae*, the first day of every month, this being the beginning of the whole year, and the night being in the Highlands reckoned as preceding the day.

Towards evening men began to gather and boys ran about shouting and laughing, playing shinty, and rolling 'pigs of snow' (*mucan sneachda*), *i.e.* large snowballs. The hide of the mart or winter cow (*seiche a mhairt gheamhraidh*) was wrapped round the head of one of the men, and he made off, followed by the rest, belabouring the hide, which made a noise like a drum, with switches. The disorderly procession went three times *deiseal*, according to the course of the sun (*i.e.* keeping the house on the right hand) round each house in the village, striking the walls and shouting on coming to a door:

A challuinn a bhuilg bhuidhe bhoicinn
Buail an craicionn (air an tota)
Cailleach sa chill,

Cailleach sa chùil,
Cailleach eile 'n cùl an teine
Bior na da shùil
Bior na goile
A challuinn so,
Leig astigh mi.

'The *calluinn* of the yellow bag of hide,
Strike the skin (upon the wall)
An old wife in the graveyard,
An old wife in the corner
Another old wife beside the fire,
A pointed stick in her two eyes,
A pointed stick in her stomach,
Let me in, open this.'

Before this request was complied with, each of the revellers had to repeat a rhyme, called *Rann Calluinn* (*i.e.* a Christmas rhyme), though, as might be expected when the door opened for one, several pushed their way in, till it was ultimately left open for all. On entering each of the party was offered refreshments, oatmeal bread, cheese, flesh, and a dram of whisky. Their leader gave to the goodman of the house that indispensable adjunct of the evening's mummeries, the *Caisein-uchd*, the breast-stripe of a sheep wrapped round the point of a shinty stick. This was then singed in the fire (*teallach*), put three times with the right-hand turn (*deiseal*) round the family, and held to the noses of all. Not a drop of drink was given till this ceremony was performed. The *Caisein-uchd* was also made of the breast-stripe or tail of a deer, sheep, or goat, and as many as choose had one with them.

The house was hung with holly to keep out the fairies, and a boy, whipped with a branch of it, may be assured he will live a year for every drop of blood he loses. This scratching and assurance were bestowed by boys on one another, and was considered a good joke.

Cheese was an important part of the refreshments, and was known as the Christmas cheese (*Càise Calluinn*). A slice, cut off at this feast, or a piece of the rind (*cùl na mulchaig*), if preserved and with a hole made through it, has strange virtues. It was called *laomachan*, and a person losing his way during the ensuing year, in a mist or otherwise, has only to look through the hole and he will see his way clearly. By scrambling to the top of the house, and looking through it down the *fàr-lus* (the hole in the roof that served in olden times for chimney and window), a person can ascertain the name of his or her future husband or wife. It will prove to be the same as that of the first person seen, or heard named. A piece of *laomachan* is also valuable for putting under one's pillow to sleep over.

In this style the villagers, men and boys, went from house to house, preceded in many cases by a piper, and drowning the animosities of the past year in hilarity and merriment.

J. G. Campbell, *Witchcraft and Second Sight*, 1902

THE OLD NEW YEAR: COUNN MORRISON, KENGHARAIR

Tha cuimhne 'am math gu leòr air Counn Morison agus 'se 'n t-Seann Bhliadhn' Ùr a bhiodh e gléidheil 's anns an am sin tha mo sheanair anns na Haunn a'coiseachd gu Ceanngharar far an robh e a' toirt a staigh a' Bhliadhn' Ùr – an t-Seann Bhliadhn' Ùr – agus tha fhios agam gu robh òran air choireigin a bh' aig mo sheanair, nuair a ruigeadh e 'n dorus bha e gabhail seo. Agus tha fhios 'am, seo aig am na Nollaig, chan eil fhios, bha *date* air choireigin ann agus dh'fheumadh, 'feòil bheag' dh'abradh iad ris, sin a' chiad fheòil a bh' aca.

Translation: I remember Counn Morison well and it was the old New Year that he was keeping and at that time my grandfather from Haunn used to walk to Kengharair, where he stayed, to bring in the New Year – the Old New Year – and I know that my grandfather had a certain song and when he reached the door he sang this. And I know that Counn Morison used to kill a sheep at that time, at Christmas time, I don't know, there was some date, and they had to have the 'little meat' as they called it, and that was the first meat they had.

Anything similar done at Christmas or Hogmanay?
They kept Hogmanay (*Oidhche Challainn*) right enough.

> Older traditions like taking the fleece, the Token?
> Peter had never heard about it.
>
> Peter MacLean, Dervaig, 2000

Notes:

1. The Gaelic word for the fleece, or token, is *caisean* in Dwelly: '*caisean* – anything curled, wrinkled or hairy: the dewlap or skin that hangs down from the breasts of cows'; '*caisean-uchd*: the breast strip of a sheep killed at Christmas or on New Year's Eve and singed and smelled by each member of the family, as a charm against fairies and spirits.' MacAlpine adds: 'In Islay at any time, but never for the sake of the fairies.'

2. 'A strip torn from the breast of a cow killed at Christmas was singed and sniffed by everyone in the household as a security against evil spirits. Alexander Forbes says in *Gaelic Names of Birds, Beasts, etc*, that a spoon made from a horn lost by a living cow was thought to heal many diseases when food was eaten from it. When the cow died the efficacy of the horn spoon ceased.' (*Mary Beith, Healing Threads: Traditional Medicines of the Highlands and Islands*, 1998)

HOGMANAY

By Hogmanay, houses had to be cleaned and tidied and all accounts had to be settled.

At the stroke of midnight doors and windows were to be opened to let the Old Year out and the New Year in. On New Year's Day neighbours visited each others' houses, the first-foot, preferably a dark-haired male, presented the housewife with a bit of coal or black bun. The traditional greeting was 'Bliadhna mhath ùr' and the response was 'Mar sin dhuit fhéin is móran dhiubh.' ('A good New Year; the same to you and many of them.') The songs which were practised in the weeks leading up to New Year were sung, and drams were drunk. New Year's Day was a holiday. The season of the year was called in Gaelic a' Challainn (the first day of the month) and Hogmanay was called Oidhche Challainn (New Year's Eve) a time when, in my father's boyhood in Lewis, young men went guizing and repeated traditional rhymes, demanding items of food from the housewives.

Donald W. MacKenzie, *As it Was*, 2000

St Bride's Day – *Féill Bride*

There are many traditions associated with St Bride's day – the first day of spring. (1st of February. O.S., and 13th February N.S.) but I have not been able to find any Mull references to this. It would be interesting to have any accounts of this important day in the old Celtic Year.

Notes from J. G. Campbell, *Witchcraft and Second Sight*, 1902, and
Ann MacKenzie, 2001

April Fool's Day

All-Fools' Day is variously known in the Highlands as 'The Day of going on Fools' Errands' (*Latha na Gogaireachd*), 'Cuckoo Day' (*Latha na Cuthaig*), and 'The Day of Tricks' (*Latha nan Car*). Its observance is on the 1st of April, N.S., and this argues its very recent introduction into the Highlands. The tricks and practices of the day are the same as elsewhere, the sending of acquaintances on sleeveless errands. Sometimes, but only rarely, there is some ingenuity displayed in taking advantage of local and passing events to throw the most suspicious off their guard, and send them on fools' messages.

J. G. Campbell, *Witchcraft and Second Sight*, 1902

Easter and Christmas

Easter and Christmas were not celebrated by special services in church as they are in most churches in Scotland today. That is to say, that the commemoration of the resurrection and the nativity was not tied to particular dates in a calendar. Easter and Christmas were eagerly awaited children's festivals. At Easter relations and friends sent us chocolate Easter eggs; at Christmas they sent us Christmas cards with celluloid transparent panels and parcels containing books, toys, games, paints, crayons and sweets. It was a time when apples and sweets mysteriously appeared in unusual places and when strange footprints of enormous size appeared in the snow if a snowfall coincided with the festive season. We hung up our stockings near the fireplace and in the cold, dark Christmas morning, half asleep but in a fever of anticipation, we pulled out little wooden and tin toys, games, an orange and an apple. At home we sang Christmas carols – 'O come all ye faithful' and 'Child in a manger', the English version of the Mull Carol composed by Mary MacDonald, 'Leanabh an Àigh'.

At Christmas, on birthdays and other special occasions my mother would make a large, fruit steamed pudding – we called it a dumpling, made, not in a cloth like the 'clootie dumpling' but in a large bowl with the top covered with muslin and placed in a large pot of water and boiled for several hours. Flour, sugar, suet, spices, sultanas and I know not what else went into the recipe to produce a rich, satisfying meal in itself when served hot. When cold it was sliced and eaten like a cake and any left-overs could be fried.

Donald W. MacKenzie, *As it Was*, 2000

HALLOWE'EN

At Hallowe'en (Oidhche Shamhna) we played games: dooking for apples and various divination games. We dipped our spoons into a large dish of mashed potatoes in which various small objects were buried. If a girl got a ring it meant she would marry; if a thimble she would remain an old maid. A boy finding a threepenny bit would become a rich man, but finding a button meant that he would always be a bachelor. Apple skins were peeled off in one piece and thrown over the left shoulder. When it landed on the floor it took the form of a letter which would be the initial of your partner to be. You put two hazelnuts side by side in the glowing embers, one representing yourself and the other an imaginary partner. You watched closely to see what would happen when they exploded with the heat: if they were driven closer to one another it augured well for the partnership; if they were driven apart, the partnership was doomed.

Donald W. MacKenzie, *As it Was*, 2000

HALLOWE'EN IN ULVA

Colin used to come to the manse at this time, where there were games – two dishes were placed in front of a person who was blindfolded; one dish with clean and another with dirty water. If you put your hand in the clean water you would get a tidy wife.

Colin Fletcher (formerly Ulva and Torloisk), Craignure, 1992

We went out with false faces (*aodainn fuadan*) and got nuts and apples. When we were older we cycled for miles visiting. Also, we played pranks, such as removing carts and gates and hiding them. Next day there were many complaints about the *droch bhalaich* (bad boys) and how harmful (*cho cronail*) they were, but we did not cause any damage, and would replace the gates for old folk.

Roddy MacNeill, Salen, 1992

HALLOWE'EN CUSTOMS

The Bonnach Salainn (salt bannock) was well known as a Hallowe'en Custom in the island of Mull. The reciter confesses to have tried it herself on one occasion when she was young. She baked it of Oatmeal and salt, in equal parts, and complied with all the conditions. After going to bed she dreamt that a man whose name was J. McL.(that was the name of the man to whom she was afterwards married), came with something soft like a pudding, in a dish, and gave it to her to drink, and as she took it from his hand, she said, 'I hope what you have got here will quench my thirst.'

On that same night, she says, she tied a Kail plant over her door, which was another Hallowe'en practice common in Mull, and the first person to come in after it was hung up was J. McL. who aferwards became her husband; and she says that many a time after she got married she thought of that Hallowe'en night, and of how true both the things turned out.

Mrs McLean, Dervaig, Maclagan MSS, from *Tocher*, no. 23, 1976

OIDHCHE SHAMHNA (HALLOWE'EN)

The Celtic year was originally divided into two seasons, Winter and Summer known as *gam* and *sam*, as in Welsh still, and afterwards extended to *Geamhradh* and *Samhradh*. The termination *ra* or *radh* was equal to the *er* in Summer and Winter, and probably meant hood or tide (summer-tide) *i.e.* a period or season . . .

Samhuinn means summer-end, old Irish *Samhfhuin* = summer-end – *fuin* being a word for ending or setting. *Oidhche Shamhna* (31st October) or Halloween is therefore the great festival which celebrated the end of the Celtic year, for *An t-Samhuinn* (1st November) was New Year's Day . . . *Samhuinn* like the other great festival *Bealltuinn* or Beltane, was sacred to the gods of light and of earth. And so we find bonfires blazing on the height, while round the hearth a plentiful supply of cakes, as well as nuts and apples, [is to hand, and the omens they offer for the future?] are discussed . . .

In crofter communities where the hill grazings are held in common *Samhuinn* or Hallowmas is an important date – as at this time each tenant's 'souming' is adjusted. In confirmation of this I cannot do better than quote from Mr. [Alexander] Carmichael's interesting paper, which appears in the appendix to the Report of the Highlands and Islands Commission (1881):

The young of most animals are changed to a new name on the first day of winter. The foal becomes a *loth* or *lothag*, filly, the lamb becomes an *othaisg*. For these things and for most if not indeed for all things of this nature 'the old people' had rhymes to assist the memory. These rhymes are invariably expressive and pithy, although now becoming obsolete. The calf changes to a stirk –

> 'Oidhche Shamhna theirear gamhna ris na laoigh,
> La 'Illeathain theirear aighean riu na dhéigh.'

> At Hallowe'en the calf is called a stirk aye,
> At Saint John's the stirk becomes a quey.

The young are separated from their mothers, and the new name is applied to them at Hallowmas, Gaelic *Samhuinn*.

Fionn, *The Celtic Monthly*, vol. 4, 1895–96

CHRISTMAS RHYMES (*RANNAN CALLAINN*)

In general the rhymes used, when seeking admittance, varied but little in different districts. Sometimes an ingenious person made a rhyme suitable to the place and people, and containing allusions to incidents and character that increased the prevailing fun.

J. G. Campbell, *Witchcraft and Second Sight*, 1902

NOLLAIG DO SPRÉIDH: THE ANIMALS' CHRISTMAS

Carmichael* records a very interesting tradition of Christmas for the stock. This was known as *Nollaig do Spréidh,* and continued, in some areas at least, until the mid-nineteenth century. For example, apparently on the island of Lismore, it was the custom to provide each animal with a special breakfast on Christmas morning. Horses and cattle were given a sheaf of corn from the stall; sheaves of corn were spread out for the sheep in the fields; the pigs and the poultry likewise had a special feast. If there was a suitable tree near to the dwelling-house a sheaf of oats was hung up on it. If not, a wooden pole was erected and the sheaf was fastened to the top of the pole – a custom reminiscent of the most archaic pagan practice. Carmichael also records that in Breadalbane the cows were believed to go down on their knees in their byres at midnight on Christmas Eve. Another very odd Highland belief was that all the bees would leave their hives at three o'clock on Christmas morning, to return again immediately.

*Alexander Carmichael, *Carmina Gadelica*

Anne Ross, *The Folklore of the Scottish Highlands,* 1976

FAIR-GROUND, DRUIM TIGHE MHIC GHILLE CHATAIN, TENGA, MULL

A remarkable series of structures is situated on open moorland at a height of 90m OD, immediately NE of a flat-topped rock outcrop which forms a conspicuous landmark at the watershed of the minor road from Dervaig to Aros. In an area measuring about 140 m from N to S by about 80 m transversely, no fewer than fifty turf-walled buildings are distributed in two main groups; the smaller occupies ground sloping NE from the rock outcrop already mentioned, while the remainder are dispersed over the summit of a low knoll separated by marshy ground from the smaller group.

The structures are of a consistent and distinctive plan-form, a typical example comprising a rectangle 6.1 m in length by 2.7 m over turf side-walls 0.6 m in thickness. In many cases one end-wall is represented by a substantial mound of turf and stone, sometimes with internal facing-stones *in situ,* while the other end is left open to provide an entrance. The narrow internal space thus formed is further diminished by a central bench or ridge of turf about 0.3 m thick and running the entire length of the building. Despite the fragile nature of the building material, the turf in most cases surviving to a height of only about 0.2 m, thirty-six of the structures identified conform to this type. The only variation is in length, one exceptional building having overall dimensions of 12 m by 3 m. Eight other structures differ only in having both ends closed, the entrance, where identifiable, being towards the end of one side-wall. Several of the remaining buildings on the site probably had internal benches which can no longer be distinguished.

Most of the buildings in the smaller group are aligned on a NNE–SSW axis, with the entrances facing downhill and away from the prevailing wind. No overall pattern is discernible in the larger group, although some of the buildings appear to line an E–W 'street' and several are so placed as to gain shelter from their neighbours. The open ends of individual buildings face in every direction except in the sector between SE and SW.

This site, which is still known locally by the polysyllabic place-name given above, meaning 'ridge of the house of the son of Gille Chatain', lies on the farm of Tenga, in the 18th and 19th centuries a property of the Dukes of Argyll. During the time when most of the cattle from Coll and Tiree were landed at the small harbour of Croig, the route from Dervaig through Glen Aros to Salen and Grass Point was an important drove-road, but with the improvement of the road through the Ross of Mull in the first quarter of the 19th century, Croig was eclipsed as a landing-place by Bunessan and Kintra. 'Druim Tighe' was identified in 1891 as the former site of the principal fairs and markets of Mull, which had been held there for centuries until within living memory, and the name 'Drimtavickillichattan' appears in the lists of fairs published in Scottish almanacs in the first quarter of the 19th century.

The fairs were held in mid-May and mid-October for cattle, and in mid-August for horses, the latter occasion being singled out by John Ramsay of Ochertyre, writing towards the end of the 18th century, as 'the most considerable [fair] in the West Highlands'. He states that 'it is held in August, upon the side of a high hill, four or five miles from any houses. Thither great numbers of persons resort from all the Western Isles and adjacent countries; and it is attended by pedlars from the Low country, and sometimes from Ireland. It lasts a week; and though it is now less frequented by the gentry, it is still a season of great festivity with the commons. People who come from a distance are obliged mostly to eat and sleep in tents or temporary huts, where droll adventures often occurred'. The extant buildings were evidently the footings of these tents or huts, the superstructures perhaps being of blankets, as at other Highland fairgrounds. Although some may have been used as taverns, their principal function was to provide shelter at night, and the central benches probably served as beds raised above the mossy ground . . .

The precise date when the site was abandoned is unknown, for in 1823 and subsequent years *The Edinburgh Almanack* gives the location as 'Mull'. By 1843 the fair was established at Fishnish, and it was transferred to Salen towards the end of the 19th century.

RCAHMS, *Argyll*, vol. 3, 1980

THE MULL FAIR

The black cattle, for the most part, are sold lean at a fair, which begins in this parish on the 13th of May yearly, and is continued in the other parishes of the island, upon 3 different days thereafter, with a day always intervening.

Revd Archibald McArthur, *OSA*, Kilninian, 1792-93

[The Mull Fair was traditionally known in the island as *an Fhaidhir Mhuileach*, more recently as *am Faidhear Muileach*.]

THE MULL FAIR

Donald first attended it when he was 14 years old. It was held in Salen on 22nd August and held in the street. People coming with horses slept outside, with their horses, near the pier (*An Cnoc*). There were no spare bedrooms anywhere. There were many horses, the cows and people came in from Lismore, Colonsay, Coll and Tiree. Fights were common and his father was once attacked. Donald also mentions that Glen Cannel was a good place for grazing horses – it belonged to the Duke [of Argyll] and had a manager. Horse dealers from the Lowlands tried to trick people and would say the horse was lame. They conspired with friends to keep prices down.

Donald goes to sell a mare (*capull*) and wanted £40. The dealer felt the mare's legs and nearly got kicked in the face. At the Salen Fair, Donald wanted £40 for his horse. He met the dealer at Allt an t-Searmoin (Salen). The dealer would not give that [£40] and he too was nearly kicked by the horse. At the Smiddy the dealer saw Donald and the horse again and complained to the police. The policeman told the dealer to keep clear. Donald got £20.

Donald Morrison, Ardtun, Mull. Notes from a recording made by
Donald MacLean and Roddy MacNeill, 1977

CATTLE DROVING AND TRADING

The trade in cattle from Argyll existed at least as early as the time of Mary, Queen of Scots, and in 1565 and 1566 the inhabitants of 'Ergile, Lorne, Braidalbane, Kintyre, and the Ilis', having complained that they were afraid to come to the Lowlands for trading purposes for fear of confiscation of their cattle, the Privy Council ordered that loyal subjects bringing cattle from Argyll to the Lowlands were not to be molested, provided, however, that goods were not taken back to Argyll. Despite this, the trade remained precarious, and in 1609 the Privy Council annulled a recent Proclamation prohibiting all trade with Mull or any of the Western Isles, MacLean of Duart having protested that the sale of 'Mairtis', horses and other goods was the only method of paying taxes to the Crown. But the troubles of the Mull cattle dealers were not yet at an end. A few years later they are again complaining, this time against tolls unlawfully exacted by MacDougall of Dunollie on cattle landed from the Mull ferries.

From early times Mull exported cattle to the mainland throughout the main droving period of the 18th and 19th centuries, and the island continued to be one of the principal sources of the Argyllshire droving traffic.

The landing place for the cattle from Coll and Tiree is vaguely described as at the back of Mull (Kintra) through Glenmore to Torosay. In the second half of the 18th century, the birch, ash and oak woods were already being cut and burned for charcoal by the

Lorn Furnace Company on Loch Etive. The Mull cattle, numbering with those from neighbouring islands as many as 2,000 per
annum, were shipped from the island at Grass Point, Kerrera, at the
Bay of Barr nam Boc. Mull possessed, in the 18th and early 19th
centuries, another ferry of some importance to the drovers. Salen,
on the Sound of Mull, had for long been a considerable cattle market
for the beasts from the north of the island and from the islands of
Ulva and Gometra and drovers found it of advantage to ferry their
beasts from Fishnish to the Morvern shore (and vice versa). A raid
by MacLean of Duart on the island of Gigha in 1579 resulted in the
theft of no less than 500 cattle and 2,000 sheep and goats.

Notes from Roddy MacNeill, Salen. Source unknown

THE MULL FAIR AND MULL HORSES

At Salen there is held every August the annual show of the Mull
and Morven Agricultural Association, at which substantial prizes
are awarded to the best exhibits. These shows which, since their
commencement, have become a craze among Mull farmers, are
giving farmers a great impetus in stock breeding. Stock of all kinds
has made rapid improvement; and breeders get the benefit in the
superior prices realised on market days. In this connection it is only
to be regretted that more encouragement has not been given to the
fostering and to the breeding of those wiry little ponies for which
Mull was once famous: so hardy and so spirited are they when
footing their way over the rough hill-tops. Very few of those clean-
boned and well-knit animals are now to be met with on the island,
though, perhaps, forty or fifty years ago, they were very numerous.
None could be more suitable for traversing the rough roads which
then intersected the island, or the sedgy moors, with their
numberless treacherous bogs. It seems a pity that this excellent
breed is gradually disappearing; for the Mull natives have been
giving more attention to the breeding of the Clydesdale type to the
exclusion of the native strain. Through the efforts of J. H. Munro-
Mackenzie, Esq., of Calgary, and the late Squire Cheape, of Bentley
Manor, the breeding of this native type of horse has been making
encouraging progress within the last few years. Tradition asserts that
these horses are a relic left by the Spanish Armada.

The Thursday* following is held the largest horse market in the West Highlands. To this important meeting congregate dealers from all parts of the country, who depart with large numbers of the hardy and well-bred horses of Mull and the neighbouring islands.

John MacCormick, *The Island of Mull*, 1923

*The first Thursday after the 20th Aug., or on the 20th Aug. if a Thursday.

TORNESS HORSE MARKET

A market, possibly only for horses, was held at Torness annually in August. There is an interesting note in the "Minutes of the Commissioners of Supply, for the Northern District of Argyll" dated 28th March 1826: "Mr Campbell, factor for Colonel Campbell of Possil, produced a Petition, complaining of the injury sustained by the Farm of Torness on account of the Horse Market being annually held on that farm without remuneration being allowed therefore." The cattle and horse markets were eventually moved to a permanent site at Balemeanach (Fishnish) given by Lochbuie. Just below the barn and fank, where the ground slopes down to the river, can be traced the market stances (whether these were benches for sales goods or sleeping bothies, opinions differ). At least eight can be found. To find these stances, follow the path that leads down to the bridge over the river and stop at a cairn. Nearby, you should find rectangular outlines of stone foundations about a foot high and measuring 8–10 feet long and 4–5 feet wide. At the time of the fair, branches and heather would be gathered to form temporary roofs.

J. LeMay and J. Gardner, *Glen More: A Drive through History*, 2001

THE MULL FAIR

In 1764 it was estimated that two thousand cattle were exported from Mull each year at an average price of £1.14.0. Most changed hands on a wide expanse of open moorland in Glen Bellart at the watershed between the rivers Bellart and Aros, *Druim tighe mhic Gille Chatain*, the ridge of the house of the son of Gille Chatain. It had been the site of one of the largest fairs in the West Highlands since medieval times. People travelled to it from all over the

Western Isles and the adjacent mainland, from the Lowlands and sometimes from Ireland, lairds, tacksmen, tenants, merchants, cattle dealers, fishermen, pipers, jugglers, ballad singers, and pedlars. It was an occasion for festivity, a chance to meet old friends, hear the news, and celebrate a break in the routine of the countryside. Those who came from a distance had to eat and sleep in tents and temporary huts, and there were numerous taverns where bargains could be sealed and fights begun; it was no coincidence that the fair was held near Aros, still the main centre for justice in Mull.* The fair took place three times a year and lasted for a week. Although an important social occasion, it was primarily a place where business could be transacted, and a market for the disposal of the surplus of the countryside. It was well situated, for *Druim Tighe* was on the drove road from Tiree and Coll, and great herds of cattle gathered there at the time of the Fair.

The problems of getting cattle to *Druim Tighe* and from there to the cattle markets on the mainland were considerable. In 1763 Donald Campbell of Airds petitioned the Commissioners of Supply in the name of the gentlemen and inhabitants of Mull for £120 to build bridges over the rivers Aros, Forsa, and Ba. This sum was to be matched by voluntary contributions from the inhabitants of Mull, Coll, and Tiree. Torloisk had made the same request ten years earlier and had claimed that the lack of bridges caused travellers to be held up for days on end. The fair in August was particularly affected, and strangers and natives had lost their lives by the lack of bridges.

The method of ferrying cattle from Mull was to 'cast them down' and tie them in boats. The practice was 'attended with great loss to the owners of the cattle'; it was also expensive. From January to the end of June, when the cattle were in poor condition, the transport of a cow cost eight pence; from July onwards, when they were fat, it was ten pence. At all times of year a bottle of whisky was given to the ferryman with each load of cattle.

Nicholas Maclean Bristol, *Hebridean Decade*, 1982

---

* There was a travelling court-house at Aros Bridge where the two-storeyed cottage now called Keeper's Cottage stands. (This building was also said to be an inn, possibly after this.) The use of this may have ceased when the court-house in Tobermory was established.

Note from Calum MacDonald, Tobermory, 2001

GAMES AT ARD DUBH

They did have Games there right enough when I was quite young, just a boy. A local thing held in Summer with running. Peter does not know who ran the Games. His uncle Willie was a very good cross-country runner. Slight prizes were given.

Peter MacLean, Dervaig, 2000

SHINTY AT CALGARY

B' àbhaist dhaibh, Là na Bliadhn' Ùire, a bhith coinneachadh aig Tràigh Calgary aig an Tràigh Bhàn, 's bhiodh iad a' tighinn a Dearbhaig, Torrloisg, Treisnis ag iomain an là sin. Cha robh ann ach dìreach cur nan còtaichean sìos air an Tràigh Bhàn agus dèanamh goals 's caiptean air gach taobh a' taghadh na daoine bha dhìth air. Ach bha sin a' dol – tha e colach gu robh sin a' dol air ais iomadh bliadhna agus sguir e uile gu léir. It was held on the ordinary New Year's Day, not the old one. It went on for a long time.

Translation: They used on the New Year's Day, to meet at Calgary Strand at the White Strand, and they would come from Dervaig, Torloisk, Treshnish to play shinty that day. There was nothing to it but putting the coats down on the white sand and making goals and a captain from each side picking the ones he needed (for his team). But that was going – it seems that was going back many years and then it stopped completely. It was held on the ordinary New Year's Day, not the old one. It went on for a long time.

Peter MacLean, Dervaig, 2000

SKATING ON LOCH FRISA AND LOCH CUAN

Peter never saw people skating on the loch, but the late Donald Paterson took a horse and cart over Loch Frisa when it was frozen over during a very severe frost.

Calum MacDonald remembers a severe frost in the 1920s when people were skating on Loch Cuan.*

Peter MacLean, Dervaig, 2000; notes, Calum MacDonald, Tobermory, 2001

*Loch a' Chumhainn = Loch of the Harbour, so called because of the harbour for galleys below Camus Cuin, Dervaig.

SPORT ENJOYED BY THE LAIRD OF TORLOISK

Soon after eight o'clock in the evening, just when the daylight was beginning to fade, everyone in the neighbourhood gathered on the shore. There is a wide rounded bay, with a fine expanse of gradually sloping sand. The Laird and his friends who were staying with him at Torloisk House were there, ladies as well as men; the farmers, their wives and daughters were there; also shepherds, gamekeepers, ghillies, men-servants and maid-servants, and the strangers within the gates.

And this was the sport. A boat was manned by three or four men, who had with them a great net, or rather they had one end of it. The other end of it was held by all on shore who could get a grip. When the boat had drawn out a sufficient distance from the beach, the crew gradually pulled along parallel with the shore, while those who held the shore end of the net walked along dragging their end, and keeping level with the boat. The boat was gradually rowed in on the beach, and then the net was pulled up on the sand, containing a struggling mass of fishes of various kinds – haddocks, saithe, flounders, and sea-trout, with perhaps other kinds. The process described is a 'scringe'. The fish were gathered up and distributed among those present. Three scringes carried on until it was too dark to see the sport any longer; and then I think the gathering proceeded to social enjoyment, being both hungry and thirsty. Part of the fun is that no one expects to keep dry, and all those who took part were most of the time that evening up to their knees in the sea.

Thomas Hannan, *The Beautiful Isle of Mull*, 1926

REGATTAS

Ann: Were there any festivals?

Roddy: No, except Salen Show, Games Day and Regattas. The regattas were with sixteen foot or eighteen foot skiffs with long sails and although brought up on an island, they [the boatmen] never learned to swim. The regattas were at Salen, Ulva Ferry, Bunessan and Tiroran with dances in the hall. People came from Dervaig, Gometra, Ulva and

Gribun. The Tobermory regatta lasted for two or three days and people came from all over. Other events were swimming, diving, for plates, Greasy Pole and a dance on the pier with the *Lochinvar* and the *Lochearn* tied alongside. This was held on a Saturday night and the dance would stop at midnight for the Sabbath. The streets were decorated with flags and there would be fireworks – it was a big day. *Latha mòr*.

Ann: When did it stop?

Roddy: There were none during the war and after the war money was not so plentiful and so no big yachts.

Roddy MacNeill, Salen, 1992

DANNSA AN RATHAID – ROAD DANCING

Dances were held in the schools when there were no village halls. They were held at Dervaig Bridge at *Samhain* (Bonfire Night), and it was not so long ago since that stopped.

Mary Morrison, Penmore, 1992

Note: Johnny Simpson, Fanmore, also mentioned that they were held at the wooden bridge at Calgary.

DANCING AT THE SMIDDY, DERVAIG

Kirsty MacGillivray said that both of the Dervaig bridges were used and also told the story of how the smiddy in Dervaig was a meeting place for dancing and they had an accordion there. It was called the Ca D'Oro, after a well-known dance hall in Glasgow.

Notes from Kirsty MacGillivray, Dervaig, 2000

Chapter 3

BIRTH, LIFE AND DEATH

AIDS FOR INFERTILITY

[On St Mary's Day in August] in Mull barren women walked around a well three times sunwise then drank the water. [St Bride's Day was also associated with customs of this nature.]

Sheila Livingstone, *Scottish Customs*, 2000

BAPTISMS

This was considered a big day (*latha mòr*) with many going to church, and there would be a big party in the house.

Roddy MacNeill, Salen, 1992

CHRISTENINGS IN ULVA

Well again, baptism was in the home. Baptism was not held in church at all. But the minister would be going (very often with his family along with him) to the house where an infant was to be baptised, and the baptism would be done in the house, and after the baptism we would have a great feast with a piper playing the pipes and drams going. A happy pleasant time it was, baptism in the house.

Donald W. MacKenzie. Recorded by Ann MacKenzie, 1992

SECOND SIGHT AND THE FORETELLING OF MARRIAGE

A native of Coll, Hugh, son of Donald the Red (*Eoghan Mac-Dhòmhnuill Ruaidh*), while serving with his regiment in Africa, said he saw, almost every evening, for a period of five years, glimpses of the woman whom he afterwards married, and whom he never saw in reality till his return from the wars. Wherever he sat, after the day's march, the figure of a woman came beside him, and sometimes seemed to him to touch him lightly on the shoulders. On each occasion he merely caught a glimpse of her. When he left the army, and was on his way home, he came to the village at Dervaig, in Mull, from the neighbourhood of which the ferry across to Coll lay.* He entered by chance a house in the village, and his attention was unexpectedly attracted by the sound of a weaver's loom at work in the house. On looking up he saw sitting at the loom the identical woman whose figure had for five years haunted him in Africa. He married her.

*Croig

J. G. Campbell, *Witchcraft and Second Sight*, 1902

RÉITEACH

In the Western Isles a 'reitach' or formal asking, was a complicated affair which usually took place after it was tacitly known that a young couple were contemplating marriage.

There was a gathering of friends at the bride's home, one of whom had been appointed to ask the bride's father in the bridegroom-to-be's stead. It was a sort of game, with never a direct reference to the matter in hand. The talk would be of other things until the friend said that he had heard there was a ewe lamb, or a boat that was needing looked after and he would be glad to arrange for this to happen. The father would agree and say that he knew it would be in safe hands.

Afterwards there was a party which might go on until the wee small hours. The mother and other relatives and neighbours contributed items of food; broth, chickens and potatoes. There would be a sit-down meal. Miraculously the fiddler and accordionist would be present as well as the best maids and bestman-to-be, although everyone pretended that it was a great surprise. On Barra the custom, slightly changed in character, is still in existence.

Sheila Livingstone, *Scottish Customs*, 2000

OIDHCHE NA RÉITEACH

This was a gathering of women before the wedding to make arrangements for the wedding feast at the home of the bride. Hens would be plucked (thus, the naming of the night), songs sung, and there would possibly be other rituals in the past. It would be interesting to hear of accounts of this from Mull and when it was last celebrated.

There is an account of one of the last reiteachs in Scalpay in the School of Scottish Studies, Edinburgh, recorded by Morag MacLeod.

Ann MacKenzie

MERCHATA MULIERUM (DROIT DU SEIGNEUR)

There is one interesting feature in Ulva's history which is worth recording, since it was here that the peculiar custom known as 'Merchata Mulierum' was practised for the last time.

According to this custom a crofter or clansman was obliged to pay the laird or chief a fine of five shillings on the marriage of the former's daughter. The last time this fee was levied was when a crofter in Ulva paid the chief MacQuarrie the customary fine when the former's daughter married.

In olden times *Merchata Mulierum* was a general custom all over Scotland, but Malcolm III. is said to have abolished it.

It is said to have been brought from France by the Normans, but Irish writers state that it was introduced into this country by the Danes.

John MacCormick, *The Island of Mull*, 1923

WEDDING CELEBRATIONS

There was a custom in Dervaig, and possibly elsewhere on Mull, continued until fairly recently, which involved the men of the village firing shots into the air as the bridal party left the church or the hall where the wedding took place. Kirsty MacGillivray, Dervaig, remembers this and says that a cannon was fired for the last time at her sister Effie's wedding. This cannon was sited on a knoll above the village called Cnoc a' Chanain and remained there until quite recently. The origins of the cannon are unclear. However, it is possible that it could be from the Crimean War and taken home by John Campbell who lived at Port na Ba, Penmore. There was a cannon on the Cannon Hill behind Penmore House which was fired for the Coronation of Queen Victoria 1837, and this may be the same cannon.

Notes: Betty Maclean, Kirsty MacGillivray, Effie MacCuaig and
Calum MacDonald, 2001

The country weddings were celebrated in a manner similar to those in the towns; only the invitations were more numerous. Sometimes the whole parish were invited; and when the company had far to ride, the cavalcade had a very imposing appearance. Many of the farmers had their wives mounted behind them, and the lads their sweethearts. The moment the bride started, all the old shoes about the house were thrown after her, fire arms were discharged, and the gridiron was rung with a thundering noise.

George Penny, *Traditions of Perth*, 1836, quoted in Margaret Bennett,
Scottish Customs from the Cradle to the Grave, 1992

There was a rush to kiss the bride, the winner often being the minister. Pistols could be fired and church bells rung, not just in celebration but to keep away evil spirits. Depending on the man's occupation, the couple sometimes passed under an arch of appropriate items as they left the church, such as sickles, boat hooks or swords. The same custom can still be seen today in the form of a guard of honour.

Sheila Livingstone, *Scottish Customs*, 2000

WEDDINGS ON ULVA

How did they keep weddings? Well, a wedding, they didn't have a wedding in church at all in my memory. They weren't keeping weddings in church. The people getting married they would, either, go perhaps to Oban and the marriage service and wedding would be in some hotel in Oban, or else, the service and wedding would be in the bride's home. That's how my father would go to weddings; he would go to the houses or to the hotels for the marriage ceremony, but they were not married in church at all.

Donald W. MacKenzie. Recorded by Ann MacKenzie, 1992

WEDDINGS

I was never at a wedding until after the war. I heard about them in the house but not church weddings. The minister went to the house to marry. There was a story about a wedding in Glen Forsa at Gaoideal with a fiddler from Salen, and on the way back they stopped at every bridge for a dance. Sometimes they had a meal and a dance in the hall [village] or a hotel.

Roddy MacNeill, Salen, 1992

PHOTOGRAPHS AT WEDDINGS

There were not many cameras. At a big wedding a photographer would come from Oban – Scrivens of Oban. There were no flash bulbs then so all photographs were taken outside. And then Kodaks, box cameras came.

Roddy MacNeill, Salen, 1992

DEATH (EXPRESSIONS FOR)

In Mull Gaelic usage, the word bàs (death) or bàsaich (die) applied to animals. Sheep and cows 'died'; people 'departed' (dh'fhalbh e) or 'travelled' (shiubhail e) or 'changed' (chaochail e).

Donald W. MacKenzie, *As it Was*, 2000

GAELIC SUPERSTITIONS CONNECTED WITH FUNERALS

Among the Gaelic superstitions connected with funerals it may be stated that it is customary to place a plate of salt, the smoothing-rod, or a clod of green grass on the breast of a corpse while laid out previous to being coffined. This, it was believed, kept it from swelling. A candle was left burning beside it all night, when it was placed in the coffin, and taken away on the day of the funeral. The boards on which it had been lying were left for the night as they were, with a drink of water on them in case the dead should return and be thirsty. Some put the drink of water or of milk outside the door, and, as in Mull and Tiree, put a sprig of heartswort above the lintel to prevent the dead from entering the house. When coffining the corpse every string in the shroud was cut with scissors; and in defence of the practice there was a story that after burial a woman's shade came to her friends to say that all the strings in her shroud had not been cut. Her grave was opened, and this was found to be the case. The relatives of the person last buried had to keep watch over the graveyard till the next funeral came. When two funeral parties met at the churchyard a scuffle frequently ensued to determine who should get their friend buried first.

The bodies of suicides were not taken out of the house for burial by the doors, but through an opening made between the wall and the thatch. They were buried, along with unbaptised children, outside the common churchyard. It was believed in the north, as in Skye and about Applecross, in Ross-shire, no herring would be caught in any part of the sea which could be seen from the grave of a suicide.

Anon., *The Celtic Monthly*, vol. 18, 1910

FUNERAL RITES

Burial customs among all nations are connected with religious ceremonies to a greater or less extent. The belief in a future existence, though crude, uncertain vague and shadowy throws a solemnity over the dead which expends itself in various rites. When once adopted the rites are pertinaceous, though the meaning, through the lapse of time may undergo a radical change, and not infrequently the original purpose is lost. A description of the rites of one age may not correspond with those of another.

Among the people of Mull, the dead body was immediately washed, dressed, wrapped in a winding sheet, and then placed on a board solely used for that purpose. Next a plate with a little salt in it was placed over the breast. Lighted candles were placed beside the bier. At the moment life became extinct the clock was stopped. From the moment of death to the burial the body was watched day and night, which practice was called lykewake, and is still prevalent in some parts of the Highlands. During the day the watch was kept by elderly persons, and at night the young were in charge. During the day the Bible was read, and devotional exercises conducted by some pious person; and during the night hours various subjects were discussed such as second sight, apparitions, ghosts, good qualities of deceased, and theological problems such as the unpardonable sin, blasphemy against the Holy Ghost, etc. The custom called 'Chesting' rose from an act of the Scottish parliament passed in 1686 ordaining that every dead body should be shrouded in linen. The object of this was to encourage the trade in that fabric. It was repealed in 1705, and woolen cloth substituted. It was also ordained that the nearest elder, with a neighbor or two should be present when the body was put into the coffin, to see that Act was obeyed. This rule took place usually on the evening preceding the day of burial, when devotional exercises were held. In the Ross of Mull one of the oldest matrons would tear off a piece of the shroud and give it to the chief mourner as a keepsake.

The whole neighborhood was invited to the funeral. There were feasting, good cheer, and sometimes inebriety during the obsequies. Prior to 1800 it was the custom of Highland lairds to take their piper with them to the funeral of a deceased friend, and when the body was committed to the grave a banquet was given in the church, and after the glass had circulated freely, then the piper would strut up and down the church making it resound with the strains of his instrument. Boswell, in speaking of his visit to Mull, in 1773 with Dr. Johnson, says: 'In the afternoon we went ashore on the coast of Mull, and partook of a cold repast, which we carried with us. We hoped to have procured some rum or brandy for our boatman and servants from a public house near where we landed; but unfortunately a funeral a few days before had exhausted all their store.'

It was believed that if any one helping to carry the corpse should slip and fall down, he would be the next to be carried to the grave. About the year 1798, a person thus engaged, in going down a steep hill to the ruinous burial place of the old church of Torosay, fell down, though only slightly hurt, he betook himself to bed, and the circumstances so preyed upon his mind that he nearly confirmed the superstition of his neighbors. However, he recovered and lived many years after.

What is known as the Highland Coronach was once common in Mull. It was a wild expression of lamentation poured forth by the relations and friends over the remains of the departed. When reduced to words it extolled the virtues of the deceased and the great love sustained by the survivors. One of the most famous Highland coronachs is that which laments the death of Sir Lachlan MacLean of Duard, Chief of MacLean and friend of the famous Montrose. The closing part is here given from a literal translation from the Gaelic, by Sir Walter Scott:

Thy dwelling is the winter house,
Loud, sad, and mighty is thy death song!
O! courteous champion of Montrose,
O! stately warrior of the Keltic Isles,
Thou shalt buckle thy harness no more.

The practice of cairn raising in honor of the dead is still observed in some districts. If a person is found dead out of doors, a few stones are collected to mark the spot, and every one who passes adds a stone. Or, if a coffin is carried to a church yard, wherever it rests upon the ground a cairn usually is erected. All funeral parties approaching the grave carried the coffin according to the course of the sun. From this many curious customs arose, such as when setting out to sea the boat was rowed sunwise.

J. P. MacLean, *History of the Island of Mull*, vol. 2, 1925

FUNERAL CUSTOMS

They have not given up feasting at funerals, though dancing is not common. After the funeral they repair to the side of a hill, and under a rock near the church, banish sorrow with whiskey. A curious account of a banquet of this kind was given me by a person who was present at the scene.

It was a custom, very lately abolished, for the highland lairds to be attended by their pipers wherever they went. A laird in Morven had taken his piper with him to the funeral of a deceased friend: when the corpse was committed to its native dust, a banquet was prepared in the church, and after the glass had circulated pretty freely, the laird ordered his piper to strike up, who, being as ready as his master, strutted up and down the church, making it resound with his melodious strains: at last he placed himself upon a tombstone, and played several airs: this so provoked a descendant of the person who was interred under the piper, who thought it an insult to the manes of his ancestor, that he went behind the musician, drew his dirk, thrust it into the wind-bag, and effectually stopped his pipe.

Thomas Garnett, *Tour through the Highlands and Part of the Western Isles*, 1811

THE WATCH OF THE GRAVEYARD (*FAIRE CHLAIDH*)

The person last buried had to keep watch over the graveyard till the next funeral came. This was called *Faire Chlaidh*, the graveyard watch, kept by the spirits of the departed.

At Kiel (*Cill Challum Chille*), in Morvern, the body of the Spanish Princess said to have been on board one of the Armada blown up in Tobermory Bay was buried. Two young men of the district made a paction, that whoever died first the other would watch the churchyard for him. The survivor, when keeping the promised watch, had the sight of his dead friend as well as his own. He saw both the material world and spirits. Each night he saw ghosts leaving the churchyard and returning before morning. He observed that one of the ghosts was always behind the rest when returning. He spoke to it, and ascertained it to be the ghost of the Spanish Princess. Her body had been removed to Spain, but one of her little fingers had been left behind, and she had to come back to where it was.

When two funeral parties met at the churchyard, a fight frequently ensued to determine who should get their friend first buried.

J. G. Campbell, *Superstitions of the Highlands and Islands*, 1900

FIGHTS AT FUNERALS

Fights were also common at funerals. They used to take a barrel of home-made whisky to a funeral until they couldn't stand. Not so much in his time but (he says) they still do that in Tiree.

Donald Morrison, Ardtun, Mull, 1977

BODYSNATCHERS AND DR MACCOLL, TOBERMORY

Dr. MacColl, who lived in Allt-na-creich, and had a surgery in
Black's Land, received bodies for which he paid £5 and then sent
them by boat in tea-chests to Glasgow and the medical school.
There is a story of a boat arriving in Tobermory, and the sailors
being short of money. So one of them, a black sailor, was placed in
a sack, delivered to the doctor, and the £5 received. As soon as the
bag was opened inside the house, the sailor sprang out, much to the
doctor's surprise, and escaped with his ship mates.

The only place on the island that had a mort box was at Kil-
patrick Cemetery, but watches were kept on the graves, and it is
said that a man called Cameron from Tobermory was guarding his
wife's grave when the robbers arrived. As he had a gun he fired on
them, and there is supposed to be the hole of a bullet in one of the
tombstones.

Other stories say that many of the graves from the Poorhouse at
Newdale, which contained people from other isles including Tiree
and Coll, and were buried at the front of Kilmore Cemetery, were
taken to the Medical School.

One of the cemeteries in the Ross of Mull, near Croggan, called
Kellean, was said to contain no bodies as a result of the grave-
robbers.

Notes taken from Calum MacDonald, Tobermory, 2001

CAITHRIS NA H-OIDHCHE (WAKE)

Two people would sit up all night for two or three nights before a
funeral. They still do this in Dervaig as they did at the funeral of
Dolly [his mother's sister].

This was an old custom (*sean chleachdadh*) to ensure that rats did
not molest the corpse.

Johnnie Simpson, Fanmore, 1992

FUNERALS ON ULVA

The funerals – the neighbours would be gathering round the house
where the funeral was to be, and the minister very often would be

standing at the door, and he was conducting the service there at the house, at the home, and then the neighbours would carry the coffin. They would walk with it, walking every bit of the distance to the graveyard wherever the graveyard might be, and they would go, six men at a time carrying the coffin. Another six would be waiting ahead, and they were going on like that all the way to the graveyard. The minister would have the service at the graveyard, and after the service what the family did was to provide whisky, biscuits and cheese. And they always had that at funerals. And I remember when my father would be coming home from a funeral, we would be going to meet him and we would be wanting the fragments of biscuits and cheese that he had in his pockets for us after the funeral.

D. W. MacKenzie. Recorded by Ann MacKenzie, 1992

FUNERALS: CARNAIN AN AMAIS

There was a stopping place on the way to funerals at Dervaig called Carnain an Amais* where refreshments were taken. The funeral bier would be carried by four men taking it in turns and sometimes a horse and cart would be used.

Ishbel Lloyd and Janet MacKeracher. Recorded for An Tobar, 1996

*Note: Charles Maclean writes in *The Isle of Mull: Placenames, Meanings and Stories*, 1997: 'At this point the Tobermory/Dervaig and Sorne (Glengorm)/Aros (Salen) routes crossed and there is a small cairn here. There is also a tradition of a minor battle here concerning cheese which in those days was important both for food and for paying rent. On the west side of Allt Na Craoibhe . . . are eight small cairns. These are funeral cairns erected by the Morrisons and have nothing to do with Carnain an Amais.'

Chapter 4

WORK

The Linen Industry in Mull

Hector Maclean of Torloisk appears to have been the first laird to promote the linen industry in Mull. In 1752 he presented the prizes at the spinning school at Torloisk on behalf of the Commissioners and Trustees for Regulating and Improving Fisheries and Manufactures in Scotland. The school attracted pupils from all over Mull, Morvern, and Tiree, and an undated report, probably written in the 1750s, describes it as being 'in a very prosperous way and bids fair for success . . . neither pains or expense is spared by Mr Maclean the undertaker or his sister the spinning mistress . . .' Yet, as the report pointed out, the industry in Mull had many problems. 'Their distance from the market subjects them to many hardships: transporting the flax from afar to that island partly by land partly by water creates an expense; bringing the yarn to Glasgow in an open boat is attended with expense and risk.' Torloisk had lost £40 on the spinning project alone, but 'still resolves to persevere'.

The linen industry in Mull appears to have collapsed during the war. Dr Walker in 1764 found no linen or cloth exported from the island and thought that its manufacture should be introduced. At about the same time Lieutenant Murdoch petitioned the Trustees for support in establishing the industry there, but he does not appear to have succeeded for he remained a linen merchant in Edinburgh until he inherited the Lochbuie estate from his cousin in 1784.

Nicholas Maclean Bristol, *Hebridean Decade*, 1982

Note 1: John MacCormick writes in *The Island of Mull*, 1923: 'With the very first good days of Spring every rock and knowe within reach of the thickly-populated hamlets were dotted with women and children gathering crotal with which to dye the worsted that had been spun and woven during the long winter evenings. The crotal, which grows on the rocks, yields a dull, brownish colour; while that produced on the barks of trees yields a more pronounced hue, approaching to a ruddy shade. Heather, again, yields a beautiful green, and was the favourite colour for Spring wear. The females were initiated in this branch of housewifery from very early years; for, when a young woman had the cares and burdens of house-keeping thrown upon her shoulders, this department devolved upon her. And more; they had to make the men's dress shirts. In every croft a rig was set apart for the growth of flax; and the women of the early part of last century were skilled in the details of the various stages in the process of linen manufacture; upon them devolved all the work from the time that the fibrous plant was first cut until the garment was ready for weaving.'

Note 2: Jean Whittaker remembers being told by Ian MacDonald (Ian Dan) of old flax beds which could be seen at Crackaig.

EMPLOYMENT IN THE SOUTH: 1850s

It was common for the young men of Mull, Lochalsh, Gigha and Applecross to go to sea, sometimes for several years on end, while domestic service was probably the most rapidly growing occupa-tion for single females. From around the Tobermory area in Mull 'a considerable number of young women go annually to seek service in Glasgow or other places in the south'.* Similar reports came from Islay, Glenelg, Colonsay and other parishes in Mull and Skye. In the early nineteenth century, Hebridean girls employed in the Lowland towns usually returned home during the winter months.

T. M. Devine, *The Great Highland Famine*, 1988

*Report to the Board of Supervision by Sir John McNeill on the Western Highlands and Islands (Parliamentary Papers 1851).

AGRICULTURE IN THE NINETEENTH CENTURY

Agriculture is here in a very low state, and though it is capable of improvement, it cannot probably be carried to the extent of supplying the inhabitants with corn. The arable land, as was before observed, lies for the most part near the shore; the soil, even there, is in general but barren, being a light reddish earth, mixed with moss, of very little depth, and very much under water. The spots which deserve a more favourable description, are in proportion very few. The common crop is a very inferior kind of oats, which the inhabitants call small oats; they are sown about the end of March, and it is generally October, and sometimes November, before they are ripe. The common return is three seeds, and so light that two bolls of oats only make one meal. Barley is sown about the end of April, and is ripe about the end of August; it generally returns from six to ten seeds; and when sown in old ground, manured with sea ware, it sometimes produces sixteen fold; this, however, is very rare. The greatest part of the barley is made into whiskey, which is much too commonly used in the Highlands. The late act obliging distillers to take out a licence, has undoubtedly diminished the number of stills in the Highlands, yet, in most of the sequestered glens, each distils his own spirits, without any fear of detection from the officers of the revenue. It is much to be wished that this pernicious poison could be banished from the country, and good malt liquor, which might be made with one-fourth the trouble, used in its stead. Surely no revenue arising from its consumption can be any compensation for its bad effects on the health and morals of society.

Potatoes grow here extremely well; they are sown in lazy-beds by the spade, and are the chief subsistence of the poor people for three-quarters of the year. Before the introduction of this useful root, for which we are indebted to America, and which is more valuable than all the gold of Mexico, all the diamonds of Golconda, or all the tea of China, the distresses of the highlanders, and particularly the inhabitants of the western islands, were frequently very great. Depending on a little meal, which constituted the chief part of their food, their hopes were frequently blasted; their corn rotted on the ground, and they were glad to drink the blood of their cattle, or bake it into cakes, to keep their families just alive. They had no money to purchase corn, even could it have been purchased. This failure of crops, through a long continuance of wet weather, happens on an average every third or fourth year; but potatoes now prove a comfortable support through the winter, when grain and meal fail. Such distress is now seldom experienced, and were the fisheries properly encouraged, would be entirely unknown.

The chief manure made use of in this island, is sea-ware, and in some parts shell-sand. The dung of horned cattle will go but little way, as the convenience for housing them is so small; but cattle are generally folded in some part of the ground, during the night, in summer and harvest; this is called teathing, and is one way in which the ground is manured. As there are few cart roads, the manure, whether sea-ware, shell-sand, or dung, is carried on the backs of horses, in baskets or creels, which wastes a great deal of time. The plough commonly made use of in this island is very rude, and is probably the same that has been used for centuries back: it is drawn by four horses a-breast. They seem to use it, because they are not acquainted with a better. There are no plough-makers, so that each farmer is obliged to make his own, which he does in the manner of his forefathers. Should any of the proprietors encourage a proper maker to settle, or give ploughs to their tenants, the advantage would soon be apparent.

But the greatest bar to improvements in agriculture, as well as to every kind of rural economy, is the want of leases; few of the lairds in the highlands, for I do not speak of Mull in particular, will let the land otherwise than from year to year, and if the tenant choose to have a house, he must build one himself. The land is generally let to the highest bidder by private offer: how then can the tenant enter upon any improvements, when the next year he will probably lose his farm, unless he himself will pay for his own improvements by an advanced rent. In this dilemma, if he does not find a hut upon his farm, he builds himself a cabin, such as has been described, scarcely sufficient to shelter him from the inclemencies of the weather. He likewise takes every thing he can off the ground, which is a great detriment to the laird. Should the proprietors grant leases of considerable length, and either build houses for the tenants, or encourage them to do it, by paying them the extra expense when they leave the farm, their lands would be much benefited, and their rent rolls in a few years considerably augmented, while the tenants would enjoy some of the comforts of life, to which, as fellow-men, they are entitled . . .

The greatest evil, however, in the highlands, is the letting large farms to tacksmen, or persons who take them for no other purpose than to subset them . . . One of these tacksmen takes a large farm of a proprietor, which he divides into a number of small ones, and lets at as high rent as he can, without any lease, his only object being to squeeze out as much money as he can from both the landlord and the poor tenants, who happen to come under his clutches, during the time he keeps possession . . .

I must not forget to mention the manufacture of Kelp, or Soda, from sea-ware, which is carried on in the island of Mull, and indeed most of the other islands, and which has added very much to the incomes of the proprietors. Upon every part of the coast there are various kinds of sea-weeds, or wrack, as it is called, which were, till lately, used indiscriminately as manures. This useful material, which has contributed so much to enrich the proprietors, and afford employment to many hands, during the season, does not appear to have been known as a manufacture in Britain, until the beginning of the present century . . .

The first introduction of the kelp manufacture, was into the island of Uist, about the year 1730 . . . The benefit of this manufacture to the proprietors will be evident, when it is known, that small farms on the coasts, which within these seven years, only paid £40 rent, have risen to £300 a year . . . I believe that not less than 500 tons are annually made in Mull, at least since the price has been so high.

Thomas Garnett, *Tour through the Highlands and Part of the Western Isles*, 1811

LAND TENURE: STEEL BOW

There is another pernicious Method of subsetting of Lands which of late, is become a very frequent Practice in Mull and some of the other Islands, and also in the adjacent Countries upon the Main Land, that is, when a Tacksman subsets his Farm, with the whole Stock of Cattle upon it. This is called setting a Farm in Steel Bow, but why it is so called does not appear. In this case, the whole Stock upon the Farm, is valued, and upon the Expiration of the Subtenants Lease, he must either produce the Stocking in the same Condition, or pay the Value of what is wanting. By this sort of

Agreement, the Tacksman always draws from the Subtenants two Rents of the Farm, and sometimes three, and has generally from 12 to 18 p. Cent for the value of the Stock upon it. These high usurious Profits, have induced very many Tacksmen, to subset their Farms in this manner. But it is plain that all Improvement must be stopt upon a Farm in this State. The subtenants never make any thing by it, and yet for want of Land of their own, and opportunity of employing their Stock otherwise, are oblidged to submit to this strange sort of Tenure.

The Revd Dr John Walker, *Report on the Hebrides of 1764 and 1771*

A CREACH

A creach was a common affair in the Highlands, and a favorite method of Mull men for obtaining cattle especially from their enemies. There was greater or less danger attending it. A party of Mull men set out for the island of Luing on a predatory expedition, and when the night was far advanced landed at Camus-cairble, with all possible secrecy. Near that port, Marquis, tenant of Baile-chuain, had a herd of goodly cattle, upon which the party laid unsparing hands. Having placed on board their barge all the cattle it would hold, they slaughtered one on the shore for immediate use. Marquis had been following them, and obtaining a good view from a height near at hand, discharged an arrow, which pierced the hand of one of the men engaged in flaying the ox. Fearing an attack in force, the marauders took to their boats, and without delay, put to sea, leaving the slaughtered animal on the shore. At the time there was a breeze of north wind blowing which rapidly moved the boat, and hugging the shore they were at an advantage. Marquis anticipating their course, crossed Cuan Ferry, hastened to the north end of Easdale Sound, where it was narrowest, and hid himself at a point ever after called, Rudha Mhic Mharcuis – Marquis Point. When the barge came within range he shot into it, arrow after arrow, with such fatal effect that not one escaped with life. He then secured the boat with all that it contained.

Another story states that in the eighteenth Century seven men set out from Crogan, Mull, on a marauding expedition and landed at a point two and one half miles south of the present site of Oban.

They directed their course inland until they arrived at Muckairn, and then proceeded to lift cattle. They first seized a white cow belonging to a poor man who resided at a place called Larach-a'-Chuodall, a short distance above a waterfall that tumbles into the river Neaunta. Driving the white cow along with them, they turned to Glenlonain where they lifted cattle as they passed along. Their spoil consisted of four cows and three stirks. The cattle being missed, five men started in pursuit, and easily traced them, as the ground was covered with snow. The party was overtaken at Gallanach-beag, some of the cattle on the shore and some in the boats. The parties immediately joined in combat, resulting in five of the marauders and three of their pursuers being slain. All the cattle were secured and taken back to their homes.

J. P. MacLean, *History of the Island of Mull*, vol. 1, 1923

CREACH OF MALISE MACLEAN

Malise MacLean was the second heir of MacLean of Torloisk, in Mull, and sometime before 1745, made the last raid into the island of Tyree, which had always an inviting prey for plunderers and pirates. The given name of Malise MacLean is a most uncommon one among the MacLeans, and also of any of the West Highland clans. The name was bestowed owing to the younger member of Torloisk's dying early in life. The sages of the country advised Torloisk to give the new addition of his family the name of the first person he met on the way to have the child baptised, which proved to be a poor beggar by name of Malise. A name thus given was deemed proof against evil. Being without prospect of an estate, Malise thought he would go to Tyree, and piece by piece he would obtain landed property for himself. He came to have the half of the township of Baile-meadhonach, married and had descendants.

One day a galley, with sixteen men on board, came to Soraba beach, the men landing and collecting every animal about the place. At the time Malise was fishing at the rocks in Kenavara Hill, and on coming home learned what had been done, and asked his neighbors what they meant to do, and would they go with him to turn the raid. All refused through fear of being killed, as the raiders were strong. He said to them, 'I prefer to fall in the attempt, rather than let my cattle be taken.' Seizing his sword he followed the marauders.

Arriving near the free-booters he was ordered to leave the road, or he would feel the consequences. He answered, 'I will not leave, and the consequences will be to you, until I get my own.' This he received, and then asked for the cow of a poor woman of the same township as himself, and getting this, he said they might do with the rest as they pleased. The robbers drove the rest of the animals to the beach, threw them down, tied their forelegs together, placed them on bearers or planks and carried them on board the boat, and rowed away. No one knew whence they had come nor whither they went.

It is a tradition in Scotland that the MacLeans of Loch Buy, Mull, were the worst cattle thieves in that country. True, they did not look upon the creach in that light.

J. P. MacLean, *History of the Island of Mull*, vol. 1, 1923

SHIELING IN ULVA

It would appear that a custom prevailed in this country, even so recently as forty years ago, of the inhabitants setting off to the hills with their flocks at the beginning of summer, and bivouacking in the vicinity of the best upland pastures, and where all the families of the district took up their residence till it became necessary to descend to the low grounds in the month of August, when the hill pasture became bare, and when their crops required attendance . . . The men occasionally visited the low grounds to attend their simple husbandry then in use, or to procure some of the delicious fish which abound along the coast; some engaged in the chase, or followed the game; and richly did they deem themselves rewarded for their toil. When returning to the family circle, the produce of the flocks and dairy were put before them, and the feast enlivened by the pure essence of mountain dew, joined to the heart-stirring strains of the bagpipe. Nor in this pastoral encampment were the women idle; much of their time was occupied in the labours of the dairy, in preparing an abundant stock of butter and cheese for winter.

New Statistical Account, Ulva, 1845

Taking Cattle to and from the Treshnish Isles

When I was a boy they used to have cattle on the Treshnish Isles. The *Princess Louise* was the name of the boat they used, an ex-trawler. The cattle were put aboard at Calgary pier and taken to the islands and put ashore there, and I think they were taken away when they were three years old [for the October sales]. A lot of people used to gather the cattle and there was always two skiffs to ferry men. They had head ropes round their horns and the cattle were taken down to the edge of the rocks and one of these boats came in close and tied a line on the head rope and threw it back to the boat and pushed the cattle over the side and towed it away to the big boat, and it was winched aboard the same way by the head rope.

There was no real landing place at Lunga. Peter does not know if there were any animals on the other islands apart from Lunga, or if there were any on Staffa as there used to be in the 18th century. Peter was never at Staffa. Sheep were taken on and off Lunga at another time and not with the cattle. Peter also told the story of how his grandfather and his grandfather's brothers used the mast of their boat to place between Lunga cliff opposite Harp Rock and this rock itself so that they could crawl along the mast onto the rock, which is a great sea bird sanctuary, and collect eggs. And on one fishing trip around the Treshnish Islands a great storm blew up around their boat and they had to take shelter on one of the islands. As they slept they both felt someone tucking the sail under which they lay, around them, and they believed this to be their mother. They both recounted this story on returning to Haunn.

Peter MacLean, Dervaig, 2000 and 2001

Puffins: *Seumas Ruadh*

Puffins were known by this name, and Peter's grandfather, Calum MacDougall, went down the cliffs at Treshnish in the summertime to collect them. The puffins were boiled but not salted. There are no puffins on the Mull mainland now, but there used to be a colony at Treshnish Point.

Peter MacLean, Dervaig, 2000

Note: Seumas Ruadh was also the Gaelic name for a puffin in Barra.

PLOUGHING MATCHES

Ploughing matches were held in different places: Glenforsa and Quinish, but Gorsten was the most regular farm. Different fields were used and the competitions were for the best pair, best mare and gelding and for the decoration and grooming of the horses as well as the three ploughing classes (ten inch, eight inch and twelve inch). Also the best rig of the field. The prizes were money and medals. At night there would sometimes be a dance.

Notes taken from Donald McNeillage, Dervaig, 1992

AGRICULTURE: SEVEN-YEAR CROP ROTATION

	Soil condition	*Crops grown*
1st year	*talamh glas* – ploughed	oats sowed
2nd year	*talamh connlain* – stubble	potatoes, turnips
3rd year	*talamh dearg* – with crop	oats, rye, clover
4th year	*talamh dubh* – soil in clement weather – free from snow	rye grass (1st year)
5th year	?	rye grass (2nd year)
6th year	?	?
7th year	?	?

This list is incomplete and it would be interesting to find details of the latter parts of this rotation.

Roddy MacNeill, Salen, 1992

HORSES AT SUNIPOL

Col. MacKenzie built a six foot wall below Cailleach Point which included remains of an evicted village called Penny ? . . . to keep his stallions from his other horses and ponies. (He was well known for Arab and Highland pony breeding.) The whole area of Cailleach up to Sunipol was devoted to this use. It is said that the men who built this wall were paid in meal.

Notes from Archie MacCuish and Donnie Campbell, Cailleach, 2001

MAKING LOBSTER CREELS

I was taught by my grandfather [Peter's grandfather went to work at fishing at the age of eight]. Saplings of hazel were taken from the wood and you bent them to the right length. One in the middle, one at each end and three across the top and that was your frame ready. Now these people made the covers. I remember first it was sail twine which was very fine but it didn't last long, but then after that they got trawler twine, tarred trawler twine which lasted much better. The net part was knitted with needles.

Ann: Did you put tar on top of it?
Peter: It was tarred already. In some places it was re-tarred. It had two eyes [*cabhuil* 'eye of a creel', usually 'creel'], one on each side. A creel [*cliabh*] was twenty-eight inches long.
Ann: What was used for bait?
Peter: Salt mackerel was the best but other salted fish were used. Single creels were set, at least sixty of them.
Ann: Other lobster fishermen in the area?
Peter: Some in Tobermory and my uncles at Quinish went as far as Mingary and Loch Tuath. There were also my Haunn cousins at Treshnish. Lachie MacNeill, Ulva Ferry, fished most of his life: he was rabbit catching in winter and lobster fishing in summer at Loch na Keal, Ulva and Gometra.

Peter MacLean, Dervaig, 2000

PEARL FISHING IN MINGARY

Travelling people used to come round about and to fish for mussels out of the river Mingary for the pearls and they were getting them too. It seems that that river was good for that. There's many a year since it stopped.

Peter MacLean, Dervaig, 2000

THE BLACKSMITH AT DERVAIG

My father was a blacksmith and so too was my grandfather, but before that the MacLeans used to build boats on Penmore [Estate] and when that happened to go they began to be millers and built the one at Penmore and they built another mill – Kellan. And I think my grandfather on my father's side, when the milling stopped, worked at the smiddy of the blacksmith they called the Black Smith. And it happened, I know that it happened, that the Black Smith had made a kind of fish trap in the river to catch salmon and the Laird noticed it and the Black Smith was cleared off and it was my grandfather that then started working at the smiddy. But, however, he had only the skill he learned from the Black Smith, and then my father who was young went to Glasgow to learn his trade, and it was pretty hard work, too, it seems, and I heard him say, I remember, that he had to make a set of horse shoes before breakfast in the morning, and when you were clear of your apprenticeship you ought to be a very good blacksmith.

And my father was a good blacksmith right enough. I remember them saying that there was somebody about the place who had a new plough and he took it to the smiddy to get something done on it, and my father looked at it: 'Straight back with it to where you got it, it isn't right!' And it seems the people that made it, they said that his remark was quite correct – the plough was faulty.

Peter MacLean, Dervaig, 2000

PUTTING IRON RIMS ON CART WHEELS

Ann: Where were all the smiddies in this area? Dervaig, Tobermory, you said there might have been one near Torloisk. Bogha na Ceàrdaich?

Peter: Ay, near Torloisk, Bogha na Ceàrdaich, 's fhada bhon a bha sin ag obair. (It's a long time since that was working.)

Ann: How did they put wheel-rims on cart-wheels?

Peter: Sin mar a bha iad cur an t-iarann air cuibhl' cairte. Well, bha duine a bha fuireach dlùth air a' cheàrdaich, anns a' Bheurla 'se *wheelwright* a bh' ann agus bha esan a' cur air dòigh a' chuibhl' agus nuair a bha i deas aige bha e 'ga toirt a nall dh'ionnsaidh far an robh m' athair. Bha cuibhl' aige agus an cearcall a bha seo dh'fheumadh e dhol mun cuairt fiodh a' chuibhle. Agus bha e dèanamh a mach, dh'fheumadh pìos de dh'iarainn, cearcall a ghearradh 's a toirt a staigh no leigeil a mach, agus nuair a bha e faotainn sin ceart, bha

àite aig a' cheàrdaich airson a' ghnothach. 'Se *ring* mór a bh'
ann de dh'iarann agus toll 'sa mheadhon airson cuibhl' na
cairte. 'S dar (=nuair) a bha h–uile nì ceart aca bha iad a' cur
an t–iarann 'na laighe air a seo agus a' cur teine mòna
dìreach mun cuairt air uile gu léir agus nuair a bha e teth,
well, bha 'chuibhl' 'ga toirt a mach agus bha a' mhòine 'ga
ciceadh air falbh agus bha 'n cearcall 'ga chur air a' chuibhl'
is uisge 'ga chur air agus mar sin bha e deiseil.

Translation: Here was how they put the iron on the wheel of a cart.
Well, there was a man staying near the smiddy, in English he was a
'wheelwright' and he was making the wheel and when it was
finished he was taking it across to the smiddy where my father was.
He had a wheel and this circle had to go round the wood of the
wheel. A piece of iron, a circle had to be cut and taken in or let out,
and when he got that right, there was a place at the smiddy for the
job. It was a big ring of iron with a hole in the middle for the
cartwheel. When everything was in order they laid the iron on this
and put a peatfire around just about the whole thing and when it
was hot, well, the wheel was taken out and the peat kicked away
and the circle was put on the wheel and water was put on it and so
it was ready.

Ann: Where did they get the peat?
Peter: Ge bith dé na daoine a bha dèanamh na cairte bha iad toirt
           a' mhòine leo airson an obair sin dhèanamh.

Translation: Whoever the people were who were making the cart
they would bring the peat with them to do the job.

Ann: Did your father ever go out to other farms, shoeing horses?
Peter: B' àbhaist dha a dhol gu Ulbha 's gu Gomastra.

Translation: He used to go to Ulva and Gometra. [MacLean of
Gometra. Everyone else would come to them.]

Peter uses the word *cearcall* 'circle' for the iron rim of a cartwheel.
Dwelly: *cearcall* = iron ring on wheel.

                                              Peter MacLean, Dervaig, 2000

MAKING IMPLEMENTS

Ann: Did he [your father] make implements?

Peter: Bhiodh e dèanamh toirsgian airson buan na mòna agus dèanamh ceaba – làn cheaba – airson toirt am mullach bho'n bhac mòna. Bhiodh e dèanamh sin agus dèanamh rudan eile cuideachd.

Translation: He used to make peat-spades for cutting the peat and spades – complete spades – for taking the top off the peat bank. He used to do that but he would be making other things also.

Ann: You said that he made gates that are still at Mingary?

Peter: Ai, geataichean iarainn agus tha iad an sin fhathast cho math 's a bha iad riamh chionn bha iad 'gan dèanamh le iarann. Na geataichean a tha iad dèanamh an diugh chan eil iad 'gan dèanamh le iarann, ach mairidh an t-iarann.

Translation: Ay, iron gates and they are still there as good as they ever were because they were made of iron. The gates they make today are not made of iron, but iron will last.

Ann: Was he the last smith in Dervaig?

Peter: Bha mo bhràthair Calum, bha e 'na ghobha an déidh do m' athair a shiubhail. An sin, fhios'ad, thòisich obair nan *tractors* agus cha robh móran guth air each no nì 's dh'fhalbh a' cheàrdaich.

Translation: My brother Malcolm, he was a blacksmith after my father passed away. Then, you know, the work of tractors began and there wasn't much talk about horses or anything and the smiddy went.

Peter MacLean, Dervaig, 2000

THE BREWERY AT TRESHNISH

Ann: And was it your great-grandfather that had the still at Treshnish?

Peter: It was . . . uncle . . . grand-uncle.

Ann: What was his name?

Peter: Allan.

Ann: And can you describe where the still is?

Peter: Where it was? It was, if you, say, go from Treshnish to
          Haunn and nearly half-way, not quite, right enough, there's
          a stream comes over the road and there's a gully goes
          straight up and they call it Allt an Fhraoich and then there
          is a flat and a wee bit cliff and below that was the brewery.
          Dlùth air a' bhriuthas sin, 'se an t-ainm a bh' air Àirigh Lag
          a' Chruinneachd, agus chì thu fhathast far an robh na
          bothain bheaga àiridh aca. Ach cha do rinn Ailean sin nì a
          riamh ach dèanamh an uisge bheatha agus bha Iain a
          bhràthair 'ga dhèanamh cuideachd. Agus bha iad anns an
          am sin . . . cha robh bàtaichean seòlaidh math idir an seo,
          cha robh móran gréim aca air an uisge. Ach co-dhiù, bha
          'phoitin air bòrd 's a' dèanamh air Eirinn, air Belfast, agus
          dh'fheumadh iad a bhith mach as, mar a chanas iad ann am
          Beurla, *territorial water*, mu'n dèanadh i là, eagal gum
          beireadh an *cruiser* orra. Ach cha robh iad a' faotainn airgiod
          idir. Cha robh iad ach a' dèanamh suaip airson mhucannan.
          Cha robh airgiod 'ga thoirt seachad idir. Anns an am sin 'se
          Gàidhlig a bh' aca 'm Belfast.

Ann: Any stories about running into the cutters . . . Coming
          across the Excise men?

Peter: Well, sin nuair a bha iad dol do Thiriodh leis an uisge-
          bheatha agus thachair gun do mhothaich iad *cutter* agus bha
          i as an déidh. Mhothaich na Tiristich seo a' tachairt agus
          bha iad deas air an tràigh, agus bha leithid ann dhiubh 's
          thog iad am bàta gu léir a mach astar mór os cionn an làin
          agus chaidh an t-uisge-beatha chur am falach.

Translation: Near that brewery, its name was Wheat Hollow
Shieling, and you can still see where their little shieling bothies
were. But that Allan never did anything but making the whisky, and
at that time John was making it too – his brother. And at that time
there were . . . the sailing boats here were not at all good, they did
not have much purchase on the water. But, however, the poteen
was on board, making for Ireland, for Belfast, and they had to be
out of, as they say in English, 'territorial waters' before daybreak, for

fear that the cruiser would catch them. But they weren't getting money at all. They were only bartering in exchange for piglets. Money was not handed over at all. At that time it was Gaelic they had in Belfast.

Any stories about running into the cutters . . . Coming across the Excise men?

Well, then, when they were going to Tiree with the whisky it happened they noticed a cutter and it was pursuing them. The Tiree people noticed this happening and they were ready on the beach, and there were so many of them they lifted the entire boat out a long way above the high water mark and the whisky was hidden.

Peter MacLean, Dervaig, 2000

Chapter 5

HEALTH

The diseases that the natives are most subject to are coughs, sore
breasts, asthmas, cancer, a dry scabby eruption of the skin, itch,
scropholous, tumors, fevers, and fluxes. The children are much
troubled with worms, for which they use an infusion of the *Myrica
gale* or Goul. The women use a decoction of the *Thalectrum minus*
for obstructions of the menses, which they are frequently troubled
with, also the girls, when they happen to prove with child,
unmarried, are said to use a decoction of the *Lycopodium selago* in
order to effect an abortion. The small pox have been inoculated on
two children here. They visit this Isle one in six or seven years in
the natural way, and are frequently mortal.

James Robertson, 1788, quoted in J. P. MacLean,
History of the Island of Mull, vol. 1, 1923

MOULD AS A CURE IN CALGARY

Long before the discovery of penicillin, people kept saucers of milk
until it grew a mould. In the Calgary area of Mull this mould was
applied as a poultice on ulcerated legs. The various moulds growing
on the walls of caves were believed to be excellent for wounds, and
'cave soil' was said to be particularly effective for damage to the
limbs.

Mary Beith, *Healing Threads*, 1998

MULL CURE FOR SWELLINGS

A swelling of the axillary glands (*faireagun na h-achlais*) is an ailment
that soon subsides or breaks into an ulcer. The 'skilful' professed to
cure it in the following manner, and no doubt when the swelling
subsided, as in most cases it did, the whole credit was given to their

magic ceremony. On Friday (on which day alone the ceremony was efficacious) certain magic words were muttered to the blade of a knife or axe (the more steel the better), which was held for the purpose close to the mouth, and then, the blade being applied to the sore place, the swelling was crossed and parted into nine, or other odd numbers or imaginary divisions. After each crossing, the axe was pointed towards a hill, the name of which commences not with *ben*, a lofty hill, but *mam*, a round mountain. For instance, in Mull and neighbourhood, the malady was transferred (*do chuids' air tha sid air, do roinn-sa air, etc.*) to *Màm Lìrein, Màm an t-snòid, Màm Doire Dhubhaig, Màm Chlachaig, Màm Bhrathadail*, etc., all hills in that island. When the swelling was 'counted' (*air àireamh*) the axe was pointed to the ground, saying, 'the pain be in the ground and the affliction in the earth'.

J. G. Campbell, *Witchcraft and Second Sight*, 1902

A FEVER BROUGHT TO THE ISLE OF NORTH UIST FROM MULL

Since the great change of the seasons, which of late years is become more piercing and cold, by which the growth of the corn, both in the spring and summer seasons are retarded; there are some diseases discover'd, which were not known here before, *viz.*, a spotted fever, which is commonly cured by drinking a glass of brandy or *aquavitae* liberally when the disease seizes them, and using it till the spots appear outwardly. This fever was brought hither by a stranger from the island of *Mull*, who infected these other islands. When the fever is violent, the spots appear the second day, but commonly on the fourth day, and then the disease comes to a crisis the seventh day: but if the spots don't appear the fourth day, the disease is reckon'd mortal.

Martin Martin, *A Description of the Western Islands of Scotland*, 1716

MOLUCCA BEANS: MEDICINAL USES

There is a variety of nuts, call'd Molluka beans, some of which are used as amulets against witchcraft, or an evil eye, particularly the white one; and upon this account they are wore about childrens necks, and if any evil is intended to them, they say the nut changes into a black colour. That they did change colour, I found true by my own observation, but cannot be positive as to the cause of it.

Martin Martin, *A Description of the Western Islands of Scotland*, 1716

The black and white *Indian* nuts are found on the west side of this isle [Mull]; the natives pulverize the black kernel or the black nut, and drink it in boil'd milk for curing the *Diarrhea*.

Martin Martin, *A Description of the Western Islands of Scotland*, 1716

The West Indian nuts are from the plant *Entada Scandens*. It was believed that if held in the hand by a woman during labour it would ease the birthpains and also ward off evil fairies. During the 18th and 19th centuries the nuts were mounted in silver and hung from watch-chains.

Eve Eckstein, *Historic Visitors to Mull, Iona and Staffa*, 1992

AQUA VITAE AND CHARMEL ROOT

This isle [Mull] is in the sheriffdom of *Argyle*; the air here is temperately cold and moist; the fresh breezes that blow from the mountains do in some measure qualify it: the natives are accustom'd to take a large dose of *aquavitae* as a corrective, when the season is very moist, and then they are very careful to chew a piece of *charmel*-root, finding it to be *aromatick*; especially when they intend to have a drinking-bout, for they say this in some measure prevents drunkenness.

Martin Martin, *A Description of the Western Islands of Scotland*, 1716

EVIL EYE

To prevent the effects of the Evil Eye, especially in young children spit was resorted to. A native of Mull stated this practice was common in that island. The method was to spit on the finger and rub an eye of the child to be protected with the moistened finger. By many this was believed to be a sufficient protection.

Another Mull woman, giving her own experience shows that spitting in healing water has actually been practised. She related that her aunt, suspecting her cow was suffering from the evil eye, sent her to the *eolas* woman to tell her about the beast, whom she found sick in bed, but on giving her the message she sent for water to be taken from under a bridge in the neighborhood, over which the living and the dead passed. It was always from this place where the healing water was taken. While repeating the incantation, the *eolas* woman would now and again spit into the bottle, which she gave to be taken to the aunt. This water was sprinkled over the cow, which recovered.

J. P. MacLean, *History of the Island of Mull*, vol. 1, 1923

CHARMS AGAINST DANGERS IN WAR

As a rule charms must be used on Thursdays or Sundays. These were of many varieties and used for many purposes. A charm used against dangers in war was given about the year 1800 from an old man in Glenforsa, in Mull. It is thus recorded:

For himself and for his goods.
The charm Bridget put round Dorgill's daughter,
The charm Mary put round her Son,
Between her soles and her neck,
Between her breast and her knee,
Between her eye and her hair;
The sword of Michael be on thy side,
The shield of Michael on thy shoulder;
There is none between sky and earth
Can overcome the King of grace.
Edge will not cleave thee,
Sea will not drown thee,
Christ's banners round thee,
Christ's shadow over thee;
From thy crown to thy sole,
The charm of virtue covers thee
You will go in the King's name,
And come in your Commander's name;
Thou belongest to God and all His powers.
I will make the charm on Monday,
In a narrow, sharp, thorny space;

Go, with the charm about thee,
And let no fear be on thee!
Thou wilt ascend the tops of cliffs,
And not be thrown backwards;
Thou art the calm swan's son in battle.
Thou wilt stand amid the slaughter;
Thou wilt run through five hundred,
And thy oppressor will be caught;
God's charm be about thee!
People go with thee!

A charm of this kind was given to a smith in Torosay, Mull, by his father. Afterwards he entered the army and engaged in thirty battles. On his return home without a wound he said, he had often wished he was dead, rather than be bruised as he was by bullets. He was struck by them, but on account of the charm they could not pierce him.

J. P. MacLean, *History of the Island of Mull*, vol. 1, 1923

CURES AND THE TRINITY

A woman in Mull, describing a cure done by herself, said: 'I remember a child I cured myself with good words that I have. It was very ill, and nearly gone when I took it and placed it in my bosom and cured it. I said the words over it, but after curing it I was very much exhausted until I got a cup of tea, and then I felt myself getting better.'

When requested to repeat the words, she affirmed they were all good words, and that it was in the name of the Trinity she did it; but she rehearsed the words in such a low voice, and indistinct pronunciation and so fast that it was impossible to follow.

In another Mull case a servant was sent for a means of cure to a woman supposed to have skill, whom she found in bed. She sat up, took a bottle containing water, put the mouth of it to her mouth, and said some words over it. The words were spoken in a low tone, and recognized to be 'good words'.

J. P. MacLean, *History of the Island of Mull*, vol. 1, 1923

TOBAR A' SGUARABHAIDH

Ann: Can you tell me about the people who came to collect
          watercress at Tobar a' Sguarabhaidh? Was it after the '45
          Rebellion?
Lachie: Yes, that was after the evictions because they were shifted
          from the glen to the shore and the only sustenance was salt
          meat, shellfish, and that sort of thing, and it developed into
          scurvy and there's a well up there. Tobar a' Sguarabhaidh is
          in Coire Gorm where *biolair* (watercress) grows.
Ann: And did they come from just in the glen or all over Mull
          for that?
Lachie: I'm not very sure. I know there was quite a demand when
          they found it was a cure. It was mostly started by the
          people around Dhiseig and Derryguaig. I can't remember
          when the last invasion they had was. People went up and
          they were given orders to kill any cattle beasts. They
          wouldn't stop to kill them, they couldn't be bothered and
          would just hock them – cut the big sinew out of the hind
          leg.
Ann: Why would they do that?
Lachie: That was the cow out of action. They couldn't breed or
          give milk, they would just die eventually, and somehow
          that was the start of the scurvy, and drove [the people] to
          the shore. They were never to cultivate anything above the
          shoreline, in fact the factor in Knock ploughed the shore at
          Knock to ensure that no-one would get shellfish or oysters.

                    Lachie Maclean, Knock. Recorded by Ann MacKenzie, 2001

THE MULL COMBINATION POORHOUSE

The Poorhouse was built in 1860 on five acres of land, about a mile
out of Tobermory on the Dervaig road, on land feued from the
estate of Aros. The sum of £20,000 was raised by local parish
councils to cover the cost. Known originally as the Combination
Poorhouse, it served the area of Mull, Morvern, Ardnamurchan,
Arisaig, Moidart, Coll and Tiree. It housed 140 people and
included a joiner's shop, a shoemaker and a smithy, as well as a

stable, byre, piggery and vegetable garden, from which some produce was sold. Much of the work was done by the inmates, and the salary list for the half-year May to November 1887 is of interest:

Governor and Matron	£50.0.0
Medical officer	£15.0.0
Chaplain	£7.10.0
Cook	£7.0.0
Porter (handyman)	£9.0.0
Secretary	£15.7.6
Servants assisting	£4.0.0

To avoid using the name Poorhouse, it was renamed Achafraoch House from a ruined croft in the area, and it later became known as Newdale.

The need for a poorhouse gradually dwindled, and the last inmates were transferred to Oban in 1922 as geriatric patients. The building fell into disrepair, and was finally pulled down in 1973, when the bulk of the rubble was transferred to Tobermory bay for the basis of the new distillery pier.

Between the time of its ceasing to function as a poorhouse and its final collapse into a ruin, it was used as residential flats occasionally.

SWRI History of Tobermory Folder, Isle of Mull Museum

THE FEVER HOSPITAL, SALEN

This was situated in a bog and held down by wires. It was inhabited by a roadman and his wife and one ward contained a hen and her brood of chicks. The late Willy Rowat was the only patient ever admitted to the hospital and that for only one night. In 1927 it was blown into the sea. Torrlochan became the Fever Hospital and the horse-drawn ambulance was kept there up to the last war 1939–45.

Charles Maclean, *The Isle of Mull: Placenames, Meanings and Stories*, 1997

ISOLATION HOSPITALS AND MEDICAL CARE

There was one in Salen, at the old pier, for illnesses like scarlet fever. Then it was at Torlochan where they had their own cows and byre far away from the road. There were also two horses and a wooden van, last seen at Gruline.

In Tobermory there was a poorhouse, *taigh nam bochd* – it was not much of a life for the wretches. Doctors travelled great distances and only the very ill – broken bones etc. – were taken to hospital in Oban.

Some people had skills with herbs. I gathered *trìbhileach* (trefoil) for two old women in Ulva Ferry which was used to prevent TB. *Copagan* (docken leaves) were rubbed on spots and *copagach Phàraig* (rat's tail) was chewed (leaf) and put on wounds to stop bleeding.

Roddy MacNeill, Salen, 1992

CURES: VIOLET LEAVES

Old women had knowledge . . . Jean Kennedy had broken her leg and something had happened to the skin on the outside of the leg. [Her grandmother] made a poultice of violet leaves and it was cured, a healing over of the ulcerated wound. [Mrs Kennedy (?), the grandmother, was from Tobermory.]

Ishbel Lloyd and Janet MacKeracher, Tobermory.
Recorded for An Tobar, 1996

A CURE FOR TRENCH FOOT

Ai . . . 'se . . . well . . . tha cuimhne 'am an déidh a' Chiad Chogadh bha Dan Dòmhnallach, bha e fuireach aig an Ard Dubh, agus bha esan 'sa Chiad Chogadh, agus tha fhios, 'san am sin bha gu leòr de na saighdearan a' faotainn dhachaidh le rud ris an abradh iad *Trench Foot* le bhith seasamh anns an uisge airson fada gu leòr. Agus thachair gu robh *ulcer* air a' chas aige 's cha robh e leighis idir.

Agus bha mo sheanmhair beò an sin, agus bha boireannach eile 's na Haunn a bha marbh roimhe sin, ach fhuair ise an eachdraidh seo bho'n a' bhoireannach. Thuirt i . . . tha cuimhne 'am gun robh m' *uncle* air ais as an Navy 's chuir i sìos e do'n chladach a faighinn crotal buidhe, agus tha fhios gun do chuir i crotal glas ann cuideachd, agus bha *dandelion* a' dol ann agus tha mi smaointinn gun robh *buttercup* agus bha bun nan copag a' dol ann, agus an duilleag eile, cuach Phàraig abradh sinn ris, agus bha iad a' cunntas gu robh

leighis mhór innte. *Well*, bha a h-uile nì air a ghlanadh 's 'ga chur
do'n phoit 's air a ghoil, agus bha i sin a' cur criomag de dh'ìm ùr
ann agus a' toirt goil air. 'S a-sin nuair a bha e fuarachadh bha i toirt
dheth an t-ìm agus 'se sin . . . agus rinn e feum do Dhan. Chiùr i e.

Ann: Who was the person who taught your grandmother these
           things?
Peter: She was dead before I knew her, but I heard of her – Ceit
           Rob,* that was her name.
Ann: Where was she from?
Peter: I don't know but she was in Haunn anyway, in a house in
           Haunn.

Translation: Ay . . . yes . . . well, I remember, after the First War, Dan
MacDonald, he was staying at Ard Dubh, and he was in the First
War and, you know, at that time there were a lot of soldiers getting
home with something they called Trench Foot from standing in the
water too long. And it happened that he had an ulcer on his foot
that wasn't healing at all.

And my grandmother was alive then, and there was another
woman in Haunn who had died before then, but she (my
grandmother) got this cure from that woman. She said . . . I
remember that my uncle was back from the Navy and she sent him
down to the shore to get yellow crotal, and, no doubt she put grey
crotal into it too, and dandelion was going in and I think buttercup
and docken roots, and the other leaf, *cuach Phàraig* we called it,
which was reckoned to have great healing in it.

Well, everything was cleaned and put into a pot and boiled, and
she was then putting a small lump of fresh butter in and bringing it
to the boil. Then as it was cooling she was taking off the butter and
it was that . . . and it did Dan good. She cured him.

                                              Peter MacLean, Dervaig, 2000

Note: Ceit Rob: Kate, daughter of Rob. Ceit Rob was a Mrs Robertson and
probably a MacKinnon before marrying.

                                        Note from Calum MacDonald, Tobermory

Crotal – 'much used in the Highlands for dyeing . . . a reddish
brown colour and so much did the Highlanders believe in the

virtues of *crotal* that, when they were to start on a journey, they sprinkled it on their hose, as they thought it saved their feet from getting inflamed during the journey. *Crotal coille* (*coille* = 'of the wood') is . . . still used by Highland old women in their ointments and potions.'

Cuach Phàdraig – Greater plantain, *Plantago Major*. Patrick's bowl or cup. Also called *Cruach Phàdraig*, Patrick's heap or hill. Another plant of the plantain family, *P. lanceolata*, ribwort, was called *lus an t-slànachaidh* 'herb of healing' and by children *bodaich dhubha*, 'black men', or *lus nan saighdearan* 'soldiers' plant'.

Dandelion – Peter does not use the Gaelic name *beàrnan Brìghde* ('notched leaf of St Bridget'). Used as a diuretic and for liver and kidney complaints.

Copag – dock. 'The roots were formerly used medicinally.'

Mainly extracted from John Cameron, *The Gaelic Names of Plants*, 1900

AILIG AN DOTAIR: DR MAXWELL AND THE PIGSKIN GRAFT

Bha Dotair Maxwell an Tobair Mhoire 's an am sin, agus chan eil fhios 'am có 'n duine a bha *accident* aige agus chaidh pàirt de'n chnuaic thoirt thar a bhathais. Thachair gun d'fhuair an dotair muc bheag agus mharbh iad i agus *stitch* e a' chnuaic aig a' mhuic air an duine seo agus ghabh e math gu leòr.

Translation: Dr Maxwell was in Tobermory at that time, and I don't know who the man was that had an accident and part of his brow was removed from his forehead. It turned out that the doctor got a small pig and they killed it and he stitched the pig's brow onto this man and it took right enough.

Peter MacLean, Dervaig, 2000

Dr Maxwell was a doctor in Tobermory until 1912. He was originally from Campbeltown. He lived in Tobermory above the Treasure shop and his consulting room and pharmacy were in the same building. He also started the lemonade factory at Barra Cottages. (See section on 'Mull and Iona Aerated Water Company', p. 117.)

Note from Calum MacDonald, Tobermory, 2001

Other remedies involving animal tissue were granulated pig's stomach as an ulcer cure and raw steak placed on cancer of the mouth (caused by using clay pipes).

Note from Calum MacDonald, Tobermory, 2001

Chicken (and fat), jelly from stag-horn, deer tallow, bacon as a cure for bruising, fish oil and skin, parts of the hare (gall, blood, skin, brain), goat (blood), frog (skin, burnt ashes, flesh), leeches (broth made from), mice (liver, whole body in concoctions), snails and slugs, snakes (head), spider, toads and worms were all used as cures.

Notes abridged from Mary Beith, *Healing Threads*, 1998

PIGS

Pigs were believed to cause ills as well as cure them. A bite from the animal was once said to induce cancer. On the other hand, an application of its blood was supposed to remove warts. Many legends about pigs may originate in their prehistoric status as a tribal totem. The Pig or Boar tribe would have had a taboo on swine-flesh except as a ceremonial dish at special feasts.

One of the tasks of the Children of Tuirenn in the legend that has been called the 'Gaelic Argonauts' was to fetch a magical pigskin renowned for curing all ills and having the rather agreeable knack of turning water into wine. Another task was to acquire the seven pigs of Easal, King of the Golden Pillars, which might be killed every night yet found alive and well again next day . . . Anyone who ate a part of the seven pigs could never again be afflicted with any disease.

Mary Beith, *Healing Threads*, 1998

ANIMAL TREATMENT IN EIGHTEENTH-CENTURY SCOTLAND

The last seven years of King William's reign 1695–1702, the 'dear years' of Scottish farming, were seven consecutive seasons of disastrous weather conditions when the harvests completely failed. This was followed, after a brief cycle of good years under Queen Anne by another harvest failure in 1709 which again produced famine. In the Hebrides during the whole of the eighteenth century, it has been estimated that one in every fourth crop was almost a complete failure.

Such recurring cycles of 'need years', i.e. years of food shortage and near famine, brought with them disease and epidemic outbreaks which were a constant and menacing burden at a time when animal care and breeding at its best was vitiated by dirt, ignorance and superstition. Ordinary safeguards, sanitation and prophylaxis were almost unknown and veterinary knowledge was of the most elementary kind.

In these circumstances, and under conditions where all rational conceptions of the causes of sickness and disease were absent, it is not difficult to see how easily the farmer, the cow-man and the stock-breeder came to be persuaded that these sicknesses and epidemics were the work of evil spirits.

An examination of the many forms of folk-cures and treatment which made up the stock of veterinary practice shows that they can be divided broadly into charm cures and amuletic cures. The distinction, however, lay not so much in the material of the cure, but in the method by which it was applied. The word charm, Latin *carmen*, means the chanting of a verse supposed to possess magical power, i.e. a spell. It has, however, a secondary significance denoting material things credited with magical properties, worn on or in close association with the object which it is designed to protect. The amulet belongs to this secondary classification of the physical charm. The words charm and amulet have thus a very wide connotation, and although they do not permit of a simple and rigid definition, it is sufficient, without qualification, to define them as follows. A charm operates indirectly and is usually expendable, while an amulet is permanent and operates directly, usually by contact.

The materials of the charm-cures covered a wide range and included remedies and prescriptions in the form of chants, pagan and christianised-pagan prayers; herbal remedies and natural elements such as salt, water and soot; and some cures derived from the belief in magical transfer. The active elements in amuletic cures were made up of natural objects, holed stones, rock crystal and coloured pebbles, and manufactured objects such as coins, ornamental pendants, prehistoric artefacts and various combinations of wool, wood and thread . . .

The belief that disease could be transferred to or from an object is very ancient and had a wide distribution. Transfer rites may take one of two main forms, transfer of a disease from an animal to an inanimate object such as water, stone or earth, and from one animal to another, occasionally through the agency of charm amulets. It was a commonly accepted belief among farmers all over Scotland that cattle ailments of every kind could be carried away and left on another farmer's land . . .

A blood disorder in black cattle known throughout Mull as the *black spauld* was thought curable by burying alive the first cow to be infected and driving the rest of the herd backwards and forwards over the pit . . .

Rock crystal balls, naturally perforated pebbles, worn, grooved and odd-shaped stones of unusual colour represent, because of their greater or more common availability, the amulet with the widest distribution. Although there appears to have been very little colour discrimination in the use of such stones, special significance seems to have been attached to the white or opaque variety.

Edward Lhwyd, keeper of the Ashmolean Museum, Oxford, in a letter written in 1699 from Linlithgow, records that in Scotland 'they have the *Ombriæ pellucidæ*, which are crystal balls or depressed ovals, which were held in great esteem for curing cattle; and some on May Day put them into a Tub of Water, and besprinkled all their cattle with the water to prevent being Elf-struck, bewitched, etc.' A fairly common name in the highlands of Scotland for a rock crystal ball used as an amulet was *Leug Loug* or *Leigheagan*, and in a letter to the Revd Robert Woodrow, quoted by Dalyell, the Scottish historian, it is defined as '*Leig*. Being a great pice of the clearest of cristall, in forme ane halfe ovall, near to the bigness of a littel hen eage: but I find it being of great use for peple that hes coues, being good for many diseases, they sik great monies for it, as forty punds Scots' . . .

As a rule, where these stones are used as cure amulets, they are either dipped in water, and the water given as a drench to the animals, or the affected part of the animal, or sometimes the whole animal, is rubbed with the stone . . .

The use of fire and smoke was frequently resorted to both as a preventive and antidote to cattle disease. Fires were made on Mid-

Summer Eve and Hallow Eve when animals were made to pass through the smoke to be rid of disease. In the event of violent epidemics, however, a special fire ritual known as 'raising needfire' was carried out . . .

Lengths of wool, thread and yarn in different compositions, combinations and colours, possessed more or less the same magical virtues. Known as 'wresting threads' and 'spraining strings', they were made up from single threads and multiple-ply yarns of various lengths. Red was the predominant colour, but often a thread of the same colour as the animal to be treated, was chosen. Where the treatment was for sprains and bone fractures, knots, either three, seven or nine, were tied in the middle and ends.

Thomas Davidson, 'Animal Treatment in Eighteenth-Century Scotland',
Scottish Studies, vol. 4, 1960

'TEIN EIKEN' (NEED FIRE)

Not only are Norse place-names in evidence in Mull, but Norse agrestic customs survive. The late Dr. George Henderson, Lecturer in Celtic in Glasgow University, describes the practice of Tein-eiginn, or rather tein eiken, in his invaluable work on 'The Norse Influence in Celtic Scotland'. Tein eiken or 'oaken fire' appears to have been performed to arrest the progress of disease in cattle. The fire was produced by the friction of an 'eiken' or 'oaken' wheel over nine oaken spindles.

Grimm gives an account of the practice of the art in Mull as late as 1767. In describing the practice of 'Tein eiken' at that period, Grimm states that, in consequence of a disease among the black cattle, the people agreed to perform an incantation although they esteemed it a wicked thing. They carried to the top of Carn Mór a wheel and nine spindles. They extinguished every fire in every house within sight of the hill. The wheel was then turned from east to west over the nine spindles long enough to produce fire by friction. If the fire were not produced before noon, the incantation lost its effect. They failed for several days running. They attributed this failure to the obstinacy of one householder who would not let his fires be put out for what he considered so wrong a purpose. However, by bribing his servants, they contrived to have them extinguished, and in that morning raised their fire. They then sacrificed a heifer, cutting in pieces and burning, while yet alive, the diseased part. Then they lighted their own hearths from the pile, and ended by feasting on the remains.

Words of incantation were repeated by an old man from Morven who came over as master of the ceremonies, and who continued speaking all the time the fire was being raised. This man was living a beggar at Ballochroy. Asked to repeat the spell, he said the sin of repeating it once had brought him to beggary and that he dared not say these words again. The whole country believed him accursed.

This curious practice disappeared from Mull long ago, and few people living on the island now know much more about it than its name; and even to that a different meaning is attached, 'Tein eiken' or 'Tein eiginn', meaning at the present day a dull, slow burning fire. 'Eiginn' has taken the place of 'eiken'.

John MacCormick, *The Island of Mull*, 1923

CURE FOR MURRAIN IN CATTLE, TEIN EIKEN/TINEGIN

Murrain in cattle had to be specially attended to. In Mull, about 1767, a hill-top was selected, within sight of which all fires were put out, and then the pure fire was produced by turning a wheel over nine spindles of wood until the friction caused combustion. Martin in his 'Western Tales' thus describes it:–

'The tinegin they used as an antidote against the plague or murrain in cattle, and it was performed thus – All the fires in the parish were extinguished, and then eighty-one married men, being thought the necessary number for effecting this design, took two great planks of wood, and nine of them were employed by turns, who by their united efforts rubbed one of the planks against the other until the heat thereof produced fire; and from this fire each family is supplied with new fire, which is no sooner kindled than a pot full of water is quickly set on it, and afterwards sprinkled on the people infected with the plague or upon the cattle that have the murrain.'

J. P. MacLean, *History of the Island of Mull*, vol. 1, 1923

SNAKE STONES (*CLACHAN NATHRACH*)

One of the commonest objects found in the debris from ancient dwellings of prehistoric man is a small circular whorl of stone or bone, perforated in the centre. These seem to have been used by the female of the species ever since wool began to be twisted into the form of thread by means of a spindle. The perforated whorls were used to give weight, and balance the wool she took off a stick called the distaff. Why then call them snake stones?

In my young days in Uig I knew an old woman who had six of these small steatite whorls tied on a string. What did she do with them? Whenever an animal like a cow or a sheep showed a swelling on one of its joints, it was taken to the house of this old crone for her to see and examine. She then took a bowl of water from a well and the whorls were taken off the string and immersed in the water, while an Abracadabra rune was said over them. I am sorry I don't know the rhyme. They were allowed to remain in the water for about an hour, then the old woman went with the bowl and washed the injured or swollen joint with the water, and she stated firmly that a snake had bitten and poisoned the joint. The remainder of the water was put into a bottle and the owner of the animal took it home and continued to bathe the injured joint with it for several days.

As a rule the animal recovered from its malady and no doubt the old lady got some gift from a grateful owner. The natives of this period got quite annoyed when you told them what these perforated discs were originally used for, and said that each was formed by a female snake twisting itself into a circular coil, and that twenty male snakes kept passing through the loop thus formed until they had left enough of the slimy mucus from their bodies to form the whorl, which was then discarded and left to harden in the sun – hence its efficacy against snakebite.

Donald Macdonald, *Tales and Traditions of the Lews*, 2000

THE MINISTER'S COW

I remember, one summer, Lena became ill and, as there was no vet in Mull at that time, we relied on those, like Colin Fletcher, who were knowledgeable about cattle, for advice. While the case was being considered, a suggested cure came from an unexpected source. Anna Dhubh, who was a frequent visitor at the manse, and who had probably the best store of traditional Gaelic lore and songs in all the parish, advised my mother what she should do: take the church key, go round Lena three times in a sunwise direction (deiseil), invoking the name of the Trinity. Millennia of religious beliefs and superstitions were encapsulated in this formula: the magical powers of iron, sun worship, the mystical power of some numbers and the comparatively recent Christian faith were all invoked to cure the minister's cow. I do not know for certain whether my mother followed Anna Dhubh's advice or if Colin had hit upon a cure, but I do know that Lena fully recovered.

Donald W. MacKenzie, *As it Was*, 2000

DOCKEN LEAVES AS A CURE FOR WHITE SCOUR

White scour in calves could be fatal and to cure this docken roots were boiled in a soup and given to the cattle. This treatment was used successfully in Mull and some of the other islands.

Archie MacCuish, Cailleach, 2000

Note: Bluestone was used as a preventative for this, by rubbing it on the green navel [remains of the cord] as the disease is said to enter the animal here.

Donald Campbell, Cailleach, 2000

BAT STONES

My being diverted as foresaid, occasioned that I had not some rare thing to send you. Receive a cylindrical white stone, and a little stone which they call bats' stones, because they heall horses of the worms they call bats. They grow out of a rock near the sea, in Mull.

John Maclean's postscript written to Robert Wodrow in relation to questions from Lhuyd's folklore questionnaire, written at Inveraray, April 1702

Revd John Maclean (Maighstir Seathan) Mull bard and genealogist who succeeded John Beaton as minister of Kilninian

J. L. Campbell and Derick Thomson, *Edward Lhuyd in the Scottish Highlands*, 1963

ANIMAL CURES

Ann: You had a story about your grandfather who had a sick mare who was dying and a woman neighbour who cured it.

Lachie: Yes. I don't know about it, whether it happened in Glenelg or Skye or Glenforsa when he came there, but I don't think it was Skye.

Ann: And what was the cure?

Lachie: The cure, there was something about a fire; about a fire and a thread, the girl was recruited to use this long thread, but what they did with it I'm not sure.

Ann: Was the thread a certain colour?

Lachie: No, I don't think I heard, but I know it was a girl that was chosen to take the thread; a long twine.

Ann: Some of them were plaited or different colours for different cures.

Lachie: I think knots were put in every so often and something was recited, and the medicine was given on one side. Everything had to move sunwise – *deiseil*, everyone attending the beast.

Ann: I think sometimes they sprinkled silver water, water that a coin had been placed in, on animals.

Lachie: Yes, that's right. At Goirtean Dhòmhnaill there is a well called Tobar a' Bhuinn Airgid, near Croggan, used for that purpose.

Ann: And what would they do, was the water just for animals?

Lachie: Yes, just for animals. I think it was sprinkling as far as I can remember, something about the head.

Ann: Did you use cures yourself when there were no vets here?

Lachie: Yes, when I started there were no vets here. One of the things I remember . . . some families were letting blood, particularly for louping ill, which is known as trembling nowadays. Triangular blades and knives were used to take off some blood and it definitely cured the beasts but the veterinarians were very against it when they came on the scene.

Ann: Was there a Gaelic name for louping ill?

Lachie: Yes, *a' chrith*.

Ann: Did people use plants for cures?

Lachie: I didn't. There was one period I can remember when
people were experimenting with cabbage. You fed a pig, it
was not a very nice cure, but it was for braxy – the beasts
used to die of it. They fed the pigs copiously with the
cabbage and the resulting excretion they gathered up and
put it in a bottle and bottled the hogs with it. Probably the
hogs were that scunnered with it they wouldn't eat it.

Ann: It didn't really work at all?

Lachie: No, they stopped, it was far too laborious. Another cure for
a sheep illness called *tart* in Gaelic [Dwelly – 'costiveness in
cattle'], a thirst or parch caused by eating dry foods like hay,
was to crush white whelks (Gaelic name *na gillean geala,*
'the white lads') and add it to a half bottle of sea-water, and
this was given to the sheep.

Lachie Maclean, Knock. Recorded by Ann MacKenzie, 2001

SMEARING

Smearing was on the wane by the end of the 19th century, and
practically ceased when it became compulsory by law in 1905 to
dip the sheep in chemicals twice a year. One farmer who
remembers his father smearing says he gave it up because it was not
only expensive but very slow work, much slower than shearing.
Another remembers her mother's consternation when the smearers
came into the house with blackened tarry hands. For the mixture
used was generally butter and archangel tar, oil or other grease. The
tar was measured into a barrel-half and the warmed butter or grease
poured into it, which made it softer to stir. Rather more grease
than tar was used; if the tar was too strong, it could burn the sheep's
skin and since the grease thinned the treacly mixture, it went
further. It took a gallon of tar, and about seventeen pounds of
butter to do about twenty-five sheep. In 1753 Kerrera butter was
selling at 4d (fresh) and 8d (powdered or salt) the pound. When the
price of wool was high and the cost of labour low, smearing was
practical, but when these conditions were reversed it was
superceded by a cheaper method.

Since the sheep had to be dry, the work was usually done under cover. In Islay there is a beautiful little 'smearing house', fern-covered, on one of the farms with arrangements for warming the mixture. Special benches were made on the farm, Bailemor had a particularly fine one. Similar to shearing benches, for which they were sometimes used, they were about four feet long, and eighteen inches high, on four legs. The bench top was the typical V-shape, twenty-eight inches at the broad end and ten inches at the narrow, with three rungs across. The worker sat astride the narrow end, with a bowl of the mixture at hand, sometimes clipped to the bench itself. If he was working on the back of the sheep her legs hung down between the rungs. With his forefinger he dipped into the mixture, and shedding the wool smeared the grease along the parting into the skin and the roots of the hair. The 'sheds' were made at one-inch intervals all over the body in a regular sequence. Since it was a slow business, working inch by inch, it was reckoned good if a man did a dozen sheep in one day. Often the work went on late into the October evenings, by the light of cruisie or candle. Smeared fleeces fetched slightly lower prices, but their extra weight usually compensated for this.

H. MacDougall, *Island of Kerrera: Mirror of History*, 1979

SMEARING SHEEP AT KNOCK

Ann: What treatments did they use for sheep?
Lachie: Well, there were no dips then, it was smearing they called it
           – *teàrradh* – and a good man could do twenty a day. They
           would shed the wool every four inches and put in tar, and
           a mixture of tar and butter and that sort of thing.
Ann: When did that stop? When did they bring in dipping?
Lachie: I'm not very sure, I think it was during the First World War
           or even the beginning of the First World War. Certainly at
           the end of the century there were sheds. I know quite a
           few farms where there was a shed called the smearing shed.
           The farm here, the Duke of Argyll used to take women in
           from Tiree to help prepare the smearing, the mixture.
Ann: Why did they come in from Tiree and why not the women
           from here?

Lachie: Well, I think they would have been . . . you see, the Duke ran Glen Cannel on a feudal system, and the people in the Ross were allowed to keep, as they called it, Leases at Will – they usually had a couple of cows and their followers; their followers would have to be summered,* and to pay for this, a man had to do a fortnight's work in the summer, and if he couldn't go his wife had to do it, a month's work, and if she couldn't go, the children went. They would have to do it all summer.

Ann: So that is why the women came, as part of the arrangement?

Lachie: It was part of . . . there's a word for this in Gaelic. I was going to say, there was one day, a storm as they left Tiree. It was three o' clock in the morning [when they arrived] at Knock, and the foreman of the women, twenty women, I think, the foreman went and said could they get a cup of tea? They were frozen stiff and wet. They [landowners/ factor] said, 'Well, this isn't the time of night to ask for tea. If they are going to get tea they might as well go and start rolling the wool in the shed.' And that was through Hugh MacNeillage's life time.

Ann: So that is really not that long ago then?

Lachie: No, that's right.

Lachie MacLean, Knock. Recorded by Ann MacKenzie, 2001

*Summered in Glen Cannel: By this arrangement the people in Tiree cut peats in Mull and stored them at Torr a' Bhlàir to ferry them back to Tiree.

Lachie MacLean, Knock, 2001

Chapter 6

PEOPLE AND PLACES

GENERAL HISTORY

Mull Names: *An Dreòllainn*

This term, used in the poetry of Iain mac Ailein, John Beaton, Alasdair Camshron and Anndra Mac an Easbuig, and in a variety of spellings, may have the meaning 'island of wrens' or be used to indicate a mystical land. In an Irish manuscript this place is given as somewhere near France but it is not usual at this period for such places to have exact locations. Later on these poetical names were attached to actual areas in Scotland: *Sorcha* with Ardnamurchan, *Ioruaidh* with Morvern, and *Tìr fo Thuinn* with Tiree.

> Notes from Ó Baoill, *Eachann Bacach and other Maclean Poets*, 1979,
> and from Calum MacDonald, Tobermory, 2001

Note: J. P. MacLean, in *A History of the Clan MacLean*, 1889, refers to Mull as having long been called 'The Island of Gloom'. I can find no reference to or explanation for this.

Aros Castle and the 'Moon'

Near Salen the ruins of Aros Castle can be seen standing on a sea cliff. This castle was once a seat of the Macdonalds, Lords of the Isles. In 1608 Lord Ochiltree, Lieutenant of the Isles for James VI, came in his flagship, the *Moon*, into Salen Bay. All the Island Chiefs were summoned to the Castle of Aros to meet him there; then all except two, whose loyalty was above suspicion, were invited to dine on the *Moon* and on arrival were informed that they were the King's prisoners. They were held prisoner for over a year, then those willing to sign the Statutes of Iona were allowed home. Eventually all signed. This is the last remembered use of Castle Aros.

> Otta F. Swire, *The Inner Hebrides and their Legends*, 1964

AN ACCOUNT OF THE DRESS, ARMOUR, AND GENERAL APPEARANCE
OF THE HIGHLANDERS AS SEEN IN MULL IN 1688

During my stay, I generally observ'd the men to be large bodied,
stout, subtile, active, patient of cold and hunger: There appear'd in
all their actions a certain generous air of freedom, and contempt of
those triffles, luxury and ambition, which we so servilely creep
after. They bound their appetites by their necessities, and their
happiness consists not in having much, but in coveting little. The
women seem to have the same sentiments with the men; tho' their
habits were mean, and they had not our sort of breeding, yet in
many of them there was a natural beauty, and a graceful modesty,
which never fails of attracting. The usual outward habit of both
sexes is the *pladd*; the womens much finer, the colours more lively,
and the squares larger than the mens, and put me in mind of the
ancient Picts. This serves them for a veil, and covers both head and
body. The men wear theirs after another manner, especially when
design'd for ornament, it is loose and flowing, like the mantles our
painters give their heroes. Their thighs are bare, with brawny
muscles; Nature has drawn all her stroaks bold and masterly: What
is cover'd, is only adapted to necessity, a thin brogue on the foot, a
short buskin of various colours on the legg, tied above the calf with
a strip'd pair of garters. What should be conceal'd is hid with a large
shot-pouch, on each side of which hangs a pistol, and a dagger; as if
they found it necessary to keep those parts well guarded. A round
target on their backs, a blew bonnet on their heads, in one hand a
broad sword, and a musquet in the other: Perhaps no nation goes
better arm'd, and I assure you they will handle them with bravery
and dexterity, especially the sword and target, as our veterane
regiments found to their cost at *Gille Crankee*.

> William Sacheverell, *An Account of the Isle of Man . . . with a Voyage to
> I-Columb-Kill*, 1702

Note: His account was written in 1688. Published 1702. He was one of the first
to attempt to salvage or to witness the salvage operations of the Spanish galleon
in Tobermory Bay. A short account of his visit to Mull is given in Eve Eckstein,
Historic Visitors to Mull, Iona and Staffa, 1992.

CLOTHING IN NINETEENTH-CENTURY MULL

Owing to the expense of shoes the country people made brogues out of skins which they tanned with the bark of a diminutive willow. They were sewed together with thongs of leather. Most of the people made a part of their clothing out of flax, which they heckled the best they could; they spun it out and wove it in the loom. Wool was used for the upper garments, which was first spun and then woven. The cloth was taken from the loom and then fulled. This was done by twelve or fifteen women, sitting round a table and rubbing hard against a board, squeezing and folding it till it had nearly acquired the requisite closeness and softness. The cloth and board were then placed on the ground, the women sitting around the cloth and working it with their feet, one against another. 'While they are engaged in this operation, they sing some Celtic songs in praise of Fingal or other heroes, often arriving at a high degree of enthusiasm.'

J. P. MacLean, *History of the Island of Mull*, vol. 2, 1925

EIGHTEENTH-CENTURY COTTAGES IN MULL

In the south-west, in Kintyre, Knapdale, and on the mainland as far inland as the Trossachs and up the coast of Argyll, with the neighbouring islands, the traditional type of building was quite different [to the cottages of the north]. The ends of the cottages were square and the gables were carried up as high as the ridge of the roof. The roof timbers rested upon the sloping walls of the gable ends. The appearance of such old cottages was much like a modern cottage, but it had the important difference that there was no flue in the gable-end. In Mull there still are a number of cottages of a hybrid type, with one end rounded and the other with a square gable. An old man told me that they used to be likened to a cow with a crumpled horn. These cottages stand in isolation but, further south, a long building with cow byre, living-room and sleeping-room joined to each other seems to have been usual. The partitions would be carried no higher than the walls.

I. F. Grant, *Highland Folk Ways*, 1961

Households in the Early Nineteenth Century

The cottages in Mull, which are generally disposed in little hamlets
without the least regularity, and which have been called showers or
sprinklings of huts, are extremely poor indeed, being little, if at all,
better than the cabins of the South Sea islanders, or the wigwams of
the American Indians. I have before described a Highland hut, but
those in the islands are much worse than any we had seen on the
main land. They usually consist, like the latter, of two wretched
apartments; one of which serves the family, like the cobbler's shop,
'for parlour, kitchen, and hall'. They are generally built of round
stones or pebbles, without any cement, and therefore not well
calculated to exclude the inclemencies of the weather; numbers in
the island are however built of earth, which I should think the
warmer of the two. The floor consists of the native ground, from
which the grass has been trodden by the inhabitants: these floors
are in general damp, and in wet weather quite miry.

In the middle of the floor, as was observed in the description of
the other cottages, they make a fire of peats, over which, by an iron
hook that comes from the roof, they hang their iron pot. In many
cottages there is a hole in the roof for the exit of the smoke, in
others not; but in every one the apartment is filled with smoke,
which finds its way out at the door: this opening, which is only
about five feet high, is generally closed by a door of boards, but in
many parts of Mull, particularly near Aros, they use a wicker door,
or osier hurdle.

In the side of the house is a small opening, about a foot square,
which serves as a window; this is sometimes closed by a thick pane
of glass, sometimes by a wooden shutter, which is left open in the
day. Round the sides of the room are ranged the little cribs for the
beds, which are generally composed of heath, with the roots placed
downward and tops upward. Above these beds are generally laid
some poles, and upon these some turf, which forms a kind of shelf,
where they can stow their lumber, and which likewise prevents the
rain that gets through the roof, from falling upon the beds.

The cottages are generally thatched with fern or heath, and
sometimes with straw; the thatch is kept on by ropes of heath
stretched by stones tied to the ends, which hang down the side of

the cottage . . . The roofs are often covered with turf instead of thatch.

The whole inside of these huts, and particularly the roof, is lined with soot, and drops of viscid reddish fluid, (pyrolignous acid, I believe) hang from every piece of wood supporting the roof. This is not the description of a single cottage more miserable than the rest, but applies pretty exactly to most of them, for we had the curiosity to enter and examine numbers of them. It is not surprizing that their cottages should be unhealthy, and particularly fatal to children, who require an air of great purity. I was informed by some of the ministers, that not more than one-third of the children born arrive at the age of twelve years, whereas in country situations in the north of England, it is not usual for one in twenty to die before that age. Little attention is here paid to the nursing of children, and the pernicious custom of giving them spirits when very young, no doubt hastens their destruction.

Thomas Garnett, *Tour through the Highlands and Part of the Western Isles*, 1811

THEFT OF GREENWOOD TREES, ULVA, 1720

Lachlan McIan Glinich, Ormsaig now in Torloisk – ane large oak tree. Forty hazel rungs John Mc Duill Vic Keallaich in Killviceoan – four large trees of oak and birch and eight kabbers of oak, birch and hazel. Adam McDugall – thirty houps and rungs

Duncan McArthur in Soribie – Two large ash trees and forty-eight rungs

Hector McQuarrie in Ulva – three trees and twelve hazel houps

SPERM WHALE WASHED ASHORE IN ULVA, JUNE 1722

The following parties were cited in connection with illegally disposing of whale oil belonging to the 'Admiral and his Deputies'. They were found liable at the rate of 2/6d per lb. of sperm oil:

Donald and Archibald MacQuarie in Kilvickeon

Archibald McArthur in Kilvickeon

Keallaich McQuarie in Ardnacallich

Angus McCurich in in Ardnacallich

John Stewart in Oskamull

Neill Rankin in Kilninian
John Gillies in Balligleich
John McErcher in Glacgallon
Alan McQuarie in Coulnish
Finlay McCormick in Gometra
John MacQuarrie in Baligartan
John McIllechalum Vic Lachlan in Balliachrach
Donald MacLean in Kilvickeown Vachtrach
Donald McEan Ghlinich
John McGhoyll Vic Keallich in Ardellum
Donald McGilespick in Arndnacallaich
Alex Lamont in Baliachrach, Gometra
Lachlan McEan Ghlineach in Torloisk

Calum MacDonald, Tobermory, 2001: from Inveraray Castle Papers

FRANCHISE AND LAW

The prestige of the laird was reinforced by the law. Only freehold-ers of land valued at a rent of at least £400 Scots were enfranchised in the unreformed parliament before 1832. In addition, lairds such as Lochbuie and Coll, whose estates had been erected into baronies, exercised civil and criminal jurisdiction over their tenants – a privilege ordinary freeholders did not enjoy. Although their power had been declining for many years, these baron courts had survived the abolition of major heritable jurisdictions in 1747. They were still used for the recovery of rent, keeping the peace at fairs, and settling civil disputes for up to forty shillings in value. Only thus could cheap, swift, and accessible justice be made available to the ordinary Scot living in the countryside.

A few landowners were also Justices of the Peace with a limited jurisdiction. Their main function was administrative: the main-tenance of roads, bridges, and ferries was part of their statutory duty, and, in addition, they supervised the revenue, adjudicated between masters and servants, and settled wages. Almost all the lairds in our area were Commissioners of Supply, although few bothered to attend the meetings. The primary task of these forebears of modern District Councillors was to settle the value of estates and to see that the cess, the land tax paid by all landowners, was collected. The Commissioners also supplemented the work of the JPs on communications and helped to supervise schools, maintain jails, and bring criminals to justice.

Nicholas Maclean Bristol, *Hebridean Decade*, 1982

RELIGION IN THE EIGHTEENTH CENTURY

The importance of religion at this period [1760s and 1770s] was very great and it is not possible to appreciate the changes in society in the Isles fully without examining the Church in Mull in some detail. The lairds, as owners of heritable property, were responsible for the upkeep of churches, provision of manses, and payment of the ministers' stipend. At the beginning of the decade, in spite of the fact that the Duke of Argyll was patron of all six parishes in the area, the local lairds and their tacksmen were the major lay influence in half of them. The dominance of the old hierarchy was equally evident in the ministry: two ministers were Macleans and a third was the son-in-law of the previous Maclean incumbent. The best example of the dominance of the old order was in Kilninian and Kilmore, the vast parish which comprised the whole of the north of Mull and had a population of over 2,000. In the year 1766 not a single elder was a Campbell.

The minister of Kilninian and Kilmore, Mr Alexander Maclean, had succeeded his father John Maclean, a distinguished poet, in 1756. Under the Macleans of Duart much of the land in the north-west of Mull had been held by the hereditary *aos dana*,* 'folk of gifts', and even in our era it had more than its fair share of poets and musicians. The high esteem in which they were held is demonstrated by the fact that at least two and perhaps three of the elders in the parish at the time of Mr Alexander's death in 1765 were the representatives of these hereditary functionaries. What is even more remarkable is that they were able to refuse the Duke's original nomination of Mr Alexander's successor. Maclean dominance in these parishes did not outlive the decade. It was eroded by the increasing interest in the Hebrides taken by the General Assembly. The post-Revolution Church had made considerable progress in the Highlands, but the change from episcopacy to presbyterianism had been gradual and had been carried out with less of the evangelical fervour seen in some other parts of the Gaidhealtachd. In 1761 there were only three churches in the six parishes: two in Kilninian and Kilmore, and one in Morvern. There were no manses, no parochial schools, and few glebes.

The Assembly was concerned over the spiritual state of the Hebrides. Few members, however, had first-hand knowledge of the islands, and the reports they received were thought to be contradictory. It was therefore decided in 1760 to appoint two ministers to visit the Hebrides. They made their report in 1761. In 1764 Dr John Walker, who had been employed by the Trustees of the Annexed Estates to visit the Western Highlands and Islands, was asked to report to the next Assembly on those places which had not been visited in 1760. It became clear from these reports that the Church's policy of 'weeding out' the Gaelic language had failed, and instead of uniting the nation under one language the reverse had happened. The people of the islands were being instructed in a language they did not understand, and to make matters worse, ministers had recently been ordered to preach in English. Dr Walker wrote: 'It is very doubtful if this measure really promotes the end it is designed to answer . . . when a minister confines his public instruction to a dozen or twenty persons which are sometimes all that understand an English sermon in a parish that contains two thousand; instead of conciliating [this] rather irritates the people . . .'

In 1767 the ban on Gaelic was repealed and the Scottish Society for Propagating Christian Knowledge (SSPCK) published the first Scottish Gaelic version of the New Testament. A large number of the works by seventeenth century Puritan divines were also translated into Gaelic. For many years these were almost the only Gaelic literature in print, but as the majority were unable to read, it was the influence these books had on the preachers that was to be important. Amongst a non-literate people who were highly sensitive to poetry and oratory, the influence of preaching cannot be overestimated, and the new interest in religion gradually replaced the Gael's affection for the tales and poetry which were passed around the fireside in winter.

Nicholas Maclean Bristol, *Hebridean Decade*, 1982

Note: Aos-Dàna, Men of Art. A collective noun which in medieval times denoted the learned orders of Gaelic society (literati). As early as 1707 it was used by Maighstir Seathan as a term applied to poets who composed in the vernacular, not classical Gaelic, and who held a position of some importance in a chief's household. A superior grade of demotic poets or bards. They were classed with the literate order of *filidh* (classical Gaelic poets).

Note from Donald W. MacKenzie, 2001

PRESS-GANGS IN MULL

The press-gangs employed by the English, for the purpose of forcing men into the army, were composed of desperate characters. They were the terror of all poor men, but well supported by the government and its officers. The infamy of the navy had reached Mull, for half a dozen maimed seamen who had been impressed lived there, and had told of their sufferings. William MacLean and his sons, Ranald and Roderic, were successful fishermen in Mull. One night the father, in company with other fishermen, prepared to smuggle some whisky from a neighboring island to the mainland. On reaching the beach they were terrified by the arrival of two boats that belonged to a ship of war in the offing, and had come for the purpose of impressing the fishermen along the coast. MacLean counseled his friends to warn at once all the fishermen to meet him at a given place to devise means for protection. He went to his own house and armed his two sons with broad-swords, and repaired to the trysting-place, where fifty men and boys were assembled. MacLean, whose terror had given place to indignation, counseled to cut off the gang, which numbered thirty men, fully armed, and led by a lieutenant. 'It is well said,' replied one of his neighbors. 'You lead us, William.'

Boys gave the report that the gang had broken into a house, and were terrifying women and children. The fishermen, led by the undaunted William, crawled upon their hands and knees, and gradually surrounded the house. At a given signal, the fishermen sprang to their feet, and in less than half an hour annihilated the entire gang. The fishermen retired to the hills, and William called upon the old laird, an old soldier, and told him what had taken place. The laird was not at all displeased, but, being apprehensive of the consequences, advised William to leave the island with his family, and gave him money to bear his expenses.

Next morning the brig signaled for the return of the boats. The commander landed, and was soon informed by Sir Archibald MacLean of the fate of the press-gang. 'I'll shoot every one of the murderers!' exclaimed the commander. 'So you may,' replied Sir Archibald, coolly, 'if you can catch them.' 'I'll land my whole ship's company, and hunt them to the death.' 'How many men have you, sir?' 'A hundred.' 'You will require a thousand,' responded Sir Archibald. 'The whole island is in arms, and mind, sir, these men are Highlanders, men who would rather fight than eat at any time.' 'Are there no civil officers here?' 'None. When a man does not behave himself he is expelled the island, and if he returns he is killed and no question asked.' 'How can you live in such a community? What safeguard have you for your life or property?' 'Safeguard enough. These wild folks are my kinsmen; there is not one of them who would not risk his life to serve me.' 'If such be your influence, then, in the king's name, I command you to produce the murderers of my boats' crews.' 'Name them, sir, and so I will.' This was the last attempt at impressment in Mull during that war with Napoleon. Taking the advice of Sir Archibald, William embarked his wife and two sons in a fishing boat, and, after much privation, landed on the island of Pomona, the mainland of the Orkneys. Here he settled upon a small farm, and changed his name to Bruce. He went upon several whaling expeditions, and was quite successful.

Quoted in J. P. MacLean, *A History of the Clan MacLean*, 1889, from *The Celtic Magazine*, vol. 7, copied from the *Boston Traveler*, 1858

THE FAMINE OF 1846 AND 1847

The great famine of 1836–7 did not awaken the nation to the real cause of this disaster, nor was the nation aroused to take preventive measures against a future recurrence. The people continued to be huddled together in motley groups upon patches of barren moors, precipices, and out of the way corners upon the sea-shore, exposed to all the casualties of the season, with no encouragement for improvement; and all of these tenants at the will of the lairds. This was a favorite scheme and adopted by all the Highland proprietors, with one or two exceptions. The potatoe had become the principal staple of food, and this substance was raised upon these most unsuitable places. Then came the potatoe failure, followed by a famine in 1846 and 1847, much greater than that of 1836–7. The severest calamities were felt along the western coasts of Argyleshire, Inverness-shire, and Ross-shire on the main-land; the islands of Mull, Tyree, Coll, the Small Isles, and the chain of Islands from the Butt of Lews to Barra-head. The cry of famine was heard beyond the shores of Great Britain.

The season of the potatoe failure was a period of woeful distress to the major part of the people. Those who could, fled from their homes and sought asylum in foreign lands. Emigrant ships arrived off the shores of Mull and carried away hundreds of the crofters, and landed some in Canada and others in Australia that they might hew out homes for themselves in the wilderness. Many succeeded and others died broken-hearted. The mass that remained, for many days, was forced to subsist upon roots and shell-fish.

J. P. MacLean, *History of the Island of Mull*, vol. 2, 1925

THE POTATO FAMINE

There are still many tales of the woe-begone condition of the islanders about the time of the great potato failure. Some people had to subsist for days upon roots and shellfish. Relief committees were started, and employment in the construction of roads was found for a large section of the people. Many of the cross roads in Mull were made by the needy, who wrought under relief committees . . . we can easily imagine what terrible privations must have been endured by a large section of the 10,064 that are returned in 1841, when their staple article of food, the only article of food of many, was a complete failure. In places where there are now very few people, or none at all, there were before the era of the potato failure large populations.

John MacCormick, *The Celtic Monthly*, vol. 25, 1917

THE POTATO FAMINE

In the same parish, the families of four cottars had been recently ejected from the farm of Ardvergnish, and two of these had taken refuge in Tobermory. I went to see them. They had taken two empty rooms in the upper flat of a back house. In one of the families there were ten children, several of whom were in the room when I entered. The mother, a woman of very respectable appearance, was making thin porridge for their supper; they had got a similar meal in the morning, and this was their whole diet. The children were very ragged, almost naked, and on this account they could not go to the Gaelic School, though admission had been offered them free of charge. In the other family there were a wife and two young children. The rooms were very bare of furniture, containing only a few things which they had carried with them over the mountains. The little infant in the second family was sleeping on the floor. The woman said that her husband had been working some time in Glasgow, that he came home last summer ill with small-pox, and had scarcely recovered when this new disaster was prepared for him. The farm on which these families lived as cottars was let at Whitsunday, soon after which time they were ejected, and their cottages pulled to the ground. For six weeks they lived in a tent during the day, but as many as could be accommodated were provided with beds by the neighbours at night. The cold of winter, however, at length drove them out: one family had gone to Greenock, another was living with relatives, and two, as we have seen, sought shelter in Tobermory. Both of the men, at the time of my visit, were absent at the herring fishing. As soon as they had seen their families safely housed, they trudged away back to Kilfinichen, to make the most of the fishing season, which had been so rudely and cruelly interrupted by their ejectment.

The results of these evictions, in a general point of view, are injurious in the extreme. They accumulate poverty and destitution in heaps. Instead of the poor being spread over their respective parishes, they are thrown together in villages, where there is no property, no agency, no resources adequate to cope with their necessities, and where, upon any unusual pressure, there is nothing but the most appalling and unmanageable destitution. The population of Tobermory has increased, in a short time, from a few families to 1,400 souls; and this increase has probably resulted more from the influx of ejected paupers and cottars from the outlying parts of the island than from the wholesome influences of prosperity.

Robert Somers, *Letters from the Highlands on the Famine of 1846*, 1848

There was a warrant search on the 24th of February, 1847, in Dervaig for a young man and his sister, who lived with their grandmother – Callaich Uistean. They had been found with three carcasses of sheep that had been killed the night before and were belonging to the Ardow (Ardhui) estate. The owner of the estate had requested that they be dealt with severely and it is probable that they were sent to Botany Bay.

Calum MacDonald, Tobermory: notes from Quinish Estate log book in Mull Museum (written by Donald Campbell, Agent to MacLean of Coll)

EVICTIONS IN MULL

I know generally the same process of cleaning away the inhabitants took place in Mull, as in our island, but not so drastically, or sudden. A slow ruthless process of eviction, still fully as effective, any one visiting the Island can fully verify this, by the remains of houses seen everywhere, and all the Lairds in it, with very few exceptions, were equally guilty in this, and as to the fact of the poor people being compelled to work at roads, drains and even piers, for a scanty allowance of the very meal and other victuals, sent gratis from America, to be distributed to the poor, to keep them alive. When these supplies came, lairds and factors got their hands into them, and compelled the people to work at improving their lands for a starvation supply of this very meal; and in some parts of Mull a large amount of drains, roads, and other improvements, were effected on the lands occupied by the factor, for this meal. Where estates were under trustees, the whole costs were demanded by the factors who pocketed the money. What grinding oppression the people were subjected to in those days, passes description, and where yet, although progress has been made, a great part of its remains exist, and will exist.

John Johnston, Coll, 1918, quoted in J. P. MacLean,
History of the Island of Mull, vol. 2, 1925

THE CLEARANCES

In many parts of Argyllshire the people have been weeded out none the less effectively, that the process generally was of a milder nature than that adopted in some of the places already described. By some

means or other, however, the ancient tenantry have largely disappeared to make room for the sheep-farmer and the sportsman. Mr.
Somerville, Lochgilphead, writing on this subject, says, 'The
watchword of all is exterminate, exterminate the native race.
Through this monomania of landlords the cottier population is all
but extinct; and the substantial yeoman is undergoing the same
process of dissolution . . . The work of eviction commenced by
giving, in many cases, to the ejected population, facilities and
pecuniary aid for emigration; but now the people are turned adrift,
penniless and shelterless, to seek a precarious subsistence on the
sea-board, in the nearest hamlet or village, and in the cities, many of
whom sink down helpless paupers on our poor-roll; and others,
festering in our villages, form a formidable Arab population, who
drink our money contributed as parochial relief. This wholesale
depopulation is perpetrated, too, in a spirit of invidiousness, harsh-
ness, cruelty, and injustice, and must eventuate in permanent injury
to the moral, political, and social interests of the kingdom . . .'

Alexander Mackenzie, *A History of the Highland Clearances*, 1883

OPPRESSION ON QUINISH ESTATE

So far as the evidence affords, one James Forsyth stands out in the
portrayal of the dark picture. Of the evictors, in Mull, he was the
most ruthless, and apparently devoid of human sympathy, or mercy,
absolutely without moral perceptions. He was not a native but a
stranger who gained valuable estates by his money. Hardly had he
been in possession until he commenced evicting, nor did he cease
until he had cleared off several townships. Some idea of this man,
and the condition of the people of north-western Mull, may be
gathered from the testimony of Lachlan Kennedy, before the
Crofters Commission, at Tobermory, August 10, 1883: 'Our
grievances may be said to have commenced when the late Mr.
Forsyth bought the Quinish estate in 1857. Before collecting the
second half-year's rent we received intimation that our rents were
to be raised. In the course of a few years it was raised a second time,
so that now we pay fully £1 more rent for our crofts than we did
when he got possession of the estate, besides being deprived of
other privileges which we then possessed. There were at that time

twenty-seven crofters in Dervaig possessing in common the hills of Monabeg and Torr, which enables us to keep fifty-six cows, one bull, and twenty-eight horses. Mr. Forsyth, shortly after entering on possession of the estate, called a meeting of us at Dervaig, at which meeting he asked us to hand him over Monabeg for the purpose of improving it, promising to restore it at the end of three years.

'We could not at the time see our way to refuse this seemingly reasonable proposal. We trusted him with full confidence on account of the implicit faith rightfully placed by us in his predecessors in this estate. It may be mentioned that this agreement was never committed to paper. During these three years Mr. Forsyth got all the ploughable ground on Monabeg turned. At the end of this period he requested half a dozen of us to appear before him at his own residence at Sorn (five miles from Dervaig), which was done. But now he had another proposal for our consideration. Instead of restoring the Monabeg on the previous terms as we expected, he could only do so on condition that we should take it on a nine year's lease at a yearly rent of £80, besides spending annually £19 in improving the soil with lime.

'This offer was refused, and we regarded it as tantamount to denying our rights to Monabeg, which turned out to be the case. Two years after taking possession of Monabeg for improving purposes, Mr. Forsyth took from us the hill of Torr, without compensating for it in any other manner or altering our rents; and now, as Monabeg was at this time in his own hands on aforementioned conditions, we had no place for grazing our cattle and horses. Having got us into this fix, Mr. Forsyth, seeing our straitened circumstances, sent his manager with the proposal that he would buy our cattle. Those among us who had no alternative gave him our cattle at his own offer, which was far below the current prices, as stocks sold by some of us the same year fetched prices equal to that given by him for our cows. It may be mentioned that one of us, who had wintering for one cow but no summer grazing, craved a summer grazing, and was told by the factor to cut her throat. After being deprived of Torr hill we tried to dispose of our horses at the first market, but the day being extremely wild, dealers were prevented from attending. We were thus compelled either to give our horses away at a mere nominal price, or make further attempt to get grazing from Mr. Forsyth. We chose the latter alternative, but were sadly disappointed. We next day went to Sorn, saw Mr. Forsyth's factor, and made our request, to which he answered by telling us to go and drown them, showing at the same time how we were to do it. As the last and only resource, the horses were turned loose on the neighboring farms.

'Naturally some of them wandered to Mr. Forsyth's grounds, where two of them were afterwards found drowned in ditches and two were found badly cut as with knives. With the loss of our horses the crofts became of much less value to us. We could no longer manure them in a proper manner, and consequently their produce decreased. At that time each crofter could have four or five bolls of meal off his own croft yearly, while at present such a thing is unknown among us. The expense of working our crofts, in so far as we are compelled to engage horses for ploughing, harrowing, and carting manure, is considerable. One of our small crofts, will take between 30s. and 40s. to the said work. Peat we have to carry these 1¼ mile on our back, or pay 1s. 3d. for each cart, which the most of us cannot afford.'

On being cross-questioned, Lachlan Kennedy further added that Forsyth bought Quinish off the laird of Coll (Hugh, Fifteenth MacLean of Coll), where all were quite happy under Coll, and the rent paid him was a little over £3, including pasture on Monabeg and Torr but now the rent, without the pasture was £4,10s. besides very heavy taxes; that the crofters had been reduced from twenty-seven to thirteen, some of whom had left, and others had become poor; that now there are no poorer people in Argyleshire; the land of Monabeg was good, and instead of improving it he had spoiled the pasture, and some of the ground has not as yet yielded grass; and all the world knows it was a bad day for Dervaig when the laird of Coll sold it.

J. P. MacLean, *History of the Island of Mull*, vol. 2, 1925

OPPRESSION AT DERVAIG

On the same day at Tobermory, before the said Commission, John Campbell was examined, and first presented the following statement; speaking in behalf of the villagers of Dervaig:

'That the true nature of our statement be thoroughly understood, we deem it necessary to divide our say into two parts. The first part embraces our history from the creation of our village about eighty years ago or so up to about 1857 or so, and the second part will bring up the history from the latter date up to the present.

'During the first fifty-seven years or so of our history we had a garden, a croft, a house and a piece of land capable of grazing twenty-six horses and fifty-two cows or so – in other words, two cows and one horse for each house – for the sum of £3, 14s. 6d. or so on an average yearly as rent for the whole. This was under the McLeans of Coll. Our houses were built by and at the expense of our forefathers. Everything rolled on smoothly during this long period on both sides; no complaints, no cause for the lairds factors and tenants pulling together. About the year 1856 we found ourselves out of the hands of the Coll family into that of an individual calling himself James Forsyth Esq., of Dunach, a total stranger to us. In the spring of 1857 he sent a message to our village that he wanted to see all the heads of our families in Sorn, at his house on the adjoining estate. We attended; he informed us that he was going to give us new titles to our holdings in Dervaig; that he intended to improve our condition or circumstances, if we would sign the paper that he presented to us. Unwilling to question him, we signed a paper that we were agreeable to accept of the new titles (as we thought). He assured us that we would be better off under the titles that he was going to give us more than before. In a short time after this we received our new titles in a printed form. His very first step in the direction of improving our condition or circumstances took the shape of a demand that he wanted a portion of our moor for three years, for (as he said) the purpose of improving it for our benefit. To agree to his demands meant the loss of some of our cattle; rather than offend him, we handed over the portion of our moor that he wanted.

'At the end of the three years, instead of handing us back this piece of land as he promised, he wanted about £40 rent for it, over and above what we were paying formerly. To make a long story short, we saw at once that we had not a gentleman to deal with; it flashed across our minds that this was the same individual who cleared off about thirty-seven families off an adjoining estate before and who did not consider it a sin to compel the poor unfortunate people to hand over to him such of their cattle as he wanted, and that on his own terms; and to prove that he was sailing under his true colors towards us, he made his cowherd gather our cattle into a corner in a certain day, sending a message to us at the same time that he wanted us at the spot where our cattle was gathered by his orders. We went and met him. He told us that he wanted to buy our cattle. He tendered his offer under the circumstances. We handed over our cattle to him at his own offer. We could not help ourselves; we had no means to keep our cattle till the drovers would come around. Such is a sample of the improvements that we received at the hands of James Forsyth, Esq. of Dunach. Were it not that he took leave of this world and all that is in it, no one can say where his improvements would end. His son, our present laird, completed what his father left undone in a masterly style. He has carried out his father's designs to a fraction as far as the management of the estate is concerned, not forgetting our new titles to our holdings. Between father and son, our holdings are at the present day about 22s. or so more than we paid McLean of Coll. Then we had two cows and one horse; today we have neither cow nor horse, and yet we pay an average of about £4,16s. or so, for what?, for about two acres of the worst land in Scotland, stony, shallow, and of a very inferior kind, turned over for the last eighty years, and so constantly it is not capable of paying the laborers who turn it over, far less yielding anything for the rent that our laird exacts from us.

'We consider it our duty to bring before the Commissioners the kind of laws that we are compelled to work under. Before doing so, it may not be out of place to mention that we have the following named officials engaged in the farming line formerly. Our catalogue embraces the parish minister, police inspector, poor inspector, collector of rates, registrar, and postmaster. Some way or other we never hear any complaints on the part of the above individuals against our lairds. Our parish minister has a croft that belonged to the village formerly in his possession; our laird is chairman of the parish School Board. We cite a few instances or cases to show the kind of crop we as taxpayers reap at the hands of our local government. In the first place, our School Board saddled this part of the parish with a new school that cost about £1000 sterling, and all the children attending the costly school at present are only about fifteen; the rest of the children in our locality are receiving their education in a school that is entirely under the control of the parish minister. This school was built about thirty-two years ago specially for the use of girls only, and free of charge of any kind or fees. Some way or other it is now open for boys as well as girls; fees are charged, but on a lower scale than the public school. How this change came about we don't know; we always understood that the terms on which the teacher in our public school was engaged was that he was to receive the fees and government grant along with a certain amount of salary. The fact that our public school is without a teacher at present suggests the very pertinent question, Has the opening of the school under the parish minister anything to do with his disappearance. Possibly the chairman of our School Board can answer this question better than any of us. We think it rather strange to see the children belonging to the Established Church in one school at reduced fees and the children of other denominations attending the public school. Whether the fact that the late teacher was a Free Churchman, and the present school mistress of the other school is a member of the Established Church, has had anything to do with it or not we cannot say. Our school and Parochial Boards are entirely in the hands of our betters, and may go a certain length to explain how our interests are looked after. A poor unfortunate who finds himself under the necessity of applying to the Parochial Board for relief has to accept such relief in the shape of goods and should the quality be plaster of Paris, there must be no grumbling. We pay our rates in coin, and we think that those receiving relief should get it in cash.

'Our inspector of poor holds many appointments. He will not give out door relief to any one in our village who occupies a house in it unless all interests are surrendered to him first. Not long ago a poor man, who was what we call well-gathered, took ill. Some way or other the inspector stepped in, procured medical attendance, nursing, etc., for this poor man, and was very attentive till the man died, when the inspector sold some of the poor man's effects by public auction on the street, acting the auctioneer himself. Whether this was done in his official capacity as inspector of poor or not we cannot say, but we have every reason to believe that this man was not in receipt of parochial relief at the time he took ill. We have no doubt, that he can give a satisfactory account of this business, but we think it strange that he should be acting the part of a broker or commission agent between our laird and a purchaser of this poor man's house. We know that he has been acting in this capacity in more than one case. Keeping in view the fact that our laird claims absolute right to our houses, we cannot understand how our inspector of poor meddles with these things unless he and our laird are in partnership. We consider that everything of this kind of work should be done above board. We cite a parallel: an old maid bordering on ninety years, and who finds herself under the necessity of applying for outdoor relief, has been told to walk into the poorhouse or want relief. Surely this poor old woman was equally entitled to receive relief as the other poor man's case that we have cited. It may be explained that this old woman would not part with her interests: this may account for his refusal to assist her, but does it justify it? Lately an old man applied for relief; before getting it he had to surrender his interest in his house.

'No one under the sun understands this sort of work but our inspector of the poor and our laird. Although our population are decreasing daily, our poor rates don't follow suit. This may be explained by the fact that Tobermory many years ago became a harbour of refuge for many that were evicted from different places, including Ireland, leaving it at the present day a seat for propagating paupers. Without public works or any other of a general kind, many of the inhabitants, through no fault of their own, are thrown on our pauper roll. Within the last sixty years or so our parish has lost 327 families of the crofter class, leaving upwards of forty townships empty at this moment. Out of twelve estates, eleven are without crofters; the twelfth, the Torloisk, has adopted another method of getting rid of its crofters – thirty-two of them have been crushed out of their holdings to enable the estate factor and others to extend theirs. Volumes could be written in connection with these clearances of a character that would not reflect much credit on those who were the sole cause of them.

'Although our loch, rivers, and streams teem with salmon and trout, and our glens, bens, and straths abound with game, we cannot shake hands with any of our old acquaintances in the passing by on account of game, trespass, fishery, and criminal laws; all other laws are almost a dead letter in our parish excepting our laird and factor laws. If any of us want a trip to Edinburgh on the cheap, we have only to look at either loch or glen and away we go. We are obliged to put up with too many laird laws. We cannot see how we can better ourselves unless we break the law of the land. We have several kinds of grievances growing among us; years ago a party came among us stating that his object was to make our condition known to the public of Britain. Without the slightest hesitation on our part, we told him all about our circumstances; fancy our surprise to find our village reported by him as dying a natural death, with the rider that we could not die too soon in the opinion of the writer.'

Glengorm Castle, is a product of James Forsyth. In order to build the house and lay off the ground he cleared off a great number of families. An old lady, who died in 1917 at the age of ninety-four, and who had been employed about the place, narrated that when the house was almost ready for occupation, Forsyth rode up to the door, and when about to enter, a bat flew out of it and into his face. Those with him remarked that the bat was the soul of one of those he had evicted; that it was a curse on him, and that he would never sleep a night in that house. He never did sleep in it. Soon after the incident he was taken ill, and died before its completion. Simply a narration of a nemesis and a degenerate.

J. P. MacLean, *History of the Island of Mull*, vol. 2, 1925

DATES OF EVICTIONS IN THE NORTH OF MULL

1829	Ensay – Proprietor *Eóghainn Mór Alasdair* (Hugh MacCaskill)
1830	Sunipol, Arine – Proprietor *Eóghainn Mór Alasdair* (Hugh MacCaskill)
1832	Inniveagh – Proprietor *Eóghainn Mór Alasdair* (Hugh MacCaskill)
1847–51	Ulva – Proprietor Francis Clark
1849	Glengorm – Proprietor James Forsyth
1857–58	Persecution in Dervaig
1858	Druimnacroish village (old name Torr Aint) – Proprietor James Forsyth
1858	Aintuim and Coireachan – Proprietor James Forsyth
1859	Ardmore, Tobermory – Proprietor Mr Steele
1867	Glac Gugairidh – Proprietor Captain George MacKay
1867	Crackaig – Proprietor Captain George MacKay

Notes from Calum MacDonald, Tobermory, 2001

AN CORRACHAN

Before the 1748 Act the control of lawbreakers was maintained by
the chiefs. Lord Teignmouth refers to the Laird of Coll, 'on the desolate brow of a steep ridge beyond Bellachroy (Dervaig) we passed
a small hamlet of about a dozen small cottages called "Siberia".'

On asking one of the inhabitants wherefore they chose so dreary
a situation for their abode, he replied, looking archly, 'Coll knows
the reason very well'. This was in fact the place to which the Laird
of Coll banished his people from the island when guilty of
smuggling and other crimes deserving exile.

They had no alternative but to accept this punishment or to fly
the country. A proof of the practical continuance under the control
of law of the heritable jurisdiction of the chiefs.

Calum MacDonald, Tobermory, 2001 (notes from Lord Teignmouth,
The Coasts and Islands of Scotland and the Isle of Man)

THE NAPIER COMMISSION

Lachlan Kennedy, the carrier in Dervaig in the north of Mull,
explained that the people had built their own houses with stone
and lime in the village and roofed them with thatch, but by 1883
most of the houses were slated. Each householder had a garden of a
quarter of an acre, a croft and the hills of Monabeg and Torr as
pasture, and between them they were able to keep fifty-six cows, a
bull and twenty-eight horses. Intent on 'improvement' the new
owner took Monabeg in order to plough it up, promising to give it
back in three years, but the rent he wanted was far too high for
them. Then he took away the hill of Torr and they, without grazing,
had to sell their animals to his manager at nominal prices. Without
stock their standard of living and way of life changed:

'We could no longer manure in a proper manner and our
produce decreased. At present a crofter can have little meal off his
own croft. The expense of working our crofts, engaging horses for
ploughing, harrowing and carting manure is considerable. One of
our small crofts will take between 30s. and 40s. for the said work.
Peats we have to carry 1¼ mile on our back, or pay 1s.3d. for each
cart which most of us cannot afford.'

The other delegate for Dervaig, John Campbell, was an ex-soldier who had been through the Crimean War and the Indian Mutiny. When he was asked if many young men from Mull joined the army today, he replied, 'Bless you, no. There are no men in our parish – nothing but sheep and game.'

Meeting in their Temperance Hall in Salen to prepare the case they would put to the Royal Commission, the crofters and cottars on the Glenforsa estate were asked a series of questions:

'How many of you present have enough of land?'

Not a hand was raised.

'How many are there who have not enough of land?'

All hands went up.

'How many on the estate of Glenforsa have enough land to live on?'

'Two.'

'How has it come about that there are so few holding land enough, and so many having so little?'

'The people have been cleared off excellent and extensive lands and sent hither and thither, some settling in Salen, some in Tobermory, some in Glasgow and some in foreign lands.'

As an example, they said the island of Ulva had had a population of 859 in 1841. (That was the population of the parish, whereas the island contained 604 people in 1837.) Lachlan MacQuarrie, now 64 and living in Salen said there were now on the island only the proprietor, and his three shepherds, besides two or three cottars. At first he himself had a large croft on Ulva at Ormaig but someone offered more rent and he had to move to a smaller croft at Cragaig. Evicted from there with his wife and three young children he had taken the couples of his house and built a hut with them on the shore. It was so close to highwater mark that the proprietor on seeing it gave him a house at £3 a year at Caolos and he had lived by catching lobsters. When he left there it was of his own accord.

'Yes, I remember when Ulva belonged to the MacQuarries (until 1835). People were comfortable then, and they were comfortable in my time. It is a pretty fertile island for raising oats and potatoes but there is no crop at all now, except what the laird grows himself.'

Fortunately, the Royal Commission's journey along the west

coast was blessed with fine weather day after day until they reached Mull. Then a great storm blew up with winds of hurricane force, driving rain and even sleet – all this in early August! The meeting they had arranged in Iona had to be cancelled because there was no chance of landing but this was almost the only disappointment on their cruise. They had sailed 1100 miles on board the *North Star* with Captain Ritchie, whom they had learned to regard as a very fine seaman. Strangely, one of the witnesses who appeared before them at Tobermory was John MacDonald, master mariner, who had been their pilot on the *Lively*. No mention was made of that unfortunate ship. Instead the Commissioners took the opportunity to enlist the exceptional knowledge he had of western harbours and record in detail what he advised on the best places to build piers and the size of boats that would be needed to allow west coast fishermen to compete on equal terms with the east coast men.

A. D. Cameron, *Go Listen to the Crofters*, 1986

THE CROFTER COMMISSION

I have walked over whole tracts of desolate country. I remember in Mull walking over such a tract with a landed proprietor who was one of the best – and the best are always those that speak Gaelic. We were passing through an old ruin of perfect desolation, and he said, 'I thank Heaven that I have not to think of that desolation on my death-bed.'

Professor John Stuart Blackie, recorded in the 'Evidence of the Crofter Commission', J. P. MacLean, *History of the Island of Mull*, vol. 2, 1925

COMMUNICATIONS: EARLY FERRIES IN NORTH MULL

Fishnish to Lochaline: Previously known as the Balemeonach to Kilcolmcill ferry, this grew in importance with the droving of cattle between Morvern and Mull from about 1760 and until the mid nineteenth century. The Mull landing was at a jetty built before 1790. It still remains about 500 yards south of the present-day ferry slip. In 1847 an improved pier was built at the Loch Aline landing close to the present ferry slipway. Fares in 1828 were: passengers 1/-, a bull 2/-, and a cow 6d.

Ardnacross to Rhemore (Morvern): This crossing of the Sound of Mull at its narrowest point was probably in use long before it is mentioned in 1794. It was still running in 1836. The Ardnacross landing was below the house at an inlet and beach about half a mile north.

Drimnin to Tobermory: In 1836 a ferry between Drimnin and Tobermory commenced, being maintained by the Gordons of Drimnin. This may have been a continuation of an existing ferry, with local hearsay claiming a landing along with an inn or dram house being sited at the Dorlinn entrance to Tobermory Bay. From the 1880s the Sound of Mull steamer called twice daily with the ferry boat being used to transfer passengers and goods ashore.

Tobermory to Ardnamurchan: In 1803 an occasional ferry was linking Tobermory with Kilchoan, with increased use by 1842. Boats from both shores could be hired. In 1846 a hired ferry with three men rowing took two hours from Glenmore Bay to Tobermory. A regular service was established later when the Outer Isles steamer service from Oban called at both Tobermory and Kilchoan Bay where landing to the shore was by rowing boat. This ceased in 1949 when a thrice-daily service by motor launch commenced between Tobermory and Mingary Pier.

Mull to Coll: In 1789 a sailing smack referred to as the 'Coll Packet' was sailing about once a week from Croig to Coll, where a small harbour was built at Arinagour. In 1805 it started carrying the mail for Coll and Tiree. In 1830 it was sailing to Tobermory in preference to Croig. It ceased about 1863–5 when the ferry was superseded by the forerunner of the present day steamer service.

SOUND OF ULVA FERRIES

The present ferry across the Sound of Ulva linking Mull with the islands of Ulva and Gometra goes back to antiquity and is mentioned frequently in eighteenth- and nineteenth-century travellers' accounts, notably in 1773 by Dr Johnson and James Boswell, and later by tourists en route to visit Staffa. A ferry from the Sound of

Ulva to Gribun across Loch na Keal served a link in a route between North and South Mull. Often a wild crossing, it is the scene of Thomas Campbell's poem, 'Lord Ullin's Daughter'. In 1774 the ferry boat overturned due to a fight on board and eight drowned.

In 1878 fares were 1/6d for one passenger, 1/- each for two, and 8d each for over three. The ferry probably ceased in the mid nineteenth century after the construction of the road under Gribun cliffs.

Ferrying Cattle between Coll, Tiree and Mull

During the eighteenth and nineteenth centuries considerable numbers of cattle for markets on Mull and the mainland were ferried from Coll and Tiree. Using the shortest crossings dependent on weather, landings were made at places like Kintra and Market Bay on the Ross and Port na Ba near Croig. A clean, sandy bay was favoured, with the boat moored afloat, and the beasts were driven into the sea to swim ashore; the sand gave a soft landing. The sea-water not only cleaned the cattle but disinfected wounds – usually goring – sustained in the ferrying.

The seven preceding descriptions of ferry services are taken from a display on 'Ferries' by Alistair Garvie at the Isle of Mull Museum.

Taigh a' Lobhain

A ferry was situated here [at the edge of the field directly opposite Killiechronan House] where boats left for Eorsa, Treshnish and Iona. There had been remains also of an inn here until they were flattened, but when this was in use is uncertain.

Notes from a recording of Lachie MacLean, Knock, 2001

The Glen Albyn Steamboat Company of Tobermory

In 1834 a notable addition to the fleet was made, viz. *Glen Albyn* . . . She was the property of the Glen Albyn Steamboat Co. of Tobermory, composed of landowners and merchants in the North and West Highlands, and was placed in service along with *Staffa*, *Maid of Morven* and *Highlander*.

C. L. D. Duckworth and G. E. Langmuir, *West Highland Steamers*, 1967

THE COLL PACKET

The packet was provided by MacLean of Coll at his own expense to run from Arinagour to Quinish, Quinish being part of the Coll Estate.

As far as I have heard, it was the little pier at Quinish that was used (not the larger pier at the late Alex Ban's House which is farther out of the loch). I never heard that the packet ran from Croig, as Croig was in the Duke of Argyll's territory, and as is well known there was no love lost between the MacLeans and the Campbells.

The packet might of course have run from Croig in its last years when Hugh, 14th Chief of Coll, went bankrupt and the Estate of Coll was run by Donald Campbell, a native of Islay and a relation of the Duke of Argyll. This man was an ex-lieutenant of the marines. He was the local Lloyd's agent in 1847 and lived in Cuin.

The packet seems to have weathered many storms, but one boat was lost with all hands in a terrible storm 'when Tiree was in six islands and Coll in three' and the skipper was *Calum Ruadh*. There is a gravestone in Kilmore: 'Alex MacLean, late Erray, Tobermory, brother Finlay drowned Coll packet 14/10/1815'. I wonder if this refers to the above storm?

A report of a severe storm 27/11/1847 says that the packet had a narrow escape. There seem to have been some crew trouble 13/2/1849 – 'Due to severe windy and wet weather, Alex Munn, Donald MacLean (Miller) and John Beaton (Penmore) declined to sail as their wives will not permit them.'

I presume that the packet would have run till 1856. That was the year that Coll was sold to the new proprietor (Stewart). I think the last packet boat was built at Ledaig, Tobermory. There was a boat-building yard on the site of the present Baptist Church/Masonic Lodge.

Calum MacDonald, Tobermory, 2000

PUFFERS

Coal for the district was delivered by puffer at Croig and they were
the last boats to use Croig Pier. From here it was taken by horse and
cart to the houses. Croig had an inn. Boats came from Coll and
Tiree and brought grain to the mill [at Penmore].

Mary Morrison, Penmore, 1992

CALUM POSTA

Among locally well known runners was *Calum Posta*, or Malcolm
the Post, who carried the mail between Tobermory on Mull and
Oban on the mainland for forty years from 1820. Even for those
days his record was impressive; in these it makes epic reading. Not
only because of his long service, but also because of his character,
and his mileage. His travels, it is reckoned, would have taken him
five and a half times round the world had his duty not kept him to
his mail route.

For twenty-five years he did the Tobermory–Oban–Tobermory
round on foot, apart from his two ferry crossings, and for the
following twenty years when his route was between Tobermory
and the Auchnacraig ferry on Mull he had a horse.

Starting with the mail at Tobermory he passed through Salen,
where his home was, through Glen Clachaig, up the thousand foot
shoulder and down to the head of Loch Scridain, where he was met
by the Bunessan-Pennygael runner from the Ross of Mull. With
this usually light addition to his load he carried on through
Glenmore to Lochdonhead, branching right down the road to
Auchnacraig Post Office and ferry. Here, perhaps, he may have
spent the night before crossing by ferry to Barr nam Boc. His route
across Kerrera took him within sight of the school, then near
Bailemor farm, and stories have been handed down how the
scholars enjoyed watching out for him – sometimes he would be
carrying something of recognizeable interest, such as a horse collar.

After crossing the small ferry to the mainland he took the hill
road to the Oban Post Office in Shore Street, where Mrs Bayne,
followed by Miss Rankin, was Post mistress. Here the letters would
be laid against the window panes, address outwards, to be called for

Above left. Roddy and Joan MacNeill and
Pibroch, Salen 1992 (Ann MacKenzie)

Above. Colin Fletcher (formerly Ulva and
Torloisk), Craignure 1992

Left. Donald W. MacKenzie (formerly
Ulva), 1992 (Ann MacKenzie)

Above left. Mrs Mary Morrison,
Penmore 1992 (Ann MacKenzie)

Above. Kirsty MacGillivray, Dervaig
(Permission requested from Gremlin
Napier)

Left. Peter MacLean, Dervaig 2001
(Ann MacKenzie)

Top. Johnnie Simpson, Fanmore 1992 (Ann MacKenzie)

Above. Calum MacDonald, Tobermory 2001 (Ann MacKenzie)

Left. Angie Henderson, Tobermory (by kind permission of Janet MacDonald)

Below left. Lachie MacLean, Knock 2001 (Ann MacKenzie)

Below right. Iain Robertson, Tobermory, 1992 (Ann MacKenzie)

Calum and Margaret MacDonald, Dervaig (by kind permission of Calum and Margaret MacDonald)

The MacKenzie family, Ulva 1920s. Author's *seanair* and grandmother, Auntie Mairi, Uncle Angus, father, Donald and Uncle Stewart (by kind permission of Donald W. MacKenzie)

Top. The MacKenzie family putting at Ulva Manse, 1925 (by kind permission of Donald W. MacKenzie)

Above. Gometra School, c. 1917. The two young men in the back row were probably students who taught during the summer months when there was no resident teacher. (The Mull Museum)

Top. Gometra School, c. 1929. Left to right: Iain MacDonald, Flora MacDonald (no relation), Jane Ann MacFarlane, (?)McPherson (by kind permission of Morag MacDonald)

Above. Salen Show, c. 1900 (The Mull Museum)

Top. Salen Show, 1922 (Miss Margaret Low Collection, Scottish Life Archive, National Museums of Scotland)

Above. Transporting horses from Mull to Oban on the *Caribineer* (Hugh Cheape Collection, Scottish Life Archive, National Museums of Scotland)

Top. Tobermory Regatta, *c.* 1900 (The Mull Museum)

Above. Tobermory regatta, 1930s/40s (The Mull Museum)

Top. West Highland ponies, a grey gelding from Mull (centre), a bay mare (right) from Barra and a dun mare from Uist (left), by William Shiels, c. 1840 (National Museums of Scotland)

Above. Christening photograph from Mull – persons unknown (by kind permission of Dr Bill Clegg)

Top. Gathering whelks, c. 1890s (MacVean Collection, The Mull Museum)

Above. Cutting seed potatoes, c. 1890s (MacVean Collection, The Mull Museum)

Top. Ploughing match, Quinish, c. 1920 (by kind permission of Mrs Effie MacCuaig)

Above. Ploughing match, Calgary, c. 1920 (by kind permission of Mrs Effie MacCuaig)

Top. Estate workers at Quinish, c. 1920 (by kind permission of Mrs Effie MacCuaig)

Above. Shearing sheep (MacVean Collection, The Mull Museum)

Top. The smiddy at Deravig, 1929. Left to right: Mr MacFadyen (Cuin), Calum MacLean, Alasdair MacLean and Hugh MacLean – three brothers from Dervaig (by kind permission of Mrs Betty MacLean)

Above left. Herdsmen from Gometra on Staffa, c. 1900 (The Mull Museum)

Above right. Donald MacKechnie cutting peat at Bealach an Sgàthain, Dervaig. This is part of a triptych of photographs taken by Dr Bill Clegg

Left. Dan MacAllister, at ninety years of age, in a sailing skiff (The Mull Museum)

Left. Filling wool sacks, c. 1890 (The Mull Museum)

Above. Washing clothes, c. 1890s (The Mull Museum)

Top. Harvest scene in Gometra near Ulva Ferry, Mull (by kind permission of Chrissie MacLennan)

Above. Boats in Gometra Harbour, c. 1928 (by kind permission of Chrissie MacLennan)

Right. Haymaking in front of Gometra House (by kind permission of Chrissie MacLennan)

Top. Mull combination poorhouse, *c.* 1920 (The Mull Museum, Peter MacNab)

Above. Torlochan fever hospital, 1930s (The Mull Museum)

Right. Dr Maxwell in Reserves uniform (The Mull Museum)

Above. Burning kelp at Inch Kenneth by William Daniell, 1818 (Scottish Life Archive, National Museums of Scotland)

Below. The Treshnish Isles from Cailleach. Left to right: Cairnburgh, Fladda, Lunga and the Dutchman's Cap (Ann MacKenzie)

Above two pictures. Cairnburgh Castle, Treshnish Isles (RCAHMS)

Top. Calgary Bay. There were many evictions from this area (Ann MacKenzie)

Above. Inch Kenneth, c. 1890s (The MacVean Collection, The Mull Museum)

Right. Mull type of thatched cottage (The Estate of I.F. Grant)

Below. Mull Weaver's Cottage, 18th Century (from J.P MacLean, *History of Mull*, 1923)

Fɪɢ. 16. South-Western type of house. (A) General view. (B) Detail of chimney in middle of roof. (C) Fastening of thatch to square gable end. (D) Mull type of house. (E) Detail of chimney at end of house.

Above. Thatched cottages, Glac na Ceardach, Tobermory c. 1920s (The Mull Museum)

Above. Tobermory, c. 1900 (The Mull Museum)

Top. Salen Pier, *c.* 1900 (?) (The Mull Museum)

Above. Calum and Margaret MacDonald and their father's mail van at Dervaig (by kind permission of Calum and Margaret MacDonald)

Top. The MacDougalls of Haunn and Counduille Rankin Morison of Kengarair (by kind permission of Mrs Betty MacLean)

Above. The wool boat at Ulva ferry, after Lady Congleton (by kind permission of Mrs J. Howard, Ulva)

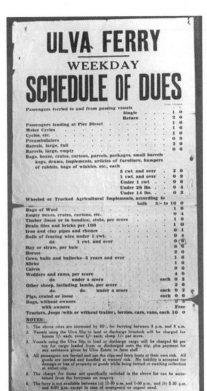

ULVA FERRY
WEEKDAY
SCHEDULE OF DUES

		Each Charge
Passengers ferried to and from passing vessels		
	Single	1 0
	Return	2 0
Passengers landing at Pier Direct		1 0
Motor Cycles		1 0
Cycles, etc.		1 0
Perambulators		0 9
Barrels, large, full		2 0
Barrels, large, empty		0 6
Bags, boxes, crates, cartons, parcels, packages, small barrels kegs, drums, implements, articles of furniture, hampers of rabbits, bags of winkles, etc., each		
	5 cwt. and over	2 0
	1 cwt. and over	0 9
	Under 1 cwt.	0 6
	Under 28 lbs.	0 4
	Under 14 lbs.	0 3
Wheeled or Tracked Agricultural Implements, according to bulk	5/- to	10 0
Bags of Wool		1 6
Empty boxes, crates, cartons, etc.		0 4
Timber (loose or in bundles), stobs, per score		1 0
Drain tiles and bricks per 100		1 0
Iron and clay pipes and rhones		0 1
Rolls of fencing wire under 1 cwt.		0 4
do. 1 cwt. and over		0 6
Hay or straw, per bale		0 3
Horses		2 0
Cows, bulls and bullocks—2 years and over		1 6
Stirks		1 0
Calves		0 6
Wedders and rams, per score		4 0
do. under a score	each	0 3
Other sheep, including lambs, per score		2 6
do. do. under a score	each	0 2
Pigs, crated or loose	each	0 6
Dogs, without owners		0 2
with owners		Free
Tractors, Jeeps (with or without trailer, lorries, cars, vans, each		10 0

NOTES:—

1. The above rates are increased by 50% for ferrying between 8 p.m. and 8 a.m.
2. Vessels using the Ulva Slip to land or discharge livestock will be charged for horses 1/- each, cows 1/- each, sheep 1/- per score.
3. Vessels using the Ulva Slip to land or discharge cargo will be charged 6d per ton for cargo loaded from or discharged onto the slip, plus payment for any assistance given by Ulva Estate or farm staff.
4. All passengers are ferried and use the slips and ferry boats at their own risk. All goods are carried and handled at owners' risk. No liability is accepted for damage or loss of property or goods while being ferried or awaiting collection at either slip.
5. The charge for items not specifically included in the above list can be ascertained from the ferryman on enquiry.
6. The ferry is not available between (a) 12-30 p.m. and 1-30 p.m., and (b) 5-30 p.m. and 6-30 p.m., except in case of emergency or urgent need.
7. Sunday journeys only by special arrangement with ferryman.

Left. Ulva ferry fares schedule (by kind permission of Mrs J. Howard and Mr J. Howard, Isle of Ulva)

Below. Wall built by Colonel MacKenzie at Cailleach Point to contain stallions (Ann MacKenzie)

by the recipients when the word went round.

Usually it was the recipient who paid the freight charge although this might also depend upon the circumstances of the writer and the receiver, but in 1840 when the Penny Post came in letters had to be prepaid by the sender with an adhesive stamp. Surely Calum must have been intrigued when he first saw a letter embellished with the portrait of Queen Victoria – the original 'Black Penny' stamp.

After collecting the incoming mail in Oban, he set off on the long journey back, making the double trip three times each fortnight.

H. MacDougall, *Island of Kerrera: Mirror of History*, 1979

POSTAL AND TELEGRAM SERVICES

In our time, the mail from the south, including newspapers, was brought by the *Lochinvar* to Salen and sorted at the Aros post office there. Aros was the postal district which included Ulva and Ulvaferry. Our address was The Manse, Ulva, by Aros. The mail for our district was collected by Sandy Black, the mail contractor, and mail for Gribun and the Ross of Mull by Johnny Cameron. Sandy Black, Oskamull, took over the mail contract from his predecessor who lived at Laggan and for whom he drove the pony and trap that conveyed the mail to and from Salen. By 1924, Sandy was the mail contractor and, instead of using a pony and trap to transport the mail, he used a motor car. He was the first person in the district to have a car for hire – a black Ford tourer with a canvas hood. The car he used for the mail run was also a Ford, Model T, with the body reconstructed into a wooden van with compartments for seating passengers and for the mailbags. The car registration letters for Argyll at that time were SB – his initials, Sandy Black solemnly assured us.

He left Ulvaferry at about 5 a.m. with the outgoing mail and returned with the incoming mail at 6 o'clock in the evening. The letters, cards and parcels were then taken by the postmen on bicycles and delivered to Ulva and Gometra in the dark, often wet and stormy, evenings between 6 and 9 p.m.

Hugh (Eoghan) the post was succeeded by his brother Lachie.

They wore uniforms of navy blue with red piping and round hats with high crowns and with patent leather skips, fore and aft. In wet weather they wore long waterproof capes and leggings. They carried their satchels or mail bags on a carrier fixed in front under the handlebars of their bicycles. The capes were sufficiently voluminous to cover the entire upper part of their bodies and also their arms and hands and the mailbags strapped to the carriers. A postman thus clad riding his bicycle resembled nothing as much as a tent on wheels. The carbide-acetylene lamp which would have been obscured had it been mounted in the usual place was mounted on a bracket low down on the right hand fork of the front wheel.

Urgent messages were passed on, before the advent of the telephone, by telegrams. Ulvaferry Post Office was also a telegraph office, and schoolboys were employed as telegram boys to deliver the decoded message written with an indelible pencil on coarse, buff-coloured paper and enclosed in an orange-coloured envelope. Lachie Beag, for instance, was given the day off school and paid half a crown (2/6 old money) for delivering telegrams to the big house of Gometra. 'Reading the telegrams' became a ritual part of wedding celebrations performed by the best man. Many of those greeting telegrams were in Gaelic – Gaelic so mutilated in the course of transmission as to render it incomprehensible.

Donald W. MacKenzie, *As it Was*, 2000

TOBERMORY

TOBERMORY DURING THE JACOBITE RISING, 1745–46

Tobermory Bay, although reported in April 1746 as being a 'bad winter Anchorage' was used to a considerable extent by navy ships in support of the Government troops. At first it was to prevent the Pretender landing from France, then to prevent the French ships giving support to the Highland army. After Culloden, in April 1746, it was used as a convenient anchorage for the ships in their search for the fugitive Prince Charles, preventing French ships assisting his escape, hunting down returning Jacobite supporters and deterring any possibility of a future rising.

The Navy ships arrived in West Highland waters in August 1745, too late to prevent the Prince's landing, but on Mull, they took action to prevent the MacLeans joining the rising, and, to discourage movement, stove in all the boats they could find in the Sound of Mull. In spite of this, upwards of 100 men under MacLean of Drimnin joined the Highland army.

By April, ships were blocking the Minch and the Sound of Mull, using Tobermory for shelter. In May, the *Greyhound* was lying in the bay with the Naval Commander on board, and the frigate *Triron* towed in a snow (a two-masted, square rigged vessel usually used for carrying despatches) which was captured off Trotternish, Skye. The sloops *Furnace* and *Terror* with the tender *Mary Anne* and the cutter *Union* embarked 200 troops of the Argyll Militia and Guise's Regiment from Fort William to search the Outer Isles. In June, General Campbell sailed from the harbour on board the *Furnace* in company with the *Terror* to search St Kilda. In July, the two-decked frigate *Glasgow* arrived with the captured French brigantine *Le Bien Trouvé* and with prisoners taken off the Summer Isles. This was followed soon after by the returning *Furnace* with Flora MacDonald on board, captured at Strathaird, Skye.

An interesting 'on the spot' account comes to us from the despatch of Captain Duff of H.M.S. *Terror*, dated 22nd February 1746, and written from 'Topar Murry'(!): 'I have destroyed every boat that could be found on the coast of Morvern in Lough Sunart, and shall sail to Mudiart [Moidart] where I shall distress and annoy the rebels by all means in my power.'

There must have been many troops in the Tobermory area at this time, with reports of them at Reraig and Erray. Captain Campbell of Skipness wrote to his Commander from his station at Mingary: 'Yesterday, 29th May, about noon, three Companies of our Militia came to Tobermory in great distress for want of meal . . . I sent them two sacks of meal and writ the officer at Dowart (who was Campbell of Ballimore) to send them some supplies as I could not spare them any more.' In July, 1746, General Campbell wrote to his son from Horseshoe Bay, Kerrera, telling him to send an order to the officer commanding at Tobermory, to return to Inveraray.

Morvern and Loch Sunart were given cruel treatment, mostly at the hands of Captain Fergusson of the *Furnace*. The principal navy ships left the area in August for the Orkneys, where French privateers were of concern, and the Prince was able to make his escape from Moidart in September.

SWRI History of Tobermory Folder, Isle of Mull Museum

Note: Two houses near Tobermory were also said to have been set afire at this time; one was a farm at Ardmore.

Calum MacDonald, Tobermory, 2001

NATIONAL FAST 1832

As a protection against cholera in 1832, a meeting of the Presbytery held in Tobermory considered a National Fast 'as a general and solemn act of humiliation, because of the rapid and daily increase of cholera and other pestilence approaching these bounds. In fasting and prayer the people may be led to prostrate themselves before the Great Disposer of every event Who is alone able to succour the afflicted of His people and to avert impending judgement from those who have as yet been mercifully exempted from its merited and afflictive visitation'. This was unanimously approved and a day of fasting was appointed in all parishes throughout the bounds of the Presbytery.

SWRI History of Tobermory Folder, Isle of Mull Museum

TOBERMORY IN 1874

Come back with me in thought to Tobermory in 1874, and we find a thriving busy town, more rural in aspect than it is today, as there were thatched houses interspersed with the slated ones in all the streets of the Upper Village, giving them a cosy, rustic appearance that they lack in their present-day sameness.

These thatched cottages were roomy and comfortable, and had in many of them an upper loft which was used for sleeping accommodation. The lower rooms were sometimes divided by partitions of latticed willow which admitted air, and could be easily washed down when soiled with smoke.

Glachnacardaich, Tobermory 1879: Glachnacardaich was a picturesque hamlet of white-washed cottages with gay fuchsia bushes growing in many of the gardens. The dwellers there were very conservative, and proud of their aloofness from Muinntir Thobarmhoire, as they called us who lived on the other side of the river; for in those days the burn flowed merrily down between fern-lined banks, and shady trees lined the approach to the little suburb, where every house sheltered a busy family, whose men-folk were sailors in foreign waters, except in the case of a widowed mother who had all the care of the upbringing of a young family, and one or two old couples whose sons had made a name for themselves in the world.

Ledaig: Going down to Ledaig we find a row of neat slated cottages extending from the Lodge to Iona Cottage with byres at the back; for nearly every householder had a cow and croft and the right to cut peats, so the peat stacks and byres and henhouses were all in a back row.

Various crafts and trades were practised with much proficiency and success at Ledaig. There were shoemakers, seamstresses, tinsmiths who made tin-ware of every description and horn spoons, and a smithy at the corner next the Eas where it has so recently been. We all had our boots and shoes made to measure in these days, and never required to send away for them; for they were beautifully made by local craftsmen of whom there were quite a number. The anvil at the smithy rang from dawn to dark; for these were the days of horse traffic, and the blacksmith – a fine, upstanding figure of a man, well over six feet – was quite a personality, intelligent and interested in volunteering and athletics and helpful in many ways in the social life of the town. His mother was an accomplished needle-woman, who specialised in patch-work, and took orders for work, ladies supplying their own material for whatever they required her to do. She also crocheted and knitted very beautiful boudoir caps and quilts. But she preferred patchwork as giving her artistic sense more scope.

The town hummed with traffic every Tuesday and Friday when the *Clansman* and *Clydesdale* made their weekly runs from North and South. Vans, carts, gigs, ponies with panniers, and waggonettes with high-stepping horses, and coachmen in livery sitting high on their boxes, came in from the country to do their shopping. Smacks came from Rhum, Canna, Eigg, Coll and Tiree, also across from Ardnamurchan and Morvern, and the bay was a pretty sight with varied craft sailing out and in.

Trades and Crafts: Trades and crafts necessary then flourished; there was a saddler with a beautiful white horse in his window which was an unfailing attraction for all boys. He also was a barber and gave all the schoolboys what he called 'the bowl clip'. He placed an inverted bowl over their heads and cut the fringe of hair that emerged round the edge. A turner who made beautiful spinning wheels was kept constantly busy. Cartwrights and boat builders had much to do, and milliners, of whom we had four, trimmed hats and bonnets in the latest fashion at all seasons of the year. One of them was in advance of our present-day milliners; for she had in her window a very beautiful mannequin. This milliner, Miss MacLean, had her shop in a small slated house behind the house presently occupied by Mr Riddoch. It faced the road and 'the doll', as we called the waist-length wax figure, was seen to full advantage by passers by. Miss MacLean's brother made boots and shoes in the shop at the other end of the building, so footwear and headgear of the most up-to-date designs could be had without descending to the lower village. Everybody loved Miss MacLean's doll, and the favourite walk on Saturday always began or ended by passing her window and looking to see if the pink-cheeked lady was wearing a new bonnet; and it used to amuse us to see the bonnet so displayed on Saturday being worn in Church next day. Only last year a long absent native asked me wistfully – 'Oh! What became of Miss MacLean's doll that gave us so much pleasure in our childhood,' but alas! I could not tell her.

In Breadalbane Street we had four handloom weavers whose shuttles flashed backwards and forwards all day long. Two brothers, Alexander and Lachlan MacDougall, were highly skilled craftsmen in linen weaving – Alexander making tablecloths of damask design, while his brother confined himself to the dam-rod or check and simpler patterns. They also wove beautiful fleecy blankets, as did also John MacLean who worked on the opposite side of the street. He was always spoken of as 'The Paisley Weaver'. I think they had all learned their craft in that town; but John seemed to intersperse his conversation with memories of what he had seen or done in Paisley. The brothers MacDougall were men of deep and sincere piety, devoted to their church, and Lachlan would have been very proud could he have foreseen that his great-grandson, John MacDougall, Kengharair, is now a diligent and successful Divinity student. The 'Paisley Weaver' sat on a high stool when working, and he welcomed us warmly when we went in to see the shuttles flying swiftly backwards and forwards when blankets or rugs were being woven. He also made rag carpets which were soft and comfortable underfoot for nurseries and bedrooms. The warp was of thick cotton, and the material, cut in long strips, was woven in at random as to colour, and the result was very pleasing and restful to the eye.

John MacKinnon came later from Dervaig, and he too never lacked work and always welcomed visitors. When making a crumb cloth for us, we as children, made it our duty to call often to see how the work progressed, and when it at length was laid over the carpet we felt we had helped to weave it, so interested had we been in its progress.

In Breadalbane Lane we had another busy smithy which still, I am glad to say, carries on. Angus Henderson, the old smith, when not too busy, used to let the boys blow his huge bellows for the pleasure of making the sparks fly upwards, and they loved the feel of the long smooth horn handle. They were always down there when cartwheel rings were being heated, and the circle of peats did their work, while the fragrant smoke ascended, and many interested spectators looked on.

Court House: Tobermory was important in these days, as the Crown officials represented by the Sheriff and Procurator Fiscal resided here, and the dignified figure of Sheriff Ross could be seen every Wednesday passing over to the Courthouse to hold his weekly Court. He was a very fine man who interested himself in everything that could benefit the Community. Being very musical, he encouraged choir singing in the churches and himself conducted a choir practice weekly in the courtroom where young men and women from all denominations went to learn hymn singing. His son John, on completing his Oxford course, thought we needed entertainment, so he enlisted the help of all the talented young men (and there were many such), and fortnightly penny readings were arranged and held in the Courtroom, the proceeds being given to local charities. There was a Mutual Improvement Society where debates were held and all the questions of the day discussed. Shakespeare was studied and much benefit mentally derived from the friendly gatherings. A Choral Union embraced all churches, and glees, part songs and community singing were taught to an appreciative class, the session always ending in a grand concert. And there was a flourishing Comunn Gaidhealach.

Churches: Our three Churches – Established, Free and Baptist – were always well attended. Long services thrice daily did not daunt us, and parents faithfully went, taking their families with them. There was no instrumental music in our churches then, and it was not required, for in all three churches the precentors were men with a knowledge of music, and fine leaders of praise.

Education: And our education was not neglected in these old days. We had four schools – the Established Church and Free Church schools, the Industrial School, where the three Rs, sewing and knitting were taught, and a Gaelic School.

Poorhouse: The poorhouse was then in occupation as an institution for the care of needy old people and children. The inmates wore a uniform of pale blue, and the school children, of whom at one time there were quite a few, used to troop in wearing their blue cloaks and white pinafores. One or two of the boys returned in manhood, gratefully remembering the care they had received there.

Weddings: Then there were weddings, celebrated in good old Highland fashion, when the gentlemen called for their lady partners, and brought them safely home again after the feasting and dancing that invariably followed the ceremony. The young couple after the honeymoon always got photographed by the local photographer, Mr Stewart, who had a sweet little studio in the front garden at Barra Cottage, where he lived.

Transport: Our steamer service was quite good, the *Clansman* and *Clydesdale* appearing with all the promptitude that the weather permitted, twice weekly.

The Bellman: We rarely troubled to announce forthcoming events by bills in the windows, preferring to make any such announcements through the medium of our local bellman, whose eloquent advertising of the arrival of fresh herring or the date of a Member of Parliament's meeting always excited the listeners' admiration.

Lighting: Autumn was a busy time in Old Tobermory. Thatchers had their hands full re-thatching cottages, housewives were extracting oil from fish livers for their cruisies, and making tallow candles before the winter days closed in.

Water Supply: Our water supply was inconvenient and inadequate, only one or two houses having private reservoirs; so we had to go to the well for all water for household use. There were many wells and springs to supply our need, and maids enjoyed going with their wooden receptacles, which were called stoups; for they met many companions similarly engaged, and gossip afterwards retailed always ended with: 'It is quite true, for I heard it at the well.'

> Marjory Mary MacKinnon, Tobermory, *1874: A Talk to the S.W.R.I.*,
> SWRI History of Tobermory Folder, Isle of Mull Museum

MULL AND IONA AERATED WATER COMPANY

What is now Barra Cottage was once a lemonade factory using water from Springbank burn; each bottle was made individually, with essence to give colour and flavour, and then gas syphons of soda water were also manufactured. The factory went out of production in 1913. It was run by Dr Maxwell, who also had an apothecary's shop where the former sweet shop was situated.

> SWRI History of Tobermory Folder, Isle of Mull Museum

OLD FARM HOUSE, ERRAY, TOBERMORY

Dr Hector MacLean (an authority on the history of the Clan Mac-
Lean) was one of the MacLeans of Gruline and was a surgeon in
Glasgow for many years. He was married to MacLean of Coll's
sister Catherine. He returned to Mull in 1767 and resided in Erray
House (now the old Farm House) with his wife and daughter
Christina.

When Dr Johnson and Boswell visited Mull in 1773, they called
at Erray House. Dr Johnson described Christina MacLean as the
most accomplished lady he had found in the Highlands. She knew
French, music and drawing, could make shellwork, and could sew
neatly and could milk cows. Also she was the first person he had
met that could translate Gaelic poetry literally.

Social snobbery was at a high pitch at this period, and an alliance
was unthinkable with someone who did not know who his 'noble'
ancestors were. Poor Christina's choice of a local swain so incensed
her father, that he locked her up in her room, and fitted iron bars to
the windows (still in position in 1999). I was told years ago by some
elderly people in Tobermory that she had died of a broken heart,
and that her ghost was said to haunt the old house. Certainly the
presence of a spirit has been reliably confirmed in recent years. I
know a couple who got married about thirty years ago and stayed
at this house as their first home, who experienced the appearance
of a female ghost in their bedroom on frequent occasions. The
bride's father, who believed in ghosts, was curious about this
information and spent a night on his own in this room. He left
early next morning and was tight-lipped and refused to discuss his
experience.

However from information received from the late Mr Counn
Morison, Ceann a' Ghadhair, Dervaig (a noted local historian), it
seems that Christina did not die of a broken heart. She moved to
Dervaig on her father's death and lived in her aunt's house (the late
Parish church Manse – Tor a' Mhanich), now called Glebe House.
She was eighty-six years old when she died, and was buried in old
Kilmore Cemetery in 1826.

Calum MacDonald, Tobermory, 2001

STEWART'S HALL, TOBERMORY

Stewart's Hall (against the cliff at the end of Back Brae and used by Mr Turner as a workshop in the 1970s) was also known as Hall na Cracionn (Hall of the Skins) which we hope we are correct in recording as 'Tinker' Gaelic, as it was used by them for storing otter skins etc. There were also Quaker meetings held there: it also served as a church on various occasions.

SWRI History of Tobermory Folder, Isle of Mull Museum

SHOPS IN TOBERMORY IN THE 1920s AND 1930s

Shops were open until 9 p.m. and were open early in the morning. Orders were taken from the houses, made up in the shops and taken round the houses in a basket carried on the boy's back.

Lists of shops: painter, grocer, Tally [Italian], paper shop, milliner, bakery, four churches, three banks, Hall, Post Office – and a shop that sold tobacco, paper and haircuts. Carmichael, the grocer (who also had a shop in Ardrishaig, Argyll), sold flour, meal, everything; wine came in barrels and was bottled and Carmichael's label put on them. A butcher, another grocer [MacFarlane] that also sold clothes and shoes, the Clydesdale Bank, a plumber, shoe repairer, Brown's that sold spades, clothes, whisky, North of Scotland Bank, chemist, shoe repairer, Italian (ice cream), grocer (Lachlan MacLean – Lachie Collach) who sold Coll cheese, Royal Bank, café, hotel, paper shop near pier. [Some of the same shops are mentioned twice here.]

There were also the shops in the upper part of the town, one a grocer. There was a coal ree near the pier and puffers came in and were unloaded into carts and taken to the ree. Coal was taken in carts and delivered to the houses from there.

Iain Robertson, Tobermory, 1992

TOBERMORY DURING THE SECOND WORLD WAR

There was always plenty of work during this time. There were warships in the harbour and wood was also needed to build ships etc. Trees were cut down in the Mull forests and taken away for timber. There were soldiers and the RAF also, and canteens for men in Tobermory.

Although no peat was used in Tobermory in his time there was in his grandfather's; there was the distillery which used peat for flavouring the whisky. It was cut near the Mishnish Lochs. The distillery was closed down during the War and was used as a barracks and ammunition store and canteen.

Iain Robertson, Tobermory, 1992

THE ISLANDS

INHABITANTS OF STAFFA

Although Staffa is now uninhabited and has been for many years, it was not always so. U. Von Troil (one of Sir Joseph Banks' companions when he visited Staffa in 1772) states in his 'Letters on Iceland', when describing Staffa, 'There is only one hut, which is occupied by a peasant who attends some cattle that pasture there. To testify his joy for our arrival he sang all night over in the Erse language, which we did not understand. He regaled us with fish and milk.'

Sir Joseph Banks erected a tent on Staffa, but the lone inhabitant pressed him so strongly to spend the night in his hut that he left his companions in the tent and slept in the hut. On leaving the hut next morning he discovered he had acquired a colony of vermin. He mentioned the circumstances to his host in terms of mild reproach. But the latter, who was touched to the quick, straightened himself up and, assuming a tone of consequence, retorted haughtily and harshly that it was Sir Joseph himself who had imported the vermin into his island and adding that he had better have left them in England.

At the time of Banks' visit the island belonged to a Mr. Lauchlan MacQuarrie. The Bishop of Londonderry, who visited Staffa several years after Banks, found the above-mentioned herdsman still occupying the island. The Bishop, being unable to speak Gaelic, told one of his guides to ask the 'Lone Herdsman of the Hebride

Isles, Plac'd far amid the melancholy main' what he most wanted. The answer was simple and moderate, 'a razor and some soap'. The worthy Prelate gave him a purse containing ten guineas, and later sent three razors and several pounds of soap, which made the poor fellow pity and despise the rest of the world till his presents were worn out and expended. It is said that when the above reverend visitor first beheld Fingal's Cave he was so impressed by its sublimity that he fell on his knees and prayed.

When in September, 1784, B. Faujas de Saint Fond, the French geologist, visited Staffa the population numbered sixteen persons. Faujas was the first geologist to visit Staffa and describe it as a volcanic island. He says in 'A Journey to the Hebrides in 1784', 'The total population at the time when I visited it, consisted of two families who lived apart in two huts, constructed of unhewn blocks of basalt roofed over with sods, and who amounted, men, women and children, to the number of sixteen persons. Belonging to these were eight cows, one bull, twelve sheep, two horses, one pig, two dogs, one cock and eight hens.' He further states, 'These huts get no light except from the door, which was only three feet high, and from the chimney, which consisted of a pyramidical opening in the middle of the hut . . .

'Only on the highest part is there a flat piece of ground covered with a poor dry turf, alongside of which is a corner of ground newly broken up, where a little oats and a few potatoes are raised. For firing, the inhabitants are obliged to make use of a bad turf, which they lift in the summer season in order to dry it. It is not a peat since it consists simply of fibrous roots of common grasses, intermixed with earth. Nothing worse in the way of fuel could be used, but here necessity reigns with absolute sway.

'The whole of the island belongs to Colonel Charles Camble of Cambletown, in Cantyre. It is let at the rent of twelve pounds sterling on account probably of its fishery, for its territorial value ought to be considered as nothing.'

Describing his reception on Staffa, Faujas says, 'The women and children of the two families did not fail to come to us, and invited us to their habitations; but being already informed of their excessive dirt, we were inflexible; and preferred on good ground to receive their civilities and their compliments in the open air.

'Finding that it was impossible to prevail with us by the most friendly gestures, they resolved to do us the honours on the small esplanade in front of their dwellings.

'The men, women and children, with much gravity, first formed themselves in a large circle in which they placed us and our seamen. Then one of the women, disgustingly ugly and dirty, brought out a large wooden bowl filled with milk, with which she placed herself in the centre of the circle. She viewed us all round with attention, and immediately came up to me, and pronouncing some words, presented the bowl with a sort of courtesy. I held out my hands to receive it, but she drank some if it before she gave it to me. I followed her example and passed the vessel to my neighbour, William Thornton; he gave it to Mr. MacDonald and so on from hand to hand, or more properly from mouth to mouth, till every person had tasted of it. Having made our acknowledgements for this kindness, they immediately appointed two guides to accompany us to Fingal's Cave and all the remarkable places of this small isle.'

Abraham Mills, a vulcanist, who visited Staffa in 1788, says:– 'There were three houses (5th July, 1788) uninhabited, and barley, oats, flax and potatoes growing near the centre of the island, and good grass in several parts. When the crops are ripe, labourers are sent to gather them in; after which thirty head of cattle are sent to winter on the island, which, with a solitary herdsman to attend them, continue till the seed time the ensuing spring.'

In the old (Sinclair's) 'Statistical Account of Scotland', 1795, the Rev. Arch. MacArthur states – 'In the mouth of Lochnankell lie the islands of Ulva, Gometra, Little Colonsay and Staffa, all of which are inhabited.'

Prof. T. Garnett who visited Staffa during the month of July, 1798, says in 'A Tour Through the Highlands of Scotland', 'Near the middle of the island we found two wretched huts, built with fragments of basaltic pillars and rude pieces of lava; one of these served as the habitation of a herd and his family, who take care of the cattle that feed on the island; the other is used as a barn or cow-house. Upon the side of a hillock near the hut we sat down and partook of our provisions, and the herd's wife presented us with some milk in a large wooden bowl so heavy that we could scarcely lift it to our mouths; they had no smaller vessels, nor spoons.

Indeed, their manner of life is extremely simple, their food consist-
ing chiefly of milk and potatoes with, now and then, a little fish.
There being no wood on the island the only fuel used by these
poor people is the sods of earth which they carefully dry.

'This family resided here both winter and summer for three
years, but in winter their situation was frequently very unpleasant;
for during storms the waves beat so violently against the island that
the very house was shaken, though situated in the middle of it;
indeed, the concussion was often so great that the pot which hung
over the fire partook of it and was made to vibrate. This so much
alarmed the poor inhabitants one very stormy winter that they
determined to leave the island the first favourable opportunity, for
they believed that nothing but an evil spirit could have rocked it in
that manner. Since that time they have resided here only during the
summer season and even at this time of the year (July) their
situation is far from enviable, for it is impossible to keep a boat in
the bay on account of the surf.'

Dr J. Leyden, the Scottish poet and friend of Sir Walter Scott,
who visited Staffa in 1800, makes no mention of the inhabitants,
but says that he saw three deer which had been placed on the island
and which seemed perfectly tame.

There were no inhabitants during the visits of Dr. John
MacCulloch, the geologist, between the years of 1811 and 1821,
and a Mr. B. Botfield, F.R.S., who visited Staffa during the summer
of 1829, describes the island as being uninhabited. The Rev. D.
MacArthur, writing in September, 1843, in 'The New Statistical
Account of Scotland', says:– 'Staffa is uninhabited', but Prof.
MacLean in his 'Report on Fingal's Cave, 1887', states:–

'A few years ago a shepherd and his family were persuaded to go
on the isle, but they soon beseeched to be removed, because the
hollow roar made by the sea through the caverns during times of
storms sounded so dismally that they became terrified. To a
superstitious people there would be something more than natural
forces in the fetch of the ocean which bursts through these pillared
portals with a sound as of artillery.'

Donald B. MacCulloch, The Island of Staffa, 1927

STAFFA

The 'Grenadier' used to call at Staffa every weekday in summer and the Gometra fishermen met the steamer and took the people ashore in their boats.

Margaret Low, *Highland Memories*, 1990

CAIRNBURG, TRESHNISH ISLANDS

This small island is the most northerly of the Treshnish Isles, situated about two miles from the nearest point on the coast of Mull, and about three miles from Ulva. The whole circumference exhibits a wall of rock perfectly perpendicular, and at its base is surrounded by a very deep sea, which there forms a furious current; thus surrounded, it is rendered by nature almost inaccessible. The only landing-place consists of steps cut in the face of the rock, which are continued in a winding staircase to the top. For over a thousand years it was used as a royal garrison. The defenses at the summit are partly cut in the solid rock and partly masonwork; the ruins of the keeper's house, the watch-tower, and guard-house are on the level within; it altogether forms a most interesting specimen of an ancient stronghold. It is said to have been originally built by one of the kings of Norway for a royal residence.

J. P. MacLean, *A History of the Clan MacLean*, 1889

CAIRN NA BURGH MORE AND CAIRN NA BURGH BEG

The two islands are separated by a narrow channel, subject to a strong tidal flow, and it is from within this channel that landings are usually made on either island by means of small boats. The main part of the castle is situated on the larger of the two islands, namely Cairn na Burgh More, the smaller one probably having been fortified largely to secure the approach to the principal stronghold. Apart from the chapel on Cairn na Burgh More, which may be as old as the 15th century, all the surviving buildings, including the curtain-walls, appear to be of 16th- or 17th-century date . . .

The castle of Cairnburgh, or Kiarnaborg, first comes on record in 1249 as one of four castles held by Ewen, lord of Lorn, from King Hakon of Norway. It continued to be regarded as a royal castle by the Scottish Crown after the Treaty of Perth (1266), and following the forfeiture of the MacDougalls of Lorn, custody of Cairnburgh was probably granted by Robert I to Angus Og of Islay. Angus's son and successsor, John of Islay, was himself forfeited by David II, but subsequently made his peace with the king, who in a charter of 1343 granted him the keeping of the royal castles of Cairnburgh, Iselborgh and Dun Chonnuill (in the Garvellach Isles).

Eleven years later John of Lorn and John of Islay came to an agreement by which the MacDougalls renounced all claim to the bulk of their former island possessions, including the three castles above named, stipulation being made, however, that John of Islay should never give custody of the castle of Cairnburgh to anyone of the MacKinnon family. In 1390 Donald of Islay, Lord of the Isles, granted the constabulary and keeping of the castles of Cairnburgh and Iselborgh, together with certain islands in the Treshnish group and lands in Gometra and Mull, to Lachlan MacLean of Duart, while about the same time the 'exceedingly strong castle of Carneborg' was included in a list of castles in the Western Isles compiled by the chronicler John of Fordun.

The identity of the castle of Iselborgh (also called Hystylburch and Isleborg) has been the subject of considerable discussion, but since early charters generally couple it with Cairnburgh and other islands in the Treshnish group, there appear to be good grounds for accepting the view that Iselborgh is an early name for Cairn na Burgh Beg ('The Cairn of the Little Castle'). The first element of the name is probably the Gaelic *iosal*, 'low', in reference to the fact that this island rises to a lesser height than its neighbour, Cairn na Burgh More ('The Cairn of the Big Castle').

During the 15th century Cairnburgh remained in the keeping of the MacLeans of Duart, but after the forfeiture of Lachlan MacLean for rebellion in 1504 the castle was besieged by a royal expeditionary force supplied from the naval base at Dumbarton. Nine years later, during a second phase of rebellion, Lachlan MacLean again seized Cairnburgh, but afterwards came to terms with the government and was reinstated in his possessions. At this period payments towards the expenses of the custody of the castle were made from royal rents in Kintyre, while grain was supplied from Tiree . . .

In 1579 complaint was made to the Privy Council against Lachlan MacLean of Duart by Donald MacLean, son of John Diurach (of the Torloisk family), on account of his unlawful imprisonment in the castle of 'Carnbulge', while a year later provision for garrisoning the castle was made in one of the articles of an agreement drawn up between John, Bishop of the Isles, and Lachlan MacLean of Duart. During this period the MacLeans of Treshnish appear to have held the hereditary constableship of the castle on behalf of the MacLeans of Duart. In the Civil War the MacLeans took the Royalist side and Cairnburgh, in common with other castles belonging to this family, was captured by General Leslie during his expedition to the Western Isles in 1647. Thereafter the castle was held on behalf of Leslie by Hector MacLean of Torloisk, with a garrison of thirty men, despite attempts at its recapture by the MacLeans of Duart. It is possible that some of the existing defences of the castle were erected at this period.

Cairnburgh also played an important part in the long struggle between the MacLeans of Duart and the Campbells during the last quarter of the 17th century, and an incident which is recorded to have taken place in 1679 probably typifies the history of the castle at this period. In the summer of that year Archibald, 9th Earl of Argyll, mounted an expedition against the MacLeans and, after capturing the castles of Coll and Tiree without resistance, issued a summons of surrender to Hector MacLean of Treshnish, who was then garrisoning 'the two rocks of Cairnbulge'. Having reconnoitred the castle and made preparations for a siege Argyll retired to Iona, whereupon the garrison made a sortie, killing two of the Earl's men and releasing three prisoners. The next day Argyll returned and anchored off Fladda, intending to parley, but after a further day spent fruitlessly circumnavigating the islands he retreated to Mull in worsening weather, leaving the castle still in the hands of the MacLeans. The castle was finally surrendered to Archibald Campbell, 10th Earl of Argyll, in 1692. Cairnburgh was held alternately by the MacLeans and by government forces during the Jacobite rebellion of 1715, following which it seems to have been occupied by a permanent government garrison.

RCAHMS, *Argyll, Vol. 3*, 1980

SAMALAN, ERISGEIR, AND EORSA

Two other islands went with Inch-Kenneth: Samalan and Erisgeir. Samalan was small and flat; it was off the east end and about half an acre in size. It had grazing on it but no fresh water, only one or two brackish pools. The farmer used to put three or four sheep there for the summer.

Erisgeir was two miles away out from the Wilderness (Burg Point). We went there that summer in the old white skiff and landed. Erisgeir is like Rockall, the top of a submerged mountain, and there is no shore. We scrambled up the rocks and walked about on the comparatively flat top. There was grass and masses of sea-pinks among the flat rocks, and puffins everywhere. I'm told in the old days six sheep could live in Erisgeir all the year round, but when we were there in 1925 the puffins had taken over and tunnelled everywhere.

That summer we also landed on Eorsa, a large hilly island in the middle of inner Loch-na Keal. It was covered with dense bracken and had the ruins of a cottage, probably used as a summer sheiling. There were wild goats on the island which we were told had been put there to kill the adders.

Margaret Low, *Highland Memories*, 1990

Note: Inch-Kenneth was bought from the Clarks of Ulva in 1900 by Mr Malloch and then sold in 1923 to Mary Low (grand-daughter of Forsyth of Quinish), who was Margaret Low's mother. Mary Low owned Inch-Kenneth for ten years, and it was then sold to Sir Harold Bolton.

Inch-Kenneth and Eorsa, formally belonging to the Prioress of Iona, became part of the Parish of Kilfinichen and Kilvickeon (Ross of Mull) and are therefore not included to any great extent in this book.

Chapter 7

TALES

Cu-Duilig MacRaing came from Ireland with Lachainn Lùbanach and Eachann Reanganach – the first MacLeans who possessed land in Mull. Clann Duiligh and the MacLeans were of the same stock. Cu-Duilig learned to play the pipes in Ireland. He was the first piper in Mull. Clann Duiligh or Clann Mhic Raing (Rankin) played on MacLean's right flank in battles. They settled at Kilbrennan, and one of them learned his art from the fairies at the Sìthein of Lagan Ulva. The fairies gave him *feadan sìthe Chloinn Duiligh* (the fairy chanter of Clann Duiligh) and taught him the 'Glas Mheur' (the Finger Lock) – a 'hidden tune'. MacRaing's daughter learned the tune and passed it on to one of her father's pupils who was courting her. When this pupil had completed his training at the piping college at Kilbrennan he had to play all he had learned before MacRaing who was so impressed by his young pupil's performance that he asked him to play more. He played the 'hidden tune' that the daughter taught him, and when he had finished, MacRaing reached for his sword and went after him. The story does not say what happened but presumably the young piper escaped.

The man of Muckairn (Taynuilt) took two men from Ireland – David, a harpist, and Robert, a blacksmith.* Robert had a son Calum who was sent to Mull to learn piping. He had a good ear but did not apply himself. One night he attended a wedding with MacRaing and drank too much. MacRaing ordered him out of the house with his pipes under his oxter at midnight. It was a dark night but Calum saw a light and made for it. There he met an old man sitting at the fire who told him that MacRaing was composing a new tune and it only needed one variation. The old man started the tune and gave it to Calum and said, 'Go, and when you are near the wedding house, play the tune.' Calum did so and MacRaing heard it, and from then on he became an attentive pupil. The 'Glas

Mheur' came from the hands of Calum. MacRaing used to play the hidden tune in a cave whose entrance was concealed by the waterfall, the Eas Fors.

There was a big competition between MacRaing and Northumberland pipers. One of them came to Kilbrennan to compete with MacRaing. The Sasunnach stood on the wall of Dun Chuagain – an old Norse fort above Kilbrennan. MacRaing played on Cnoc nam Pìobairean at the end of his own house where his pupils used to play on summer evenings. MacRaing won. Next year the Sasunnach came again and this time he won. The third time he lost, but the contest was so close MacRaing was afraid that if he came back the next year, the Sasunnach might beat him, so he went after him and caught up with him at Achadashenaig at a little field at the other side of the river opposite Aros Castle. MacRaing offered swordplay and killed him. He buried him where he was and put a stone over him. When the main road between Salen and Tobermory was being made 120 years ago the Cairn was dismantled and human bones were found under it. Ever since, this field is known as Dail an t-Sasunnaich.

An Irish nobleman used to come to Duart every autumn. He usually came with only one companion – his piper – and was always certain to be in Duart on the night of the meeting. MacRaing and the Eireannach (Irishman) were alone in a room by themselves. The Irishman was good at the pipes and played tune for tune with MacRaing. When MacRaing finished, the Irishman changed hands on the chanter, right hand up and left hand down – very difficult to do. MacRaing tried it and could do it with all his fingers except with his little finger. He was so mortified, he cut off his little finger. The lord and his piper exchanged news of all that happened every day and the Irishman told him what had happened. The lord took fright and said that if Duart heard of it he would kill them. When all was quiet at night the two fled. When Duart rose next morning he enquired of his guests and they were gone. He suspected there was something wrong and off he went after them. He was told that they had taken the road to Tobermory, but they had already gone and were in Ardnamurchan. He followed them to Kilchoan where he caught up with them. He killed and buried them both there. MacRaing composed a beautiful lament for them, 'Lament for the Lord of the Meeting' (*Cumha Moraire na Coinneimh*), now forgotten, or else it goes by a different name. John Johnston, who died in the Isle of Coll a few years ago, heard his own uncle playing it in Canada when he went out to learn piping from him.

Neil Rankin Morison (Kengharair), *Transactions of the Gaelic Society of Inverness*,
vol. 37, 1934–36, translated and abridged by Donald W. MacKenzie

*Notes

1. A song common in the Lethir Thorrloisg (the coastal strip of Torloisk) is about Robert the blacksmith. The song is given in the text.

2. Burial place of Clann Duiligh. The burial place is at Kilninian. There are three flat stones (*leacan*) resting on their graves. The first one is a smooth (not carved) one. On the second one intertwined foliage is carved and on the third is a fully armed warrior with a hound at his feet. Those last two are exactly similar to the old gravestones to be found on Iona. This in itself shows us how ancient the family was – 500 years – they belonged to the beginning of the 15th century.

3. In Thomson's *Companion to Gaelic Scotland*, Alan Bruford says of Counnduillie Rankin Morison (1856–1943): 'Of Dervaig, Mull. Authority on Mull Traditions. Contributor to *MacLean Bards* (A. MacLean Sinclair 1898–1900). Manuscripts of songs, including waulking songs, collected locally by "Counn" and other Morisons now deposited in the School of Scottish Studies.'

THE SPANISH PRINCESS (A LEGEND OF MULL)

The following highly romantic and thrilling traditional tale may possibly throw some light on the cause of MacLean's waning love for his fair spouse, which formed the subject of my sketch in last issue. It is a long story, but the gist of it is somewhat as follows:–

A daughter of the King of Spain, named Clarssaina Viola, one night had a vivid dream, in which she beheld a hero of such a noble form and stately mien as to fill her whole heart with the most ardent love. She knew that he was not of her own people, but wist not what his race, his language, nor his country was. She had no rest by night nor by day seeking for the noble-looking hero of her dream, but sought for him in vain.

At length she resolved to visit other lands, and got a great ship built, with four masts, and sails as white as snow one night old. She then left her native shores, and sailed to many distant foreign lands, and when she entered a port or harbour she sent invitations to all the nobility and chiefs of Highland clans in the surrounding country to come on board the great ship with the four masts and snow-white spreading sails, where they were royally entertained. All were pleased and glad to be her guests, and many gave her the warm love of their hearts, but among them all she found not her love, the hero of her dream. She sailed from one kingdom to another, and from harbour to harbour, and made feasting and music wherever she went. Around her all was gaiety and gladness, but within her heart all was dark, cold, and empty.

At length, while returning from the far-distant north, and passing the land under the wave – the flat island of Tiree – she came near the kingdom of Sorchi – Ardnamurchan, and after this to 'Mull of the great mountains', to the harbour of all harbours, curved like a bent bow, and sheltered from all the winds that blow. Here the great ship with the four masts and the white sails cast her anchors, and here, as in all other ports, the beautiful, dark-eyed Spanish Princess sent invitations to the nobility of the neighbouring country to visit her on board her ship. Here many a brave swordsman who rejoiced in the field of slaughter, and many a leader of numerous hosts who never turned their faces from the foe came on board; but all were strangers to her until at length the gallant, handsome Lord of Duart, the chief of the numerous, the warlike, the renowned MacLeans, shone upon her sight. Then did her heart leap with joy, and soon turned to rest in gladness, for he was the hero of her bright dream, in quest of whom she had travelled to so many lands.

It was then that there was the magnificent entertainment. There was music of sweetest sound. The daughter of the King of Spain had a sunbeam in her heart and lightness in her countenance. The Lord of Duart was so completely blinded with her great beauty and nobleness that he saw not the great black gulf that lay before him. He surrendered himself entirely to her loveliness, and great was the happiness of their converse. He quite forgot that in the strong, dark-frowning Castle of Duart he had left a youthful fair spouse. On board the great ship days passed like moments in the midst of unalloyed enjoyment; but not faster flew the happy days on board than rumours flew to Duart proclaiming to the forsaken lady of the castle the faithlessness of her lord. The colour left her usual rosy cheeks, sleep departed from her eyes, gnawing jealousy entered her heart, and fierce revenge filled her whole mind. Often as she turned on her pillow, as often turned a new plan in her head for the destruction of her who had robbed her of her love, but none of these did satisfy her.

At last she resolved to take into her counsel and confidence a noted Mull witch named *Cairistine Chrubach-a-Ghlinn* – *i.e.*, Cripple Kirsty o' the Glen, who, after listening to the lady's doleful tale, immediately summoned to her assistance all the weird sisterhood in the island, including *Ealasaid Ruadh-Claon-fiar-shuileach* – *i.e.*, Squint-Eyed Betsy, but it is needless to give the long Gaelic names of the others, as they were all as Hielan' as Mull. They immediately set about the fearful and uncanny job they had taken in hand, namely, to sink the great Spanish ship with the four masts and snow-white sails, then riding securely at anchor in Tobermory Bay. They first made a wax figure of the beautiful, dark-eyed Spanish Princess, which they hung before the fire in order to melt it slowly down, every now and then piercing it with sharp-pointed needles. They then tied a stout rope to a charmed stone, and passed it over the highest joist of the house; all seized the rope, and pulled with might and main, and as the charmed stone rose the wind rose, but with all their united strength they could not raise it high enough.

At length, seeing their work was like to fail, they called on *Seumas mór làidir*, the strongest man in Mull, to come to their assistance, and hold the rope, and keep the stone from falling to the ground. *Seumas mór* seized the rope in his powerful grasp, and held the stone up firm and fast close to the rafters. Several of the weird sisters then mounted their swift broomstick steeds, and flew to different distant places for assistance – one to Tiree, one to Kintyre, and one to Lochaber, to plead for the assistance of the celebrated *Morag Mhor-Cham chasach* – *i.e.*, Big Morag with the bowly legs, whose marvellous power was known to be more than any one of the sisterhood. She yielded to the pressing request of *Cairistine Chrubach*, and no sooner did she mount her favourite broomstick, and fly through the air, than a tempest began to blow the sea into roaring, curling white sea-horses. Morag-Mhor soon reached the great ship with the four masts and snow-white sails in Tobermory Bay, in the form of a huge grey cat, larger than was ever seen before, with a strong grey beard, every hair the size and sharpness of a tooth of a lint heckle, and a prodigious long tail. She at once scrambled up the rigging to the very pinnacle of the highest mast, and was immediately joined by her companions on evil deeds intent, numbering thirteen all told, and began to scramble hither and thither amongst the rigging, muttering their incantations and mystic charms.

The wind now veered suddenly round to the north-east, blowing straight from Lochaber, and across the dark, heather-clad hills of Morven with great velocity. Tobermory Bay being less protected from the north-east blasts than from any other point of the compass – Calve Island, which forms its breakwater on the north-east side, being comparatively low, probably less than twenty feet at its highest point – so the great ship, with its lofty masts and rigging, was exposed to the full force and fury of the terrific hurricane, and soon began to lurch and stagger hither and thither on her heavy iron chains, the tall masts bending and creaking, the wind whistling with an eerie, ominous, noisy sough amongst the rigging.

At last the great ship with the four masts and snow-white sails heeled over on her broadside, and began to sink – the piercing shrieks of those on board mingling with the howling, weird moan of the fierce storm. Several clinging to the sinking ship threw themselves into the raging waves, but the great suction of the huge vessel as she gradually disappeared drew them all after her – down, down, down to the bottom, so that all on board the great Spanish ship with four masts and snow-white sails perished in Tobermory Bay. The evening preceding the sad disaster the Lady of Duart had contrived a well-laid scheme, which proved successful, to induce Duart, and him alone, to withdraw from the doomed ship.

Some two weeks after the sinking of the great ship the disfigured lifeless body of a female was found along the dark, ragged, rocky beach of Mull, which was readily identified as the mortal remains of the beautiful but unfortunate Princess by the numerous precious jewels with which her person had been adorned. Duart at once engaged some masons or stone cutters, and had a strong stone coffin prepared, into which the remains were carefully laid, and one evening shortly after sunset the coffin was put on board Duart's galley, and conveyed across the Sound of Mull to the Morven shore. From thence it was carried up a long steep brae to the ancient kirkyard of Cill or Columb-Cill, where, as some say, rest the mouldering dust of the Holy Saint Columba.

The coffin was laid down at the base of the beautiful Iona Cross, which still stands outside the parish burying-place of Morven, and notwithstanding its great antiquity is in a wonderful state of preservation. The coffin, after resting for a short time at the foot of the stone cross, was then carried three times – according to the course of the sun – round it, then taken to the consecrated ground within the ancient chapel, and there committed to the dust, silently and secretly during the dark midnight hours, without priest or prayer or solemn hymn of repose. The spot has ever since to this day been known and pointed out to strangers as the tomb of the unfortunate Spanish Princess.

Malcolm Ferguson, *The Celtic Monthly*, vol. 3, 1894–95

GYPSIES

At a recent talk of mine a woman came up at the end. She said she was brought up in Glasgow and that her mother, a Gaelic-speaking native of Mull, would reproach her for bad behaviour as a girl, saying, 'It's the gypsy coming out!' She explained that local belief held that the Tobermory galleon of 1588 had gypsy women aboard who survived the shipwreck, came ashore and married local men.

Information from Roy Palmer via Margaret Bennett

A TORLOISK LEGEND

Torloisk appears to have always been a Maclean possession, and the founder of the Torloisk branch is generally given as a son of the famous Sir Lachlan Mor Maclean of Duart, who was killed at the battle of Traigh-Gruinneirt in Isla, in 1598 – the same chief who figures in the story of the treasure ship. So that date may be roughly taken as the beginning of the Torloisk Macleans as a separate branch.

But there is a legend which puts the establishment of the Torloisk Macleans three generations farther back. It is told by Dr McArthur* at considerable length in the *New Statistical Account* as a traditional story; and as I have not found it elsewhere it is worth recounting as a legend – one of those stories told at great length in Gaelic round the peat fires in the long winter nights.

The Maclean of Duart had an intrigue with a beautiful young woman of his clan, and she bore him a son. Because the child was born in a barn he was called Allan nan Sop,† which means 'Allan of the Straw'. McArthur does not give the name of the chief, but the name of the son fixes the chief as Lachlan Cattanach, who was a warrior troublesome to James IV about the year 1504. There was already a Maclean of Torloisk, and he married the boy's mother. Allan often visited his mother at Torloisk, but was not made very welcome by the Laird. One morning, as the lady of Torloisk saw her son approaching the house, she began to bake him a cake; and when he entered the house the old Laird put it suddenly into the boy's hand, burning hot, pressed his hand upon it, and said, 'Here is a cake for your breakfast, Allan.' Allan resented the injury and insult and did not return for many years.

When he did return it was with a little fleet of Danes among whom he had served with distinction. He wanted to see his mother who, however, was now dead. But the old man was much alive, and not a little afraid. So he professed great love for his stepson; and as he had a grudge against his neighbour, Macquarrie of Ulva, he recommended Allan to attack Macquarrie and seize his goodly island.

Allan crossed to Ulva, but was so well received that he could not find it in his heart to do what he had intended. Instead, he told Macquarrie of his ill purpose, and Macquarrie turned the tables on old Torloisk by suggesting that Allan should apply the treatment to him. So Allan returned, and said to his stepfather: 'You hoary old traitor, you instigated me to murder a better man than yourself; have you forgotten how you burned by fingers with a hot cake twenty years ago? The day has come when that breakfast must be paid for.' With which uncomfortable words he cleft the old man's head with his battle-axe, and took possession of Torloisk. And that is the origin of the Macleans of Torloisk.

There was a bloody bridal once at the Castle of Torloisk, and
that was in the time of Sir Lachlan Mor Maclean, and in the very
year in which the *Florida* took refuge in Tobermory Bay. Duart had
a feud with the Macians of Ardnamurchan, a branch of the Clan
Donald. Duart's mother was an attractive widow, being a daughter
of an Earl of Argyll and possessing a good jointure. Macian decided
that it would end the feud, and be to his advantage in other ways
besides giving him a charming bride, if he could obtain the lady in
marriage. And Duart at last agreed. The historian did not think it
necessary to record the lady's willingness, but the progress of the
tale makes that evident.

The chief of Ardnamurchan was invited to Mull for the nuptials,
which were duly celebrated at Torloisk. There were great festivities.
At last the bridal pair retired to their chamber, while the gentlemen
and servants of Macian retired to a barn in which they were to rest,
close to the house. In the dead of night the Macleans attacked the
barn, and a hideous massacre of unarmed men ensued. Duart
himself with some followers proceeded to break into the bridal
chamber to kill the Chief, who had been aroused by the clamour
and was ready to sell his life dearly. But on the intercession of his
wife his life was spared. He and two of his followers who had
escaped massacre were thrown into the Duart dungeons, where it
was said that the Macleans daily tortured Macian. In the following
year, however, he and his companions were exchanged for Macleans
whom the Macians had held as hostages, and there is reason to
believe that the course of true love ran smoothly – perhaps more or
less – from that time.

Thomas Hannan, *The Beautiful Isle of Mull*, 1926

* Kilninian and Kilmore in *N.S.A.* was drawn up not by Dr McArthur, who was
the minister, but by Francis William Clark of Ulva.

† Derick Thomson says of Ailean nan Sop (d. *c*.1552) in *The Companion to Gaelic
Scotland* (1987): 'Son of Lachlann Catanach of Duart and half-brother of
Eachann Mór of Duart. Brought up in Carnaburg Castle in the Treshnish Isles.
Noted pirate on Scottish and Irish seas; his last plundering expedition was
known as Creach na h-Aisne. Buried in Iona. The song "Caismeachd Ailean nan
Sop" is attributed to An Cléireach Beag.'

WITCHES DELAYING THE BIRTH OF AILEIN NAN SOP

This infernal cantrip was played by means of a ball of black worsted thread in a black bag, kept at the foot of the witch's weaving loom, where it might not be detected. If the ball was taken away the plot fell through. In proof of this, there is a story told that a child was once kept twenty-two years in its mother's womb by means of witches, and when born it had hair, beard, and teeth, like a person of that age.

The mother of a celebrated West Highland freebooter, 'Allan of the Faggots' (*Ailein nan Sop*),* was a servant maid who became pregnant by a married man. The man's wife, when she heard of the scandal, got a *bone* from a witch, which, she was assured, would, as long as it was kept, delay the birth of the child. Allan of the Faggots was thus kept in his mother's womb for fifteen months beyond the usual time. The husband got word of his wife's doings, and took a plan to defeat her. He made his Fool one day come home, pretending to be very drunk, staggering about, and smashing the furniture. On being called to task, the Fool said he had been in a house down yonder (that of the servant-maid), where a child had at last been born, and had got a dram, which went into his head. The wife, on hearing this, thought the witch had deceived her, and threw the bone into the fire. It disappeared in blue smoke, and knocked down the chimney! Allan was then born, with large teeth.
*Also known as Allan of the Straw.

J. G. Campbell, *Witchcraft and Second Sight*, 1902

ÀIRIGH CHREAG NA NIGHINN, THE SHIELING OF THE GIRL'S ROCK, ULVA

A dairy-woman accused a girl who was helping her of having stolen something [a 'caboc' or cheese], and the girl, who was a relation, denied it. The woman tried to force a confession by tying a plaid round the girl's neck and lowering her over a neighbouring rock. Unfortunately, the plaid tightened and the girl was strangled. Neighbours flocked to the scene, and finding the girl dead, they took the dairy-woman, tied her up in a sack, and placed her on a rock to be covered and drowned when the tide came in. And the rock has been called 'Sgeir Caristina' ever since.

Thomas Hannan, *The Beautiful Isle of Mull*, 1926

MacIan Ghiarr

MacIan Ghiarr, an Ardnamurchan thief, stole so many cattle from MacLean of Duard, that the chief became an enemy. On one of his roving expeditions he passed at midnight the chapel of Pennygown, in Mull, and seeing a light in the church, he entered, and witnessed three witches sticking pins in a clay body, intended to represent the chief of Mac Lean. As each pin was stuck in, MacLean would be seized with a pain in that part of the body which corresponded to the injured place. Only one pin remained and that was intended for the heart, and would cause death. MacIan scattered the witches, took with him the clay body, and made his way to MacLean, whom he found at death's door. In the presence of MacLean, one by one he took out the pins, and when the last one was withdrawn MacLean jumped up a hale man, and ever after remained a warm friend of MacIan Ghiarr.

J. P. MacLean, *History of the Island of Mull*, vol. 1, 1925

The Black and White Boat

He was one of the MacIans of Ardnamurchan. Now the name, he's a man Mac Iain Gheàrr. That wasn't the name the old people had for him. They called him Mac Iain Ghiar (pron. *year*). Now you would gather from that that Ciar was the name of the place that the old man came from. It wasn't Ciar (=dun-coloured) but Ghiar, Mac Iain Ghiar. Now, many stories are told about him. A saying, you know – he was a great robber at sea, you know. There was nothing he wouldn't lift, cattle or ponies or anything he could take for himself. The lads had a saying, 'a black side and a white side like Mac Iain Gheàrr's boat'. He would go up the Sound of Mull when he was going around on those raids, his boat would be white, painted. It was white. And you would swear that a boat had gone up, and maybe in the evening a boat would come back, and it was black on the other side, you know. He had his alibi right away. It wasn't the same boat at all. Mac Iain Ghiar, he was no slouch!

Alexander Cameron, Tobermory, recorded by Donald Archie MacDonald and Alan Bruford, transcribed and translated by Morag MacLeod, 1968, in *Tocher*, no. 52, 1996

The Crofter and the White Horse of Ulva

During the evictions in Ulva one of the crofters who lived near Starvation Point owned a very fine white horse. The factor had threatened that if he did not remove the roof of his house, he would shoot his horse. As the crofter refused to do this, and the horse was killed, the crofter predicted that when a sapling growing nearby died, the family line of the landlord, Francis William Clark, would also die out. The sapling was struck by lightning, and one of the Clarks was killed in action in Italy in 1944, although the family line continued.

Dr Thomas MacIntyre, Tobermory: as told by Dr Bill Clegg

The Broch at Kilbrennan – *Dùn nan Gall*

The field where this is situated is reputedly cursed and an archaeologist, while exploring the entrance to the broch and camping on the site, sent his son to Salen for provisions. When the son returned with chocolate containing hazelnuts, the archaeologist, possibly being allergic to them, choked and died. A nurse attending to him was believed to have seen an apparition sitting on the dickie seat of the car shaking his head as if in response to this.

Dr Thomas MacIntyre, Tobermory: as told by Dr Bill Clegg

The Grizzly Lad's Leap

The following may be accepted as the traditional account of certain incidents which are more or less authenticated by Gregory and other historians.

At one time (about 1450) the Laird of Coll (*Iain Garbh*) and MacNeill of Barra were at deadly feud, or as the *seanachie* graphically describes it – '*an rùn na biodaig d'a chéile*'. It would appear that when Iain Garbh was an infant his mother married MacNeill of Barra, who thought he might attach the island of Coll, seeing the heir was a mere child. Iain Garbh and his nurse fled to Dowart and MacNeill took possession of Coll. In course of time Iain Garbh decided to gain possession of his ancestral estates and having raised a following of some fifty clansmen, he sailed from

Mull for Coll, and landed at a creek or bay known as '*An Acarsaid Fhalaich*' – the Hidden Anchorage. Fortunately he met a woman who knew who he was, and she gave him information regarding MacNeill and his movements. She told him that MacNeill was at the time residing at Grisipool House, but as he was living in daily dread of the lawful heir making an attack upon him, he kept up daily communication with Breacachadh Castle – the messenger always riding on a grey horse.

'And there he goes,' continued the garrulous dame, shading her eyes with her hand as she looked in the direction indicated – 'He rides in haste to acquaint MacNeill of your arrival, and unless you checkmate him you and your men will be taken prisoners.'

Among Iain Garbh's followers was a young man from Dervaig, Mull – called '*An Gille Riabhach*' – or the Grizzly Lad. He being swift of foot offered Iain Garbh to stop MacNeill's messenger, and bring back his head, on condition that he received from Iain Garbh the lands of Dervaig, Mull, which, at that time, formed part of the Coll estate. Iain Garbh willingly consented, and the *Gille Riabhach* taking advantage of certain short cuts reached a place called '*Bealach na foille*', or Pass of Deceit, before the messenger. Resting himself by the wayside he carelessly enquired of the messenger what his news was. 'Important news,' answered the messenger, 'Iain Garbh and his followers have landed and are proceeding towards Grisipool, and I must make haste so that MacNeill may not be taken unawares – I see him and his men in the distance.' 'Is there any sign,' enquired the *Gille Riabhach*, 'by which MacNeill knows when he sees strangers in your company, whether they are friends or foes?' 'Oh yes,' responded the messenger, 'if foes, I keep apart from them, but if friends I and the grey horse move in their midst.' 'I have heard enough,' said the *Gille Riabhach*, and instantly springing up, pulled the messenger off his horse and cut off his head. Iain Garbh and his men soon came up, and the *Gille Riabhach*, throwing the head of the messenger to his master, mounted the grey horse and rode in the midst of the followers of Iain Garbh, and so deceived MacNeill and his men. A conflict ensued, and it is said that MacNeill, engaged in a hand-to-hand fight with Iain Garbh, was getting the better of his adversary, when the *Gille Riabhach* came to the assistance of the latter and wounded MacNeill severely. Before the *Gille Riabhach* was aware, he was sorely pressed by MacNeill's foster brother. The *Gille Riabhach* was in an awkward position, being hemmed in by the banks of the stream which passes Grisipool House, and he was obliged, in order to avoid a deadly blow from his adversary's battle-axe, to leap backwards and upwards across the stream, and the place is still known as '*Leum a' Ghille Riabhaich*' – the Grizzly Lad's Leap. Such was the force of the blow aimed at the head of the Grizzly Lad that the axe went into the ground, and before MacNeill's foster-brother could defend himself the *Gille Riabhach* leaped back and cut off his head.

MacNeill was killed and Iain Garbh took possession of the island. He fulfilled his promise to the *Gille Riabhach* by giving him the lands of Dervaig, in Mull.

Fionn, *The Celtic Monthly*, vol. 8, 1899–1900

Note: Interesting variants of the foregoing story will be found in *Clan Traditions and Popular Tales* by the Revd John G. Campbell, Tiree, and at p. 152 of Charles Maclean's *The Isle of Mull: Placenames, Meanings and Stories*. (Another tale connected with Dervaig is given at pp. 151–52 of the latter.)

REVD JOHN FRASER'S ACCOUNT OF SECOND SIGHT

The second instance is after this manner. I was resolved to pay a visit to an English gentleman, Sir William Sacheverill, who had a commission from the English Court of Admiralty, to give his best trial to find out about gold or money or any other thing of note, in one of the ships of the Spanish Armada that was blown up in the bay of Topper-Mory in the Sound of Mull.

I decided upon the number of men that were to go with me, one of the number was a handsome boy that waited upon my own person. About an hour before I made sail, a woman that was also one of my own servants spoke to one of the seamen and bade him dissuade me from taking the boy along with me for if I did, I should not bring him back alive. The seaman answered that he could not tell me such unwarrantable trifles. I took my voyage and sailed the length of Topper-Mory and having stayed two or three nights with that liberal gentleman, I then took my leave of him. In the meantime, my boy grew sick of a vehement bloody flux – the winds turned cross so that I could neither sail or row. The boy died with me on the eleventh night from his falling ill. The next morning the wind made fair and the seaman to whom the matter was foretold, related the whole story when he saw it verified. I carried the boy's corpse aboard with me and after my arrival and his burial, I called for the woman and asked her what warrant she had to foretell the boy's death. She said she had no other warrant but that she saw, two days before I took my voyage, the boy walking with me in the fields, sewed up in his winding sheets and that she had never seen this in others but that she found that they shortly thereafter died and concluded that he would die too and that shortly.

The Revd John Fraser, Minister of Coll and Tiree, *A Discourse on Second Sight*,
1707, quoted in Betty MacDougall, *Folklore from Coll*, 1978

MacFadyens of Garmony

Lochbuy first belonged to the Macfadyens. Maclaine . . . having obtained a grant of the place from the Lord of the Isles, deceitfully asked Macfadyen for a site for a sheep-fold (*crò chaoraich*), and, having obtained a hillock for the purpose, proceeded to build a castle. When the place was sufficiently fortified he shot an arrow from it at Macfadyen, who sat at some distance picking bones (*spioladh chnàmh*) at his dinner. In the end Macfadyen had to leave his own land and go to Garmony (*Gar'moin' an fhraoich*), where he supported himself by coining gold, gathered in *Beinn an Aoinidh*, Mull, whence his descendants became known as 'the Seed of the Goldsmith's' (*sìolachadh nan òr-cheard*).

J. G. Campbell, *Witchcraft and Second Sight*, 1902

Hugh of the Little Head (*Eoghan a' Chinn Bhig*)

The ghostly rider of the black horse (*marcaich an eich dhui*), crosses the seas in discharging his task. When coming to Tiree (where there are now but two or three persons claiming to be of the sept of the Lochbuy Maclaines), he takes his passage from *Port-nan-amhn*'* near *Ru-an-t-sléibh*, in Treshinish, Mull. About fifty years ago a Mull woman, living there, insisted that she had often, when a young woman, heard him galloping past the house in the evening and had seen the sparks from his horse's hoofs as he rode down to the shore on his way to Tiree.

J. G. Campbell, *Witchcraft and Second Sight*, 1902

*Haunn

HUGH OF THE LITTLE HEAD AND THE STRONGMAN

On the high road between Calachyle and Salen in Mull, a strong man of the name of Maclean was met at night by Hugh. The horseman spake never a word, but caught Maclean to take him away. Maclean resisted, and in the struggle caught hold of a birch sapling and succeeded in holding it till the cock crew. The birch tree was twisted in the struggle, and one after another of its roots gave way. As the last was yielding the cock crew. The twisted tree may still be seen. The same story is told of a twisted tree near Tobermory, and a similar one is localised between Lochaber and Badenoch.

J. G. Campbell, *Witchcraft and Second Sight*, 1902

MURDER IN GLENBELLART

Hugh Cameron, farmer at Frachadil, Calgary, was at Salen Fair along with David Thorburn, farmer, Sunipol. Having sold their stock and no doubt in possession of large sums of money, they were observed drinking at the Salen Inn (now Hostel) before proceeding up the glen on horseback.

They were attacked by a band of men near the bridge beyond Cranich (recently constructed). Cameron's saddle straps were cut and he was thrown into the river and killed. It was said that Thorburn, having a better horse, escaped unharmed.

It was generally believed at the time that the assailants were from the mainland, as many who attended the horse fair came from all over Britain and Ireland, and were likely to have had some vagabonds in their company. However some years ago, I was told by an old resident of Salen that she had heard that the murder had been carried out by some natives of that village. Thorburn was also suspected of being implicated in some way in the crime, and it was reported that he was under observation by the judiciary for a long time after the murder had been committed. He was known to be a very avaricious man. He also had the reputation locally of treating his farm servants harshly, even by the times, and did not allow them to have milk with their porridge, only whey. As far as I know no one was ever arrested for the crime.

Hugh Cameron is listed in Slaters directory as a farmer in Frachadil in 1867 but not in 1878. He was an uncle of the late Donald Cameron, butcher, Tobermory, who retired in the 1950s.

David Thorburn was a native of Wigan, Lancs., and the family farmed in the Isle of Muck before moving to Mull. He retired from Sunipol farm about 1899 and built a new house in St Mary's, Tobermory. He resided there in 1900.

Calum MacDonald, Tobermory, 2001

DÒMHNALL ÒG CHOLLA: DONALD MACLEAN 'YOUNG COLL' (1752–74)

Donald MacLean was the son of Hugh MacLean the Laird of Coll. He was greatly beloved by his father's tenants and there was universal grief when he tragically met his death in the year 1774.

On Sunday the 25th of September 1774, he and a few companions left Erray House (now the Old Farm-house), Tobermory, then occupied by Dr Hector MacLean (1704–86), and proceeded on their journey to the Island of Inch-Kenneth where Sir Allan MacLean was in residence. There being no public roads at that period of time, they followed a path which took them first into Glen Bellart where they called at the house of Eachan O'Muirgheasain (Hector Morison) at Achadh na Sabhal (above Druim-na-croise) who was MacLean of Coll's ground officer at Quinish. In his conversation with Mr Morison, Dòmhnall Òg remarked that he was very displeased with young Lochbuie's conduct during their journey across the hill – the latter had been shooting game birds all the way over.

The party left Achadh na Sabhal and proceeded up Glen Bellart until they reached the footpath which crossed the hills to Lagan Ulva. On arrival at Lagan House, then occupied by Gilleasbuig a' Lagain (Archibald MacLean), a brother of MacLean of Torloisk, young MacLean of Lochbuie made arrangements to have some of the birds he had shot cooked. When the birds were placed on the dining table, Dòmhnall Òg rose up and threw them in the ashes of the fire-place and refused further food.

The company then left, and continued their journey to the ferry, but alas they never reached Inch-Kenneth. Dòmhnall Òg and young Lochbuie must have come to blows in the boat, which overturned, and the eight persons on board were drowned. The only body recovered was that of Dòmhnall Òg, and he had a wound on his face.

It seems that there was considerable enmity between the two MacLeans, as both courted Sir Allan MacLean's daughter, and it was reported that she much preferred Dòmhnall Òg to Lochbuie's son. After Dòmhnall Òg's body was recovered, she came over to the ferry at Ulva and asked for his watch from which she extracted a small piece of paper. It was presumed that this was a betrothal agreement which she and the deceased had made.

Calum MacDonald, Tobermory, 2001: as told by Niall Mac'ille Mhoire
(Niall Mór), 1938

FAMOUS CAILLEACHS

The legend as I heard it was:– That the Cailleach gathered the stones and carried them in a 'gad' on her back with an 'iris-mhuineal' to erect a bridge over Caol Muile. The 'iris-mhuineal' broke, the stones fell, and there they lay to this day, to prove the enterprising spirit of the Cailleach. If the 'iris-mhuineil' had not broken, no doubt the old Cailleach would have carried the 'carn' to the narrowest part of the Caol and there build so desirable an erection. Whether the Cailleach of the 'Carn' was the Cailleach Bheur of Gleann Cainneil or not is a matter of doubt, evidently there must have been many a celebrated 'Cailleach' in Albain. There was the Cailleach whose neglect of covering her well originated Loch Odha; there is Rudha-na-Cailleach in Mull: she went 'a dh'iarraidh maorach' [to gather shellfish], and the tide cut her off from the path back, and she would have been drowned had she not scaled the precipitous cliffs of the Rudha, praying to God for help, but when she achieved the ascent she said, 'Chaidh agam air a dh' aindeòin Dhia is dhaoine' (I managed it, despite God and men), and, Chaidh a tiunndadh na carra cloiche far an do sheas i (she was turned into a pillar of stone where she stood). I was shewn this Carragh, but I failed to see any semblance to a Cailleach in it. Then there is Beinn na Cailleach, near Broadford, an t-Ath-leathann, Isle of Skye. Some legend is attached to it connected with the Fianntaichean. And the ever-memorable Cailleach Bheur. Where is a 'Muileach' that has not heard of her and Tobar na-h-òige? Mr. McFadyen is in error, for in my youth no one knew for certain where it was, for it was supposed to disappear. After the Cailleach fell 'na cuaill chnamh aig an tobar' [a heap of bones at the well] – not ashes. After meeting the shepherd and his dog that barked, the Cailleach Bheur said to the shepherd:–

'S moch an diugh a ghoirr an cù,
Maduinn chiùin os cionn loch Bà.

[Early today the dog barked
On a calm morning above Loch Ba.]

Then the shepherd asked her –

A Chailleach bheur bheadarach
Gu dè d' aois?
'Nuair bha 'n fhairge ghlas na coill
S ann bha mis am mhaighdainn óg.

[Shrill, sportive Carlin
How old are you?
When the ocean was a forest
I was a young maid.]

When the shepherd enquired where she was born she replied –

Cnoc an fhir léith
Airidh bhealaich
Dui-leitir nan cabar cama
'S ann a bha mi og am leanabh.

[The hillock of the grey man
The shieling of the brae
The black slope of the bent rafters.
Is where I was young as a child.]

Duileitir is on the west side of Loch Frisa, the Leitir or Leth-tir is on the east sides. In Duibh Leth-tir I cut 'cabair chama' in 1851 for '*fiorach tarsuinn*' [cross timbers] for a boat.

Note: *gad* = a large basket; *iris-mhuineil* = shoulder band of a creel.

Donald Beaton, Queensland, *The Celtic Monthly*, vol. 13, 1904–05

CELEBRATED WITCHES

The best-known names seem to have been merely nicknames, given perhaps to more than one old woman. 'Blue-eye' (*Gorm-shùil*) is said to originate from the witch having one eye black or brown and the other blue. It is, however, a corruption of *Gormla*, an ancient and pretty Gaelic name, usually rendered Dorothy. *Gormla Mhòr* from Meigh, Lochaber, was stronger than all the witches of Mull, and gave the finishing stroke, as already detailed, to Capt. Forrest's ship. She met her death when astraddle on a mountain stream, to intercept a salmon that had made its way up to spawn. A large fish made a rush, knocked her backwards in the water, and drowned her. There was a Gormshuil in the village of Hianish, Tiree, a most notorious local witch, and one in Cràcaig in Skye, equally notorious. 'Brindled-Headless-Stocking Foot' (*Cas a mhogain riabhaich*) and 'Rough Foot-gear, the Herdsman's daughter' (*Caiseart gharbh ni'n an Aodhair*) were anywhere but where the person who is telling about them comes from himself. Shaw, the Lochnell bard, makes them sisters dwelling in Glenforsa in Mull, when Ossian was a little boy, and contemporaries of Mac-Rùsluin. 'Sallow Spot' (*Ball Odhar*) was from Kintra (*Ceann-trà*) in Ardnamurchan; 'Yellow Claws' (*Spòga buidhe*) from Maligeir on the east side of Skye; *Doideag-un* is the well-known name of the Mull witches, and is given by children to the falling snowflakes, which they are informed are the Mull witches on their journey through the air. Big Kate MacIntyre in Fort-William was extensively known some forty years ago as a person skilled in divinations and possessing mysterious powers.

                         J. G. Campbell, *Witchcraft and Second Sight*, 1902

MULL WITCHES

From time immemorial Mull was famed as the nursery and home of a race of witches, some of whom were singled out as possessing wonderful powers. The times were favorable for the belief in witch-craft, for such views were entertained from the king down to the humblest peasant, and it also entered into the laws of the nation, – as in fact into the laws of all nations. The witches of the Highlands had their unhallowed powers, but being little of the repulsive or horrible. No mention is made of their midnight meetings and dances with the devil, nor riding through the air on a broom-stick. Those usually regarded as witches were old women, destitute of friends and means of support, and some of them did cater to the idea in order to eke out a living, and even worked upon the fears of those more prosperous. They were supposed to inflict their punish-ment by means of types, the usual method being the preparation of a clay or wax image of the person or object to be acted upon; and when the witches prick or punch these images, said persons experience extreme torment.

Rising out of the myths of Mull are two witches, who in power and in personage tower above all others of that isle. One of these is called Cailleach Bheur, whose home was in the Ross of Mull, near a point on the southwest, close to the sea-shore, where a huge natural quadrangle formed of immense granite rocks, in a wild rocky place, exposed to the full force of the western gale, with the ceaseless roar of the ocean. She closed her career of thousands of years in Gruline, on the banks of Loch Ba. At intervals of a hundred years she would immerse herself in the waters of that loch, in order to obtain newness of life. But if she should fail to bathe in this, to her, elixir of life, in the morning before the birds or beasts greeted the early day, then the charm would lose its potency. One morning, just as the cycle was about to close she descended the slopes beyond the loch, and just as she had gained the bank, and was in the act of taking the plunge, which would have changed her haggard form into a handsome maid, the distant bark of a shepherd dog welcomed the first gray streaks along the eastern sky, and re-echoed among the mountains and hills. The charm was broken. The witch stood, listened, reeled, staggered, and dropped dead. Back in the ages a Mull bard put into Cailleach Bheur's mouth at the last moment a lament, in which was this expression which was her favorite:

> Crulochan, deep, dark, and gloomy,
> The deepest lake in all the Universe;
> The Sound of Mull would only reach my knees,
> But Crulochan would reach my thighs.

The other of the two most famous of the witches, and reputed to be the most powerful was called Doideag Mhuileach, and made her home on lofty Ben More. She is quite prominent during the latter part of the sixteenth century. The most celebrated story concerning her relates to a Spanish princess. It is mixed up with the destruction of the Florida, belonging to the Spanish Armada. Similar to nearly all other tales it has many variants. One rendering states that Bheola, daughter of the King of Spain, dreamed of a remarkably handsome man, and made a vow she would find him. She fitted out a ship, and in the course of her inquiries, sailed into Tobermory harbor. Here she saw Sir Lachlan Mor MacLean, who proved to be the man she had seen in her dream. Although knowing he was married, yet she fell violently in love with him. His wife, in a jealous rage caused the vessel to be blown up, the agent making his escape and reaching Pennygown, a distance of ten miles, before the actual explosion. The cook was blown to Srongarbe, near Tobermory, where there is a cleft, still called Cook's Cave. The princess fell in the Sound, from whence she was taken and interred in Lochaline burying-ground, Morvern. Upon the news of this disaster reaching Spain, another vessel was dispatched to seek vengeance by taking the right breast of every Mull woman. When this ship arrived the Lady of Duard sent for Doideag, and by her means, with assistance procured from neighboring witches, the ship was sunk before the following morning. Doideag shut herself up in a house alone at Rutha Ghuirmein, near Duard Castle, and there made her incantations. A rope was put through a hole in a rafter, and all night long the hand-mill was hoisted up to the beam, lowered and hoisted again. To this a native of Tyree added:

'Having come that evening to Doideag's house, was compelled by her to hoist and lower and hoist and lower the millstone all night without rest or refreshment, while the witch went her way to Tyree and elsewhere for help. On her return she said that when in Tyree she had been detained a little in extinguishing a fire, which had been caused by a spark falling among the fodder in the stirk-house belonging to the man who was her unwilling assistant. As the quern was raised a gale sprang up, and increased in fury as the operation went on. At the same time gulls (others say hooded-crows, others black cats) appeared on the yard-arms of the devoted ship. The captain knew the Black Art himself and went below. As the word was brought him that another gull had appeared in the rigging, he said, "I will suffice for this one yet." He could keep the ship against some say eight, others nine, witches, but "ere a' the play was play'd" there were sixteen, some say, eighteen, on the yards. All the Mull witches were there, and the most powerful of the sisterhood from the surrounding districts. Nic-ill'-Domhnuich from Tyree is commonly mentioned. All accounts agree that when Big Blue-eye from Mey, the powerful Lochaber witch, came, the ship sank. Shortly before the captain told a sailor to look up and see how many gulls were on the yards. On being told eighteen, he said, "We are lost." In the morning Doideag was told her house had been unroofed in the gale, but she was comforted by being told the dreaded ship had gone down.'

It was Doideag who destroyed the ill-fated Spanish Armada. When she discovered that this fleet was about to swoop down upon England, she determined to thwart its purpose and to accomplish its destruction. When it was announced that the fleet had entered the British waters, she raised a great storm at sea, and then taking with her the clay image of a ship, she went to the sea-shore, and placing her model on the water, she kept whirling it about, and as often as it sank, down went one of Philip's invincible men of war.

Doideag was ever faithful to the MacLeans. Among her last acts was the protection of the clan in 1675. In that year the earl of Argyle set out with two thousand men to invade Mull. The army embarked and set sail for Mull; but Doideag raised a dreadful storm which raged for two days, driving back the fleet and disabled some of the vessels. She had promised the Chief of Mac Lean that as long as she lived the earl should not enter Mull.

J. P. MacLean, *History of the Island of Mull*, vol. 1, 1923

THE *CAILLEACH MHÓR*

It was here on the northern end of Mull, some say near Ardmore Bay, that the *Cailleach Mhor*, Hag of the Ridges (Winter), found her last refuge. She fled there to die after her defeat by Spring in the Cuillins of Skye. Songs still commemorate her coming, for she was one of the Great Ones and may not be forgotten. The Hag arrived in Mull furiously angry and one cannot help having a little sympathy with her. After all, she was driven out of her own Scotland, which she had made, by the young upstart Spring of the red-gold hair who was aided, of course, by the Cuckoo . . . and was left to die, homeless and helpless, on Mull.

Here, accounts differ. One story tells how the Cailleach landed at Ardmore and sang a song so bitter that the young grass withered and died and the trees wilted but that, charmed by the beauty of the island, she rested and slept and while she slept Spring came in peace, while others claim that Spring killed her in Mull, or that she died of rage at his doings and that her grave may still be seen there, a stone cist as in a prehistoric burial mound. Before she died she wandered all over the island crying and lamenting, and her voice can still be heard, a wailing in the wind of late winter. The raven, the grey crow and the black-backed gull carried the news of her death to her consort, a great beast who came out of the sea to lament for her.

The Hag herself became a cormorant, or sea-raven, still ill to meet at sea and presager of storm. The Hag is believed to have been quite alarmingly ugly in life and in Mull was credited with having one long blue tusk. Despite this she evidently appreciated beauty when she saw it, for a more beautiful spot for a burial place than this north head of Mull would be hard to find.

Otta F. Swire, *The Inner Hebrides and their Legends*, 1964

WITCHES (*NA DOIDEAGAN*)

Na Doideagan was used as a collective name for the people of Mull just as other islands and areas had their own: Lewis *na bioraich* (the dogfish); the Ross of Mull *na gamhna* (the stirks, calves); Iona *na h-eich* (the horses); west of Ross-shire *cearcan* (hens); Glenelg *ðisgean nan casa caola* (first year ewes = hogs of the small feet); Kerrera *na h-eireagan* (pullets); Ardnamurchan *na cnòdain* (the gurnets); Lorn *na losgainn* (toads or frogs); Lismore *na h-ðisgean* (ewe hogs).

Adapted from Fionn, *The Celtic Monthly*, vol. 19, 1911

DEROGATORY TERMS: DERVAIG BEARS

The people of Dervaig were reputed to have been thus named after a travelling entertainer from Germany who brought a dancing bear to the village and was not well paid for his show. He retorted, 'Just 3¼ pennies – there must be plenty of bears in Dervaig.'

Calum MacDonald, Tobermory, 2001

WITCHES' PARAPHERNALIA

The crook or pot-hanger seems to have been an important article of the witch's paraphernalia. A shepherd in Mull, coming in late from the hill, with his feet wet, placed his stockings to dry on the pot-hanger. An old woman present pulled the stockings down again, saying to the shepherd, 'Don't do that; remember you are a person that travels the hill night and day.' . . . He never could ascertain what she meant.

J. G. Campbell, *Witchcraft and Second Sight*, 1902

WITCHES AND THE SEA

A witch, who left home every night, was followed by her husband, who wondered what she could be about. She became a cat, and went in the name of the devil to sea in a sieve, with seven other cats. The husband upset the sieve by naming the Trinity, and the witches were drowned. So the Skye story runs. In the Sound of Mull the witches went on board the sieve, 'against the name of the

Father, and the Son, and the Holy Ghost'; and the husband upset
the concern by putting his foot on board in the name of the Father,
and the Son, and the Holy Ghost. In Tiree the unfortunate women
were passing Kennavara hill in egg-shells on their way to Ireland,
when the husband of one of them, seeing the fleet, wished them
God-speed. Instantly the egg-shells sank, and the women were
drowned.

J. G. Campbell, *Witchcraft and Second Sight*, 1902

THE WITCH AND THE THREE-KNOTTED STRING

A boatman from one of the southern islands was long detained in
Lewis by adverse winds. He was courting a witch's daughter, and
applied to her mother for a favourable wind. He gave her a pound
of tobacco, and, assisted by neighbouring witches, after three days'
exertion, she produced a string with three knots upon it. The first
knot was called 'Come gently' (*Thig gu foill*), and when he loosened
it, as he left the shore, a gentle breeze sprang up. The second knot
was called 'Come better' (*Teann na's fhearr*), and on its being untied
the breeze came stiffer. As he neared the harbour, he out of
curiosity loosened the last knot, the name of which was 'Hardship'
(*Cruaidh-chàs*). A wind came 'to blow the hillocks out of their
places' (*séideadh nan cnoc*), and sent the thatch of the houses into the
furrows of the plough-land, and the boatman was drowned. In
Harris, they say the boat was drawn up on land and secured before
the last knot was untied. She was capsized and smashed to pieces.

J. G. Campbell, *Witchcraft and Second Sight*, 1902

THE THREE-KNOTTED HANDKERCHIEF AND FISHING BELIEFS

I remember one of the MacAllisters in Tobermory, there was an old
woman, a relation, and when he was going to fish she would give
him a three-knotted handkerchief (*nèapaigin le trì snaoim*). You
opened the first knot if there was no wind, and the second if there
was not enough, but no way would you open the third! Heaven
would fall down! This still happened after the Second World War.

Peter MacLean, Dervaig, 2001

WITCHES AS RATS AT THE TRESHNISH ISLES

A Tiree boatman, bringing a load of peats from the Ross of Mull, was met at the Treshinish Isles by two rats sailing along on dry cowsherds. As good luck did not direct him, he threw a piece of peat at the rats, and upset their frail barks. A storm sprang up, and with difficulty he got to land. The rats were witches, and he should not have meddled with them.

J. G. Campbell, *Witchcraft and Second Sight*, 1902

CLAY CORPSES – *CUIRP CHRÈADHA*

The greatest evil that witches can do is to make, for a person whose death they desire, a clay body or image (*corp creadha*), into which pins are stuck, to produce a slow and painful disease, terminating in dissolution. Waxen figures for the same purpose, and melted by exposure to a slow fire, were known to Lowland superstition. In the Highlands wax was not accessible to poor bodies, and they had to make clay serve the turn. It is said that when a person wants [lacks] a limb he cannot be destroyed by witches in this manner.

MacIain Ghiarr, the Ardnamurchan thief, stole so many cattle from MacLean of Dowart that he made that chief his deadly enemy. On one of his roving expeditions he was passing at midnight the chapel or burying-ground of Pennygown (*caibeal Peighinn-a-ghobhan*), on the Sound of Mull. Seeing a light in the chapel, he entered, and found three witches sticking pins in a clay body (*corp creadha*) intended to represent MacLean of Dowart. As each pin was stuck in, MacLean was seized with a stitch in the corresponding part of his body. Only the last pin remained to be stuck in. It was to be in the heart, and to cause death. MacIain Ghiarr scattered the witches, took with him the clay corpse, and made his way to MacLean, whom he found at death's door. He took out in his presence the pins one by one, and when the last was taken out MacLean jumped up a hale man, and remained ever after the warm friend of MacIain Ghiarr.

J. G. Campbell, *Witchcraft and Second Sight*, 1902

THE GLAISTIG OF ERRAY

There is one tale of this kind which is told of a house near Tobermory. It is the tale of 'The Glaistig of Erray', to be found in *The Superstitions of the Scottish Highlands*, collected by John Gregorson Campbell, Minister of Tiree. The Glaistig, according to Campbell, is a female occupying a middle position between the Fairies and human beings. The name is made up of two words – *glas*, meaning grey or pale green; and *stig*, which means a crouching or hiding object. She is described as a woman who had received a fairy nature. Apparently from the fact of her former humanity she retained a desire to be always about a human habitation, and to take part in the domestic work. But in the nature of things this is impossible when the people of the house are about during the day. Accordingly, the glaistig gets busy at night. She sweeps the floor, moves the furniture about, and does a variety of other things. Sometimes she does real tidying, but very largely her indoor work gives satisfaction only to herself. In some cases she leaves everything in confusion. But she also takes a hand at doing outdoor work at night, watching over the cows and the dairy, and apparently seeing that nothing goes wrong in these directions, so long as her industry is recognised by leaving out some milk for her own use at night.

Erray, according to Campbell, is from *an Eirbhe*,* meaning the outlying part of a farm; and Erray House is about a mile north of Tobermory. The land must have been a farm at one time, whatever it may be now. On this farm there was a glaistig who seems to have specially attached herself to the barn. The 'herd', or farm-servant, often heard trampling in the barn while he himself slept in the 'byre', or cowhouse, which adjoined it. Everything left in the barn at night was found in confusion in the morning.

A curious and pathetic feature is that the glaistig is generally represented as a former mistress of the house, but laid under a spell which gives her the fairy nature.

Thomas Hannan, *The Beautiful Isle of Mull*, 1926

Note: The Revd John Gregorson Campbell points out in *Superstitions of the Highlands and Islands of Scotland* (1900) that 'in olden times a wall (of turf) was commonly built to separate the crop land from the hill ground, and was known as *Gàradh bràgh'd*, or Upper Wall. The ground above the *Gàradh bràgh'd* was known as the *Eirbhe*.'

THE GLAISTIG OF ARDNACALLICH, ULVA

The Glaistig of Ardnacallich, the residence of the Macquarries of Ulva, used to be heard crying 'Ho-hò! hò-ho! Macquarries' cattle are in the standing corn near the cave! The bald girl has slept! the bald girl has slept! hò-hò, ho-hò.' The 'bald girl' was no doubt a reference to her own plentiful crop of hair.

J. G. Campbell, *Superstitions of the Highlands and Islands*, 1900

THE GLAISTIG OF COIRE-NA-SHEANCHRACH

The Glaistig of *Coire-na-sheanchrach*, a valley on the Mull coast, half way up the sound between that island and the mainland, met a poor fisherman of the neighbourhood every evening, when he came ashore from the fishing and always got a fish for herself. One evening he caught nothing but lithe, and when the Glaistig came and looked at them, she said, 'They are all lithe tonight, Murdoch.' Whatever offence was taken by her in consequence she never came any more.

J. G. Campbell, *Superstitions of the Highlands and Islands*, 1900

THE GRUAGACH

A supernatural female who presided over cattle and took a kindly interest in all that pertained to them. In return a libation of milk was made to her when the women milked the cows in the evening. If the oblation were neglected, the cattle, notwithstanding all precautions, were found broken loose and in the corn; and if still omitted, the best cow in the fold was dead in the morning. The offering was poured on 'clach na gruagaich', the 'gruagach' stone. There is hardly a district in the Highlands which does not possess a 'leac gruagaich' – a 'gruagach' flag-stone – whereon the milk libation was poured. [There follows a list of all the places where they have been seen, including Mull and Iona.] All these oblation stones are erratic ice-blocks. Some of them have a slight cavity into which the milk was poured; others have none, the libation being simply poured on the stone. In making the oblation the woman intoned a rune.

Alexander Carmichael, *Carmina Gadelica*, vol. 2, 1928

THE NINE-HEADED MONSTER OF STAFFA

Staffa's chief title to fame is its wonderful caves with their basalt columns. The largest and best known of these is Fingal's Cave and in it lived at different times a variety of giants. The first known to have inhabited it was a most horrible nine-headed monster with an appetite commensurate with the number of his mouths. He was credited with using the cave as a cage in which to fatten his unfortunate captives, whom he then preserved in vinegar and malt whisky until he had nine of them. Then he would lay them out carefully on enormous platters of wood suitable to his size, one on each of his nine tables, the Islands of Staffa, Iona, Jura, Oronsay, Colonsay, Scarba, Lismore and Kerrera. After that he would dine in leisurely comfort, seated in his chair – Ben Mhor of Mull – with one unfortunate human for each of his nine mouths. It is said that he came to a bad end when the great Irish hero Cuchulainn, on his way to Skye to join Sgàthach's 'School for Heroes' there, got wind of his activities and called in when passing. For many centuries his cave remained empty and then another and very different type of giant (with only one head) took up his abode there. This was Fingal, a noted giant claimed by some as the ancestor of the Macdonald Clan and by others as that Finn who once built a church in Sutherland for St. Laurence with disastrous results. Be that as it may, Fingal dwelt here with his wife and family and gave the famous Fingal's Cave its name. His spirit, it is said, still haunts it and can be seen, when moon and tide are right, moving from one basalt pillar to another like some enormous white bird of light.

Otta F. Swire, *The Inner Hebrides and their Legends*, 1964

MULL FAIRIES

The mythical creation known as *fairy* occupies a prominent position in Scottish Highland superstition. It is known under the name of *sith*. In popular belief the fairies were a race of beings, the counter parts of mankind in person, occupation, and pleasure, though ordinarily invisible, noiseless, and having their dwellings underground, in hills, and green mounds. Their nature was such that man must be on his guard against them. Generally the fairies had some personal defect. Those in Mull had but one nostril, the other being imperforate. Everywhere the red deer are associated with them, and in Mull were said to be their only cattle. They lived in colonies or communities, and in Mull these were located near the extreme headland of Bourg, a green mound near Pennygown, in the parish of Salen, and one on a hillock near Duard Castle. All these colonies were active in their dealings with their human neighbors, and many tales are still current concerning them. A fairy tale of Bourg states that an industrious housewife had collected a quantity of wool to be manufactured into cloth for the family. According to custom she invited her neighbors to bring their spinning wheels and help spin the wool for the weaver, and she jocularly remarked that she 'wished the people of the hill, would come and take part in the labor'. Immediately every corner was filled with these little beings who began to sing in Gaelic:

> Combing, mixing,
> Carding, spinning,
> A weaving loom quickly
> And the waulking water on the fire.

The words uttered represented the different stages of the manufacturing process from 'combing' to 'waulking' of the cloth. Simultaneously with the pronouncing of the word that process was completed. Then the fairies crowded around the table expecting the customary meal. For this the woman was wholly unprepared. She desired them to go, but they refused. She went to the door and called an old man and made known her trouble. The old man said, 'Stand outside the door and cry as loud as you can "Dun Bhuruig ri theinidh, Dun Bhuruig ri theinidh", which is Burg is on fire! Burg is on fire! No sooner had the woman cried out the warning than the fairies rushed out, all crying and yelling in great distress, 'M'ruird is m'inneinean, mo chlann bheag's mo mhuirichean, obh! obh! obh! obh! Dun Bhuruig ri theinidh,' which means, 'My hammers and my anvils; my little children and my offspring; Burg is on fire. Alas! Alas!' They disappeared at the entrance of their home, and the woman saw them no more.

J. P. MacLean, *History of the Island of Mull*, vol. 1, 1923

APPEARANCE OF MULL FAIRIES

Generally some personal defect is ascribed to them, by which they become known to be of no mortal race. In Mull and the neighbourhood they are said to have only one nostril, the other being imperforate (*an leth choinnlein aca druid-te*).

J. G. Campbell, *Superstitions of the Highlands and Islands*, 1900

RED DEER AND FAIRIES

Everywhere, in the Highlands, the red–deer are associated with the Fairies, and in some districts, as Lochaber and Mull, are said to be their only cattle . . . 'I never,' said an old man (he was upwards of eighty years of age) in the Island of Mull, questioned some years ago on the subject, 'heard of the Fairies having cows, but I always heard that deer were their cattle.'

J. G. Campbell, *Superstitions of the Highlands and Islands*, 1900

Note: There is also a tale about a deer killed on the lands of Scalasdal that turned out afterwards to be a woman.

PROTECTION AGAINST FAIRIES

In Mull and Tiree the pockets of boys going any distance after nightfall were filled with oatmeal by their anxious mothers, and old men are remembered who sprinkled themselves with it when going on a night journey.

J. G. Campbell, *Superstitions of the Highlands and Islands*, 1900

PENNYGOWN FAIRIES

A green mound, near the village of Pennygown (*Peigh'nn-a-ghobhann*), in the Parish of Salen, Mull, was at one time occupied by a benevolent company of Fairies. People had only to leave at night on the hillock the materials for any work they wanted done, as wool to be spun, thread for weaving, etc., telling what was wanted, and before morning the work was finished. One night a wag left the wood of a fishing-net buoy, a short, thick piece of wood, with a request to have it made into a ship's mast. The Fairies were heard toiling all night, and singing, 'Short life and ill-luck attend the man who asked us to make a long ship's big mast from the wood of a fishing-net buoy.' In the morning the work was not done, and these Fairies never after did anything for any one.

J. G. Campbell, *Superstitions of the Highlands and Islands*, 1900

Fairies Stealing Women and Children

A shepherd, living with his wife in a bothy far away among the hills of Mull, had an addition to his family. He was obliged to go for assistance to the nearest houses, and his wife asked him, before leaving her and her babe alone, to place the table beside the bed, and a portion of the various kinds of food in the house on it, and also to put the smoothing-iron below the front of the bed and the reaping hook (*buanaiche*) in the window. Soon after he had left the wife heard a suppressed muttering on the floor and a voice urging some one to go up and steal the child. The other answered that butter from the cow that ate the pearl-wort (*mòthan*) was on the table, that iron was below the bed, and the 'reaper' in the window, how could he get the child away? As the reward of his wife's providence and good sense the shepherd found herself and child safe on his return.

J. G. Campbell, *Superstitions of the Highlands and Islands*, 1900

Throwing the Arrow in Glen Cannel

A weaver at the Bridge of Awe (*Drochaid Atha*) was left a widower with three or four children. He laboured at his trade all day, and when the evening came, being a hard-working, industrious man, did odd jobs about the house to maintain his helpless family. One clear moonlight, when thatching his house with fern (*ranach*), he heard the rushing sound of a high wind, and a multitude of little people settled on the housetop and on the ground, like a flock of black starlings. He was told he must go along with them to Glen Cannel in Mull, where they were going for a woman. He refused to go unless he got whatever was foraged on the expedition to himself. On arriving at Glen Cannel, the arrow was given him to throw. Pretending to aim at the woman he threw it through the window and killed a pet lamb. The animal at once came out through the window, but he was told this would not do, he must throw again. He did so, and the woman was taken away and a log of alder-wood (*stoc fearna*) was left in her place. The weaver claimed his agreement, and the Fairies left the woman with him at the Bridge of Awe, saying they would never again make the same paction with any man.

She lived happily with him and he had three children by her. A beggar came the way and staid with him that night. The whole evening the beggar stared at the wife in a manner that made his host at last ask him what he meant. He said he had at one time been a farmer in Glen Cannel in Mull, comfortable and well-to-do, but his wife having died, he had since fallen into poverty, till he was now a beggar, and that the weaver's wife could be no other than the wife he had lost. Explanations were entered into, and the beggar got his choice of the wife or the children. He chose the former, and again became prosperous in the world.

J. G. Campbell, Superstitions of the Highlands and Islands, 1900

DONALD THRASHED BY THE FAIRY WOMAN

A man in Mull, watching in the harvest field at night, saw a woman standing in the middle of a stream that ran past the field. He ran after her, and seemed sometimes to be close upon her, and again to be as far from her as ever. Losing temper he swore himself to the devil that he would follow till he caught her. When he said the words the object of his pursuit allowed herself to be overtaken, and showed her true character by giving him a sound thrashing.

Every night after he had to meet her. He was like to fall into a decline through fear of her, and becoming thoroughly tired of the affair, he consulted an old woman of the neighbourhood, who advised him to take with him to the place of appointment the ploughshare and his brother John. This would keep the fairy woman from coming near him. The fairy, however, said to him in a mumbling voice, 'You have taken the ploughshare with you to-night, Donald, and big, pock-marked, dirty John your brother,' and catching him she administered a severer thrashing than ever.

He went again to the old woman, and this time she made for his protection a thread, which he was to wear about his neck. He put it on, and, instead of going to the place of meeting, remained at the fireside. The Fairy came, and, taking him out of the house, gave him a still severer thrashing. Upon this, the wise woman said she would make a chain to protect him against all the powers of darkness, though they came. He put this chain about his neck, and remained by the fireside. He heard a voice calling down the chimney, 'I cannot come near you to-night, Donald, when the pretty smooth-white is about your neck.'

J. G. Campbell, *Superstitions of the Highlands and Islands*, 1900

DOGS AND FAIRIES

1.

Two men from Mull were engaged building a march dyke across the hills in Kintail. To be near their work, they took up their residence by themselves in a hut among the hills. One night, before retiring to rest, they heard a horrible screaming coming in the direction of the hut. They went out with sticks of firewood in their hands. Though they could see nothing, they knew something was approaching. The shrieks came nearer and nearer, and at last a large dark object passed. A little dog, 'Dun-foot' by name, which accompanied the men, gave chase. When it returned there was no hair on any part of it but on its ears, and no hair ever grew after but a sort of down.

2.

A man in Mull was sent on a journey after nightfall, and about midnight, when crossing the hills from Loch Tuath (the North Loch) and Loch Cuän (*Loch Cumhan*, the narrow loch), saw a light in the face of a hillock. He was accompanied by his dog, and before long he heard the noise of dogs fighting, mixed with sounds of lovely music. He made off as fast as he could, and, on arriving at the house to which he had been sent, was offered supper. He was unable to take any. Before bed-time his dog came with every hair on its body pulled off. It smelt its master's clothes all over, lay down at his feet, and was dead in a few minutes.

J. G. Campbell, *Superstitions of the Highlands and Islands*, 1900

FAIRIES AND IRON

In Mull, a person, encountered by a *Bean shìth* [banshee], was told by her that she was kept from doing him harm by the iron he had about him. The only iron he had was a ring round the point of his walking stick.

J. G. Campbell, *Superstitions of the Highlands and Islands*, 1900

FAIRIES AND CHANGELINGS

In Mull, a mother whose baby has actually been stolen by the Little People and a changeling* left in its stead should place the changeling on the shore below high-water mark and there leave it. When it becomes clear that she means to leave it to drown, the Little People will rescue it and leave in its place a human baby, which the mother must then take and bring up. The snag is that it may not be her own baby she gets back but some other stolen child, which, nevertheless, if she does this she is bound to accept and care for.

Otta F. Swire, *The Inner Hebrides and their Legends*, 1964

*Note: The changeling left by the fairies is usually an old wizened fairy or elf. There are many tales in J. Gregorson Campbell's and in Otta F. Swire's books about their discovery and subsequent removal.

SALEN *TAMHASG* (THE SHADE OR DOUBLE OF A LIVING PERSON)

Near Salen, in Mull, a workman, when going home from his employment in the evening, forgot to take his coat with him. He returned for it, and the apparition (*tamhasg*) of a woman met him, and gave him a squeezing (*plùchadh*) that made him keep his bed for several days.

J. G. Campbell, *Witchcraft and Second Sight*, 1902

THE ERRAY MAN AND THE *TAMHASGAN*

Alexander Sinclair, from Erray, in Mull, was grieve at Funery in
Morven. Two, if not three, of the servant women fell in love with
him. He had to cross one night a bridge in the neighbourhood,
between Savory and Salachan, and was met by the apparitions of
two women, whom he recognised as his fellow-servants. One, he
said, was the figure of a dark little woman, and lifted him over the
parapet. The other was that of the dairymaid, in the house in which
he was, and it rescued him. The adventure ended by his marrying
the dairymaid.

J. G. Campbell, *Witchcraft and Second Sight*, 1902

THE LEDMORE *TAMHASG*

A man, going home at night to Ledmore (*Leudmòr*), near Loch
Frisa, in Mull, saw the kitchen-maid of the house in which he was
at service waiting for him on the other side of a ford that lay in his
way. Suspecting the appearance, he went further up the stream to
avoid it, but it was waiting for him at every ford. At last he crossed,
and held on his way, the apparition accompanying him. At the top
of the first incline, the apparition threw him down. He rose, but
was again thrown. He struggled, but the figure, he said, had no
weight, and he grasped nothing but wind. On the highest part of
the ascent, called *Guala Spinne*, the apparition left him. After going
home, the man spoke to the woman whose spectre had met him.
'The next time,' he said, 'you meet me, I will stab you.' This made
the woman cry, but he was never again troubled by her apparition.

J. G. Campbell, *Witchcraft and Second Sight*, 1902

TAIBHS (PHANTASM OR SPECTRE)

A *taibhs* could also be treacherous. A young labourer from Mull was
given a pair of knitted gloves by a fellow servant which he wore for
the first time when crossing a mountain pass on his way home to
his family. At the most dangerous point he was joined by the *taibhs*
of the maid who had knitted the gloves. As she was on the safe side
of the path, he was terrified that she would push him over the

precipice. Praying hard, he continued in safety until he reached level ground. Then he took off the gloves, flung them at her and said, 'That is all the business you have with me.' On his way back to work, he noticed the gloves on the path, but he did not touch them. The vision never returned.

Elizabeth Sutherland, *Ravens and Black Rain*, 1985

Note: The original of this story appears in J. Gregorson Campbell's *Witchcraft and Second Sight,* and involves a man called Henderson from Glenbeg in Ardnamurchan who was in service at Kilfinichen.

THE WATER HORSE AND LOCH FRISA

The water-horse – *Each Uisge* – inhabited the fresh water lochs, and could be seen passing from one lake to another, mixing with horses, and waylaying belated travellers. It was highly dangerous to touch or mount it. The most widely celebrated tale of this class relates to a tenant of Aros, in Mull, five versions of which have been preserved. The heir of Aros was a young man of great personal activity, but dissolute, and believed there was no horse that he could not ride. He was taken by a water-horse into Loch Frisa and devoured. This occurred after his espousal of marriage. His intended bride composed a lament, which was long a popular song in Mull. It appears to be a fact that the young man was dragged into Loch Frisa by a mare he was trying to subdue and was drowned. By the lament his body appears to have been recovered.

One account states that a remarkably handsome grey mare came among the horses belonging to the tenant of Aros, then pasturing on the rushes at the end of Loch Frisa. One day his son haltered and mounted it. The mare stood very quietly until the young man had mounted it, and then rushed into the loch. Another version says the young man found a mare in the hills which he took to be his father's. He caught and mounted it intending to ride it home, but the mare rushed with him into Loch Frisa where he was devoured by water-horses. A third tradition says the water-horse was kept all winter, with a cow shackle about its neck, and remaining quiet and tractable, the shackle was neglected. One day the son rode it to the peat-moss followed by three horses behind in usual form, when it suddenly rushed into the lake, neither the son nor the horses were ever seen after, save their livers. The fourth account says, one spring several men went to the hill to catch a young horse, but were unable to do so, the following morning the son of Aros went with them; caught the horse wanted, and vaulted on its back. The horse at full speed rushed to the loch, but the young man could not throw himself off. Next day the horse's liver came ashore, the supposition being that the water-horses tenanting the lake had devoured it on catching the smell of a man off of it.

Another narration states that Mac-fir Arois was twice taken by the water-horse. The first time he managed to put a foot on either side of a gate, in passing through, which allowed the horse to slip from under him. The second time, a cap which hitherto had kept the horse, was forgotten. In the terrible speed to the loch, the young man clasped his arms around its neck, but could not unclasp them. His lungs floated ashore next day.

J. P. MacLean, *History of the Island of Mull*, vol.1, 1923

MER-FOLK AND CALGARY BAY

Mull like all other islands knew the Mer-folk and Calgary Bay was reputed to be a favourite haunt of theirs. Island girls not infrequently married mermen, just as their brothers might wed a mermaid. In either case the marriages were quite frequently happy.

Mer-folk who became mortals had, of course, to shed their tails. One of these was found by an adventurous boy in Calgary Bay. He tried it on, fitting it with a belt of oarweed, and went to sea. He soon learned that there is more to swimming than borrowing a tail, however, and was just sinking for the third time when he felt hands holding him up and found himself in the arms of a mermaid who 'slipped him into the curl of her tail' and carried him safely ashore. Then she went away, taking the spare tail with her.

The 'ordinary' mer-folk were kindly on the whole; they would protect from the Little People mortals who sought their help, and below high-water mark no fairy dare touch a mortal.

Luran, Luran black,
Betake thee to the black stones of the shore,

cried a Wise Woman to her son who had angered the fairies and was being pursued by them. Should you chance to find a merbaby and are kind to it, the mer-folk will give you anything you ask or they think you would like, but should you find one and harm it you will be drowned if you are lucky: if not, you will be cursed, and the curse of the mer-folk is something to go a long way to avoid.

But Mull knew another type of mer-folk also, the fallen angels, who were spirits of fire and air, for their misdeeds condemned to live in the sea lest they corrupt others. A Mull man once found and tried to wear a tail belonging to one of these sea-folk. It was too tight at the waist, so, drawing out his father's knife, he slit it down one side as if gutting a fish. Instantly a terrible scream was heard and he found himself enveloped in living flame. No one could approach to help him, so great was the heat, and he was burnt to death. He had found the temporarily discarded tail of one of the fallen angels (or so it was believed) and they had fire in their veins instead of blood. It was well known that if one was wounded (they rarely were) he would bleed fire and burn to death. The man in cutting the tail had wounded the Spirit and let loose fire, burning the tail, its real owner and himself.

Otta F. Swire, *The Inner Hebrides and their Legends*, 1964

TAGHAIRM

This superstition was an awful ceremony and was generally known among old men as 'giving his supper to the devil'. It was sometimes celebrated when an important question concerning futurity arose. It was then that a shrewd person was selected who was wrapped in the warm hide of a newly slain ox or cow, and then laid at full length in the wildest recess of some lonely waterfall. Here he lay for some hours, and whatever impression was made on his mind, was supposed to be the answer. But the term also conveyed a different meaning and procedure, which consisted in roasting cats alive on spits till the arch-fiend himself appeared in bodily shape, and was then compelled to grant whatever wish the persons who had the courage to perform the ceremony preferred, or to explain whatever question was asked. Tradition has preserved three instances of this performance. Once it was performed by Allan, the cattle-lifter, in Lochaber; another time by the 'children of Quithen', a small sept in Skye, and the third and last time was in the big barn at Pennygown, in Mull, towards the close of the sixteenth century, the characters said to have been Allan MacLean, son of Hector, of the family of Loch Buy, joined by Lachlan MacLean, son of Donald, son of Neill, the first MacLean of Ross. Lachlan was an exceedingly daring and warlike man and governor of Duard Castle, under his chief Sir Lachlan Mor, and fought in all the battles of that chief. Allan and Lachlan were faithful companions. At the time of the celebration of the rite, both were young, unmarried, resolute, determined. The rite then consisted in roasting cats alive one after the other, as a sacrifice to the devil, during four days, without intermission or tasting of food, at the end of which time they were entitled to any two boons they might crave. The ceremony commenced between Friday and Saturday, and had not long continued, when infernal spirits, in the form of black cats, began to enter the barn in which the rite was being celebrated. When the first cat entered, it darted a furious look at the operator and exclaimed, 'Lachlan Odhar, thou son of Neill, that is bad usage of a cat.' Allan, who was master of ceremonies, cautioned Lachlan that he must not fail to turn the spit, despite whatsoever he might see or hear. The cats continued to enter, and the yells of the cat on the spit, joined by the rest, were fearful. At last there appeared a cat of enormous size, and informed Lachlan if he did not desist before his great eared brother arrived, he never would see the face of God. Lachlan replied he would not flinch until his task was finished, even if all the devils of hell should make their appearance. By the end of the fourth day, there was a black cat at the extremity of every rafter on the roof of the barn, and their yells were distinctly heard beyond the Sound of Mull, in Morvern. At last the rites were finished, and the votaries should now demand on the spot their reward. Allan was agitated by the fearful sights he had witnessed but was able to make use of two swords which meant wealth. Lachlan, although the younger, had greater firmness and never lost his wits, asked progeny and wealth, and each literally obtained what he had asked.

When Allan was on his death-bed, his pious friends advised him to beware of the wiles of Satan. The dying man replied that if Lachlan Odhar (who was then dead) and himself were to have the use of their arms, they would dethrone Satan, and take up the best berths in his dominion. When Allan's funeral procession approached the churchyard, the second-sighted persons present saw Lachlan Odhar at some distance in full armor, at the head of a party in sable attire, and the smell of sulphur was perceived by the people. The stone on which Cluase Mor – the cat with huge ears – the fiercest of all the cats, sat, is still exhibited, with the mark visible in small pits upon the surface.

J. P. MacLean, *History of the Island of Mull*, vol. 1, 1923

AFTER THE *TAGHAIRM*

The two men obtained their desires, but were obliged (some say) to repeat the *taghairm* every year to keep the devil to the mark.

When Dun Lachlan was on his deathbed his nephew came to see him, and in the hope of frightening the old fellow into repentance, went through a stream near the house and came in with his shoes full of water. 'My sister's son,' said Lachlan, 'why is there water in your shoe?' (*a mhic mo pheathar, c' arson tha bogan a'd bhróig?*) The nephew then told that the *two* companions who had been along with Lachlan in the performance of the *taghairm*, and who were both by this time long dead, had met him near the house, and to escape from them he had several times to cross the running stream; that they told him their position was now in the bad place, and that they were waiting for his uncle, who, if he did not repent, would have to go along with them. The old man, on hearing this melancholy message, said, 'If I and my two companions were there, and we had three short swords that would neither bend nor break, there is not a devil in the place but we would make a prisoner of.' After this the nephew gave up all hopes of leading him to repentance.

A native of the island of Coll and his wife came to see him. Lachlan asked them what brought them? 'To ask,' said the Coll man, 'a yoke of horses you yourself got from the devil' (*dh' iarraidh seirreach each fhuair thu fhein o'n douus*). Lachlan refused this and sent the man away, but he sent a person to overhear what remarks the man and his wife might make after leaving. The wife said, 'What a wild eye the man had?' (*Nach b' fhiadhaich an t-sùil bh'aig an duin' ud?*) Her husband replied, 'Do you suppose it would be an eye of softness and not a soldier's eye, as should be?' (*Saoil am bi suil an t-slauchdain, ach sùil an t-saighdeir mar bu chòir?*) On this being reported to Lachlan, he called the Coll man back and gave him what he wanted.

J. G. Campbell, *Superstitions of the Highlands and Islands*, 1900

THOMAS THE RHYMER AND KENGHARAIR

The Highland tradition is, that Thomas is in Dunbuck hill (*Dùn buic*) near Dunbarton. The last person that entered that hill found him resting on his elbow, with his hand below his head. He asked, 'Is it time?' and the man fled. In the outer Hebrides he is said to be in Tom-na-heurich Hill, near Inverness. Hence MacCodrum, the Uist bard, says:

> Dar thigedh sluagh Tom na h-iubhraich,
> Co dh' eireadh air tùs ach Tòmas?

> When the hosts of Tomnaheurich come,
> Who should rise first but Thomas?

He attends every market on the look-out for suitable horses, as the Fairies in the north of Ireland attend to steal linen and other goods, exposed for sale. It is only horses with certain characteristics that he will take. At present he wants but two, some say only one, a yellow foal with a white forehead (*searrach blàr buidhe*). The other is to be a white horse that has got 'three March, three May, and three August months of its mother's milk' (*trì Màirt, trì Màigh, agus trì Iuchara 'bhainne mhàthar*); and in Mull they say, one of the horses is to be from the meadow of Kengharair in that island. When his complement is made up he will become visible, and a great battle will be fought on the Clyde.

> Nuair thig Tòmas le chuid each,
> Bi latha nan creach air Cluaidh,
> Millear naoi mìle fear maith,
> 'S theid righ òg air a chrùn.

When Thomas comes with his horses,
The day of spoils will be on the Clyde,
Nine thousand good men will be slain,
And a new king will be set on the throne.

J. G. Campbell, *Superstitions of the Highlands and Islands*, 1900

THE SHARK AND THE ORANGES

Ai, ai. 'Se seann eachdraidh tha seo an am nam bàtaichean siùil. Bha brùid de searc a' leanailt a' bhàta seo agus, O, cha robh e còrdadh ris a' chriù idir, agus bha iad a' smaointinn gur e fior dhroch chomh- arradh a bh' ann agus 'Feumaidh sinn stad a chur air.' Thachair gun robh luchd de dh'oranges 's a' bhàta agus fhuair iad bocsa agus thilg iad far na cliathaich e agus thàinig an searc a nuas agus shluig e siod. O, well, cha robh e stad, bha e 'cumail an déidh a' bhàta 's thuirt iad, 'O, well, tha seann sofa seo. Feumaidh sinn an seann sofa seo chur far na cliathaich.' Agus mhothaich an searc e agus shluig e sin sìos 'na bhroinn. 'S bha e fhathast 'leanailt a' bhàta agus, well, bha seann chailleach air bòrd agus thuirt iad, 'Tha i gu bhith deiseil co- dhiubh. Tilgidh sinn far na cliathaich i.' Rinn iad sin agus thàinig an searc a nuas agus shluig e 'chailleach.

Ach, co-dhiubh, bha e 'leanailt a' bhàta agus 'O,' thuirt iad, 'feuchaidh sinn rud eile.' Fhuair iad . . . Rinn iad dubhan mór de dh'iarann agus chuir iad ròpa làidir air agus fhuair iad pìos de mhuc bho 'n chòcaire agus leig iad sin far na cliathaich agus shluig an searc e.

An sin bha e an greim aca agus chum iad greim air agus chluich e e fhéin gus an robh e sgìth agus fhuair iad 'obrachadh gu cliathaich a' bhàta agus an sin chuir iad ròpa m'a earball agus winch iad air bòrd e.

Agus bha e sin air an deck agus mharbh iad e. Ach, an sin thuirt iad, "S fheàrr dhuinn 'fhosgladh feuch de tha 'na bhroinn.' Agus sgolt iad a' bhrùid searc sìos agus a' chiad rud a chunnaic iad 'se a' chailleach a' suidhe air a' sofa 's i 'g ithe na h-oranges!

Translation: Ay, Ay. This is an old history in the time of sailing boats. A brute of a shark was following this boat and the crew didn't like it at all and they were thinking that it was a very bad omen and said, 'We must put a stop to him.' It happened that there was a cargo of oranges in the boat and they got a box and they threw it over the side and the shark came up and he swallowed that. O, well, he didn't stop: he kept on behind the boat. 'O, well, there is an old sofa here. We must put this old sofa over the side.' And the shark noticed it and he swallowed it right down into his belly. He was still following the boat and, well, there was an old woman on board and they said, 'She is about done for anyhow. We'll throw her over the side.' They did that and the shark came up and he swallowed the old woman.

But nevertheless he kept on following the boat. 'O,' they said, 'we will try something else.' They got . . . they made a big hook of iron and put a strong rope on it and they got a piece of pork from the cook and let it go over the side and the shark swallowed it.

Then they had a hold of him and they kept a hold of him and he played himself until he was tired and they got him manoeuvred to the side of the boat and then they put a rope round his tail and winched him on board.

And there he was on deck and they killed him. But then they said, 'We had better open him to see what's inside him,' and they split the brute shark right down and the first thing they saw was the old woman sitting on the sofa eating oranges!

Peter MacLean, Dervaig, 2000

THE STORY OF THE OLD MAN AND THE CAT

On a wild stormy night, the old man was cooking fish and potatoes in a pot. When the fish was cooked he put the two pieces on the edge of the pot and waited till the potatoes were ready. A big ginger cat comes in through a hole in the door, all soaked. It sees the fish and eats one piece. 'Take the other one too,' says the man. The cat eats that and sleeps while the man eats his potatoes with butter. The next day the cat is gone.

In spring the man needs seed potatoes (*pòr*), and at last, is directed to Ceit Ruadh. She welcomes him and gives him a dram and food and seed potatoes and says, 'You were good to me that wild night when I went through your door and had two fishes.'

Angie Henderson, Tobermory, in BBC radio programme
'Sgoil Eòlais na h-Alba', 1993

IAIN BODHAR

Iain Bodhar, 'se seòladair a bh'ann an am nan soithichean seòlaidh agus 'san am sin cuideachd bha fior dhroch dhaoine a' seòladh a' chuain dh'an abradh anns a' Bheurla 'pirates'. Agus thachair gu robh iad as déidh a' bhàta a bha Iain Bodhar ann. Agus ghlac iad i 's chaidh iad air bòrd agus bha iad a' marbhadh a h-uile duine de'n chriù gos a robh mu dheireadh ach Iain air fhàgail. Thuirt e riutha, "S mise an duine mu dheireadh. Am bi sibh cho math mo chur ann an togsaid agus toll beag fhàgail air a' cheann fiach am faigh mi aidhear?'

Agus rinn iad sin 's thilg iad Iain Bodhar thar na cliathaich. Agus O, an ceann lathaichean chaidh a chur air tìr thall 's an Ros Mhuileach. Agus thachair gur e là teth a bh' ann, agus bha iad a' smaointinn gun tachradh, far an robh crodh bhiodh iad a nuas a' coiseachd anns an t-sàil 'gam fuarachadh fhéin agus rinn iad sin an latha seo agus bha tarbh leo. Agus mhothaich an tarbh an togsaid.

Ach co-dhiubh, nuair a bha e air thighinn air tìr, bha sgian phòcaid aig Iain Bodhar airson an toll a dhèanamh nas motha gus am faigheadh e 'làmh troimhe. Agus thòisich an tarbh bualadh an togsaid le adhaircean agus nuair a bha e dol seachad rug Iain Bodhar air earball aige. Mach a ghabh an tarbh leis an eagail a fhuair e agus chum Iain Bodhar greim air gus a chum e mach astair os cionn àirde 'n làin agus chualaig iad Iain Bodhar anns an togsaid agus chaidh a shàbhaladh.

Ach 'se nuallan a' chuain a dh'fhàg Iain Bodhar bodhar.

Translation: Iain Bodhar (Deaf John), he was a sailor in the time of sailing vessels and at that time too there were very wicked men sailing the ocean who were called in English 'pirates'. And it happened that they went in pursuit of the boat in which Iain Bodhar was. And they captured it and they kept killing all the men of the crew until at last there was only John left. He said to them, 'Since I am the last one would you be so good as to put me in a hogshead leaving a little hole at the top to see that I can get air?'

They did that and threw him overboard. And, oh, after many days he was beached over in the Ross of Mull. And it happened that it was a hot day, and what happened, where there were cows they used to come down to walk in the salt water to cool themselves and that's what they did this day and the bull was with them. And the bull noticed the hogshead.

But, however, when he had landed Iain Bodhar had a pocket knife to make the small hole larger so that he could get his hand through it. And the bull began to strike the hogshead with his horns and when he went past Iain Bodhar caught him by the tail. Off went the bull with the fright he got and Iain Bodhar kept a grip of him until he kept him out a distance above the high-water mark and they heard Iain Bodhar in the hogshead and he was rescued.

But it was the roar of the ocean that left deaf John deaf.

Peter MacLean, Dervaig, 2000

THE KING, THE PRIEST AND THE *AMADAN*

There was a priest in Scotland and he did something wrong, and gave great offence to the king – it was one of the Jameses. And he was to be executed. But the king allowed him a chance: if he came to see him in his palace at Scone, and answered three questions the king would put to him, he would go free. And he knew well enough that there were some questions he couldn't answer because of the way someone had framed them – that there are questions that nobody at all can answer if they are put in a certain way – no one else. Well, this was worrying him a lot, and he was just pacing up and down the house day and night, and his brother, who lived with him and was a simpleton – everybody just called him 'the fool' – he said to him:

'What's bothering you now?'

'Och, what use is it for me to tell a fool like you?'

'Oh, but I might be able to do something, give you advice, or something or other like that.'

Well, he told him how it was, that he was condemned to death, but he had one chance: if he could answer the three questions the king put to him in his own palace, then he would get off.

'Well, there are questions,' said his brother to him, 'that you couldn't . . . that you *can't* answer.'

'And what am I going to do?' said the priest.

'Well, I'll go in your place.'

'Oh no. What's a fool like you going to do?'

'Well, look here. What will happen to me if you are executed? I'm just going to be a fearful idiot wandering through this world, making sport for everyone. Won't you let me go there: if I'm executed, it won't make any difference at all.'

Well, the priest agreed that his brother should go, and he put on the priest's habit, took the priest's staff and set off. He came to the king's palace in Scone; he knocked on the door; a big man came to it beautifully dressed in a fine blue and red uniform and asked him who he was; he told him that he was the priest, and all that, and:

'What do you want?'

'I want to see the king.'

'Come in, he's expecting you.'

He was taken to the king's room, and the king was sitting there on a big throne, with gold chains round his neck and wearing lots of beautiful things.

'Come in.'

He went over to him and took off his hat. The king said to him: 'You know the reason why you are here.'

'Yes,' he said.

'Well, well, then, we might as well just begin now. First question, then – where is the centre of the world?'

'It is right here,' said he; he knocked with his staff on the middle of the floor.

'Oh well, I must let you have that. You know, yes, I believe that the world is round like a ball, and anywhere will do for its centre. Heh, I'll give you that one. Next question, then – what am I worth sitting on the throne here? Just what am I worth in money?'

'Well,' said the man to him, 'you're not worth any more than thirty pieces of silver, anyway.'

'Why do you say that?'

'The best man who was ever born in the world was sold for thirty pieces of silver.'

'You've got it. I must give you that one too. The third one – if you can answer this, you're really damned good,' said he. 'Do you know of anything I'm thinking . . . the king is thinking at the moment, and he's entirely wrong?'

'Yes,' said he.

'What's that, then?'

'You're talking . . . you think you're talking to the priest, and you're talking to the fool, his brother.'

'Well,' said the king, 'anyone who has a brother like that, and that brother a fool, deserves to get off. Away you go!'

Angie Henderson, Tobermory. Recorded in Gaelic by Alan Bruford, and published in *Tocher*, no. 5, 1972

Chapter 8

SUPERSTITIONS

In our belief system, Christian and pagan beliefs sat easily alongside each other; the worldly and otherworldly merged and the line between the natural and the supernatural was blurred. Anna Dhubh's cure for Lena, described earlier, is a classic example of this merging and blurring; the stories about fairies and the Each Uisge were other examples that were comfortably accommodated within our view of life and the world – a view more compatible, I think, with that of St Columba and the Celtic Church than that of John Knox and the Church of the Reformation.

Donald W. MacKenzie, *As it Was*, 2000

CHILDHOOD BELIEFS: EELS GROWING FROM HORSE HAIR

The omission of any science subject from the curriculum left a void that we sought to fill by observation, experiment and listening to folk tales . . . We believed that the wild cat had a barb in its tail which could inflict a serious wound on anyone rash enough to touch it.

I once decided to put another bizarre piece of country lore to the test. I was told that if you placed a hair from a horse's tail in a sluggish stream, with one end anchored in place with a stone, it would in time develop into a live eel. Not having access to a horse's tail, I tried out the experiment with a hair from Lena's tail and kept watch. After some time, as it became covered in slime and wriggled with the slow-running movement of the water, it did, indeed, give every appearance of being a live eel, but I was not convinced that it was the real thing.

Donald W. MacKenzie, *As it Was*, 2000

It is still a very common belief in the Highlands that eels grow from horse hairs. In a village of advanced opinions in Argyllshire, the following story was heard from a person who evidently believed it:

'In the island of Harris, in a time of scarcity, a person went out for fish, and succeeded only in getting eels. These animals are not eaten in the Highlands and his wife would not taste them. The man himself ate several. By and by he went mad, and his wife had to go for succour to a party of Englishmen, who had a shooting lodge near. On arriving with loaded guns, the sportsmen found the eel-eater in the fields fighting a horse. He was so violent that they had to shoot him. On inquiry it turned out that the cause of his madness and fighting the horse was that the eels he had eaten had grown from horse hairs!'

J. G. Campbell, *Superstitions of the Highlands and Islands*, 1900

COIRE BHROCHAIN

O, Coire Bhrochain. Bha sin . . . seann chleachdadh a bha sin o shean aig, anns a' Bheurla, Treshnish Point. Tha bearradh àrd, dìreach dol a sìos do'n mhuir agus tha Coire an sin, Coir' a' Bhrochain, abraidh iad ris, agus anns na seann lathaichean, 'fhios 'ad, bha iad – móran dhiubh, a' trusadh feamainn airson leasachadh, agus bha iad a' dèanamh seo an urram Mana, dia a' chuain, agus bha iad a' dèanamh poit mhóir de bhrochain, agus chan eil 'fhios 'am dé là a bh' ann, chan eil cuimhne 'am 'n e Diar-Daoin a' Bhrochain Mhóir abradh iad ris, roimh Chàisg, agus bha sin air a dhèanamh agus bha e 'ga chopadh thairis a' bhearraidh do'n mhuir, agus bha iad a' smaointinn an sin, '*Well*, nì seo feum. Gheibh sinn gu leòr de bhàrr dearg air a thilgeil air tìr.'

Translation of above and further discussion:

Ann: The other thing you told me, that was interesting, was about Coire Bhrochain . . .

Peter: O, Coire Bhrochain.

Ann: . . . and what they did there for the god Mana.

Peter: Yes. That was an old custom that was of old at, in English, Treshnish Point. There is a high, steep cliff going down to the sea and there is a corrie there, Coire Bhrochain (Porridge Cauldron), they used to call it, and in the olden days, you know, they were, many of them were collecting seaweed as a fertiliser, and they were doing this in honour of Mana, god of the sea, and they were making a big pot of porridge, and I don't know what day it was, I can't remember if it was Thursday of the Big Porridge they used to call it, before Easter, and that was made and it was couped over the cliff into the sea, and they were thinking then, 'Well, that will do good. We will now get plenty of red tangle cast on the shore.'

Ann: And when do you think that was done?

Peter: O, long before my time, it was done. It must have been. That's why it was called Coire Bhrochain.

Ann   You said there was another place near Gometra associated with Mana.

Peter: Ah, well. Manaisgeir. Manaisgeir. That's a skerry off the point of Gometra.

Ann: That must be a very old custom?

Peter: O, yes; very ancient.

Peter MacLean, Dervaig, 2000

Notes:

1.   *Bàrr dearg* – red seaweed, tangle (*laminaria digitata*), chewed when tobacco was scarce, a remedy against scorbutic and glandular diseases, main source of kelp.

John Cameron, *The Gaelic Names of Plants*, 1900

Also from the same book:

'The inhabitants of the Isle of Lewis had an ancient custom of sacrificing to a sea god called Shony at Hallowtide (i.e. All-Hallows, 1st November). The inhabitants round the island came to the church at Mulvay (St Mulvay), each person having provisions with him. One of their number was selected to wade into the sea up to the middle, and, carrying a cup of ale in his hand, standing still in this position, and crying out with a loud voice, "Shony, I give you this cup of ale, hoping you will be so kind as to send us plenty of seaware for enriching our ground for the ensuing year." He then threw the cup into the sea. This was performed in the night time; they afterwards returned to spend the night in dancing and singing. Shony (Sjone) is the Scandinavian Neptune. This offering was a relic of pagan worship introduced into the Western Isles by the Norwegians.'

Although he does not say so, Cameron, I am sure, has taken this account from Martin Martin's *A Description of the Western Islands c. 1695*.

2. Manaisgeir. On maps spelled Maisgeir (O.N. *mai* 'sea mew' + *sgeir* 'skerry'). But MacQuarrie (*The Placenames of Mull*) suggests that Mai is a personal name.

3. Martin Martin, in *A Description of the Western Islands c. 1695*, describes a libation of ale to a sea god called Shony by the people of Lewis to promote bountiful casting of seaware on the shores for use in fertilising the land.

4. Charles Maclean, *The Isle of Mull: Placenames, Meanings and Stories*, Dumfries, 1997, provides some notes at pp. 148–9 on Coire Bhrochain. He says: '(a) This is a cliff edge from which porridge was thrown into the sea as an oblation to the sea god Shony (Senaidh) on Maundy Thursday . . . if the usual drift of seaweed, Barr Dearg, was behind time in being washed up. (Dwelly p. 333). (b) Grant [I. F. Grant, *Highland Folk Ways*, London, 1961] p. 5. In . . . Iona . . . people living in 1840 could still remember that an offering of porridge used to be poured into the sea to the God of the Ocean to induce him to produce plenty of sea-wrack. Also Grant p. 297. On Lewis and on Iona an offering of porridge used to be thrown into the sea to induce a mysterious being called Shoney to send plenty of seaware . . . Could this just be Seonaidh or Johnny? (c) Watson [W. J. Watson, *The Celtic Place-Names of Scotland*, Edinburgh, 1916] p. 200. Here Brochan is applied to a mixed up "through-other" sort of place or to soft sludgy ground.'

5. Dwelly's Dictionary, p. 333, referred to by Maclean above, reads: 'Diardaoin a' Bhrochain mhóir, *Maundy Thursday*. It was at one time a custom in the Long Island, if the usual drift of seaweed were behind time, to go on Maundy Thursday and pour an oblation of gruel on a promontory, accompanying the ceremony by the repetition of a certain rhyme.'

6. Miranda J. Green, *Dictionary of Celtic Myth and Legend*, London, 1992, describes Manannán mac Lir as a sea god, protector of Ireland, also a master of skills, wisdom, tricks and magic, traditionally associated with the Isle of Man, of which he was the first king. The Gaelic for the Isle of Man is *Eilean Mhanainn*.

Big Porridge Day – *Là a' Bhrochain Mhóir*

In the Western Islands, in olden times (for the practice does not now exist anywhere), when there was a winter during which little sea–ware came ashore, and full time for spring work had come without relief, a large dish of porridge, made with butter and other good ingredients, was poured into the sea on every headland where wrack used to come. Next day the harbours were full.

This device was to be resorted to only late in the spring – the Iona people say the Thursday before Easter – and in stormy weather. The meaning of the ceremony seems to have been that, by sending the fruit of the land into the sea, the fruit of the sea would come to land.

J. G. Campbell, *Superstitions of the Highlands and Islands*, 1900

FAIR-DAYS – *DIAR-DAOIN A' BHROCHAIN*

Thursday of Easter Week was a popular fair-day in pre-Reformation times. In Gaelic it was generally known as *Diar-Daoin a' Bhrochain* ('Gruel Thursday', 'Porridge Thursday') from the gifts or sacrifices made to Bannan, Manannan or St John on that day.

Ronald I. M. Black, *Scottish Studies*, vol. 33, 2000

FOLKLORE TAKEN DOWN BY EDWARD LHUYD (IN WELSH) FROM THE REVD JOHN BEATON

(Minister of Kilninian Parish Church *c.* 1670–1701, and a member of the famous medical family of Beatons of Pennycross)

1. DEATH, SECOND SIGHT AND FUNERALS: HASTENING DEATH

When a man is on the point of death, their custom is to open all the windows, and after that one man goes out and puts his head in through a hole, and speaks thus:

An dig thu no an déid thu,
No an d'ich thu feòil churra?
(Will you come or will you go, or have you eaten heron's flesh?)

Note: In J. G. Campbell's *Superstitions of the Highlands and Islands*, p. 240, under the heading 'Killing those too long alive': 'If a person is thought to be too long alive, and it becomes desirable to get rid of him, his death can be ensured by bawling to him thrice through the key-hole of the room in which he is bedrid,

Will you come, or will you go?

Or will you eat the flesh of cranes?'

Corpse Candles: They have corpse candles &c. as in Wales [candles lit at night during the wake (*caithris*)]:

1. *Coinneal Mhairbh*, this is of a fairly green colour
2. *Coinneal Feòla*, rather red
3. *Coinneal Éisg*, very white or of a pale colour

Prognostication of Death and Other Future Events: The men with the second sight see a man with a light like the light of the glow-worm, or with fish [scales] over his hair and his clothes, if he is to be drowned; bloody, if he is to be wounded; in his shroud if he is to die in his bed; with his sweetheart on his right hand if he is to marry [her], but on his left hand if he is not to win his sweetheart.

Contemporary Visions: In Mishnish in Mull there was a man who was said to see a man carrying a creel-ful of cheese from his house, although he was 8 miles from home; and since he recognized him, he went back [and] caught hold of him.

Other Omens of Death [The manuscript here is unfortunately badly torn on the left-hand side]:

. . . they see the candles regularly; and

. . . a fortnight to a day or two

. . . there will be a dead man in the house or there will come

. . . fish to it.

Water-Bulls and Water-Horses: They believe that there are in the freshwater lochs creatures which they call *tarbh-uisge* (or *tarbh-feirigh*) (water-bulls) and *each uisge* (water-horses); and that these serve the (ordinary) cows and mares; and the calves that come from them are hornless (lacking ears), but what ears there are, are red. This bareness they describe as *corc-chluasach*, otherwise *corc a' feirigh*.

The above-mentioned water-horses used formerly to change their shapes, and to disguise themselves as men, &c. There are stories similar to these in Wales. One of these horses was wont to come out of Loch Frisa in Mull, to help a man to plough, returning to the sea at night.

2. DOMESTIC ANIMALS

Cattle. Unusual Behaviour . . . Theft?: If the cattle are bellowing and [? herd] together, they expect that enemies [intend to?] steal [them?]. [The edges of the manuscript are torn here.]

Protecting Heifers: In spring-time they are wont to tie withes to the ears of the heifers, because they are unruly.

Note: This is not clear. Does it refer to some form of *snàithlin* or thread such as was tied to cattle, &c., to protect them from the evil eye, or from elf arrows?

Rowan Used to Guard Cattle, Protect the Churn and the Plough: They are wont to put either a wedge or a nail, &c., of mountain ash in the plough. They are wont also to tie a piece of it to the tails of cattle, to guard against the bewitching of the produce of the milk; and for the same reason, when churning, a little of it [i.e. mountain ash] is put into the churn, with Hypericon leaves along with it.

Note: Hypericon is St. John's Wort, . . . *Achlasan Chalum Chille*. It had protective powers against witchcraft; but rowan was even better.

Method of Predetermining Sex of Calves: If a cow is wont to give birth to a male calf, it is necessary only to turn the afterbirth inside out, and the next calf will be female, and *vice versa*.

The Horse:

(1) It is not permitted to give corn to a horse in a *criathair* (that is, a sieve), for fear that the horse comes in contact with it, since, if that is done, no —— is obtained from it.

Note: The edge of the manuscript is torn. The sieve was used for raising the devil.

(2) When baking bread, they are wont to give the little cake, or a part of it, to an owner of horses, so that they may be successful for him. This cake must . . .

Note: The edge of the page is not torn. There is no full stop after ['must';] the sentence is left unfinished. There is a passage in Pennant's *Tour*, pp. 111–12, which may throw some light on this. Pennant describes how on the first of May the herdsmen of each village used to bake a special cake of eggs, milk, butter, and oatmeal.

> Every one takes a cake of oatmeal, upon which are raised nine square knobs, each dedicated to some particular being, the supposed preserver of their flocks and herds, or to some particular animal, the real destroyer of them: each person then turns his face to the fire, breaks off a knob, and flinging it over his shoulders says, *This I give to thee, preserve thou my horses; this to thee, preserve thou my sheep;* and so on.

(3) If you cut a willow rod to drive your horse, it is necessary first of all to strike it three times on the ground, otherwise it will be as heavy for the horse as the horseman.

(4) It is not permitted to put a rope made from the hair of a horse that died of disease, about the head of another horse.

(5) Hair from a dead horse can be used for fishing and for making fishing-lines, but one ought not to put cords made of that around the head of a live horse.

The Dog: . . . in the name of St. Columba concerning . . . the barking of dogs.

Note: The manuscript is torn on the left-hand side. The two lines appear to be a single entry, but it is not easy to think of a piece of folklore linking St. Columba with dogs. The entry follows two torn lines about a raven and a dog . . . St. Columba was frequently invoked to protect (e.g.) cattle . . . Barking of dogs at something unseen was considered an evil omen and a sign of approaching death.

The Cock: When a cock goes to its perch, if it crows at that time, or before the usual time, it signifies either the death of the man of the house, or of some other [well-known] man. When they hear it crowing they look where its head is, and from there [i.e. from that direction] they [expect?] the news. And the soles of its feet will be [wet?] if the news comes from over the sea . . . in the country they expect it.

3. WILD ANIMALS

Red Deer: If a stag is wounded it lies on *ùrach* (? *odharach*) *bhallach*,
that is to say *morsus diaboli* (devil's bit scabious); and it is that which
draws the darts from its body.

The Roedeer and the Hare: There is neither hare nor roebuck on the
Isle of Mull, and there were none on the adjoining mainland
[? Kintyre] until recently. If they encounter hares on the high
ground . . . it is a sign of misfortune.
Note: The hare was used for simples by the Arabian medical school and its Gaelic
followers . . . The hare also figures prominently in the folklore of shape-shifting.

The Otter: Whosoever eats part of the liver of an otter, he can
prevent a blister forming on any burn in the world if he licks the
burnt spot three times. *Madu* (*madadh*) *uisge* is what they call an
otter, but *dobharchù* is what they call the king of the otters.
Note: For the king of the otters, cf. Martin, p. 211: 'The hunters say there is a big
otter above the ordinary size, with a white spot on its breast, and this they call the
king of otters; it is rarely seen, and very hard to be killed. Seamen ascribe great
virtues to the skin; for they say that it is fortunate in battle, and that victory is
always on its side.'

The Badger: They say that the badger has a hole in his bottom for
every year of his age.
Note: [The badger] is known in Gaelic oral tradition and gnomic literature. We
have not come across another instance of the idea recorded here.

The Stoat: The stoats (ermines) are white a little before snow, and
when there is snow; and (some say) they change their colour with
every [new] moon.

4. WILD BIRDS

The Golden Eagle: The eagle kills a stag by alighting on [its] horns
and blinding it, and after that it (the stag) loses its proper senses, and
becomes frenzied,and kills itself on the rocks.
Note: Martin also makes this observation on the eagle in North Uist, p. 140.

The Osprey: Whenever they see an *eun fionn* (a kind of white-tailed buzzard, grey in colour) they expect a change of food before night.
Note: General Sir Philip Christison . . . tells us . . . that *eun fionn* was the Mull name for the osprey, and suggests that the prognostication about food may have referred to the run of the sea trout which begins about the same time that the migratory ospreys used to arrive in Mull each year.

The Raven: If the raven cries in the morning before the hoodie crow (viz. *feannag* the grey crow) it will be a fine day, but if it is the hoodie that cries first, they expect bad weather. [If] . . . neither raven nor dog take flesh and bread from the hand . . . soon after that he will be dead.

The Magpie: The piet calles much about a house before strangers come & if there be Fî-folk in ye house.
Note: 'Fî-folk' probably stands for 'fey folk', persons doomed to die shortly or to be unlucky . . . It is probable that magpies were known in the Highlands only as pets. The reference here seems to be to a pet magpie.

The Wren: There are twelve feathers in a wren's tail, and one of them is very lucky, but they do not know which one. And in one wing there is a lucky one, and in the other an unlucky one, but it is not known which wing, or which feather.
Note: There is a considerable amount of folklore connected with the wren, cf. Rev. C. Swainson, *The Folklore of British Birds*, pp. 35–43, but we have not come across any reference to what Lhuyd noted there or elsewhere. Swainson refers to the hen's feathers being used for the purpose of divination by herring fishermen.

The Swallow: Pulling down a swallow's nest [will be unlucky].
Note: The left-hand side of the page is badly torn . . . The swallow was considered a lucky bird in many countries.

Sea-birds: When the sea-birds go to the mountains, they expect [bad weather].
Note: Sea-birds coming inland is a well-known sign of approaching bad weather.

5. REPTILES

The Adder; Cure for Snake Bite: The custom of the men in the Highlands is to run into the nearest water as swiftly as they can when they are bitten by an adder . . . They have in the Highlands a charm against an adder's bite: they blow on water, saying it [the charm]. This water they pour on the wounded one.

[*Note*: Accounts of this are also given in J. Gregorson Campbell's *Witchcraft and Second Sight.*]

Sword Used to Kill an Adder Hisses in Water: Also, after killing an adder, their custom is to run with the sword or the other weapon that killed it, to the water, and the old scholar (John Beaton) says that this weapon hisses in the water as if it were hot.

[*Note*: Also referred to in Pennant.]

Old Adders become Dragons: They believe that old adders become winged dragons. *Dragún* is what they call a dragon, whence (? perhaps) Uther Pendragon.

Note: We have not found an instance of this idea in works on Highland folklore, but it existed in Spain . . . Uther Pendragon figures in the mythological pedigree of the Campbells.

The Stone in the Head of the Adder: They say also that there is a stone in the head of an adder, and it has the power of enticing a lark from the air to descend into its jaw; and there is a young man, still alive (says the old scholar [i.e. Beaton]) who saw the lark alighting within the jaws of an adder, while she stood half a yard erect, with her mouth open to receive it. A charm in which they believe also in India. ?True?

[*Note*: There is reference to the lark and the serpent in Pepys's diary and there are many references to serpent stones in folklore.]

6. INSECTS

The Butterfly:

> Dealan, dealan, dealan Dé
> Beannachd uaim-se go Mac Dé,
> Is beannachd eile hugad fé'.

> Butter, butter, butterfly,
> A blessing from me to the Son of God,
> And another blessing to yourself –
>> say the children to a butterfly.

Note: Miss Annie Johnston, Castlebay, Isle of Barra, remembers this verse being said by children in her childhood . . . 'In those distant days we firmly believed that a butterfly was a holy thing, perhaps an angel, or a messenger from heaven, and to kill a butterfly was a crime.'

A Fiery Circle called a Butterfly: Children when shaking a stick of fire say 'Butter, butter, butterfly'.

Note: In Dwelly's Dictionary *dealan Dé* is defined as the appearance of a burning stick waved in a circle.

> J. L. Campbell and Derick Thomson, *Edward Lhuyd in
> the Scottish Highlands*, 1963

SUPERSTITIONS ABOUT ANIMALS

When a place is infested to a troublesome extent with rats or mice, and all other means of getting rid of the pests have failed, the object can be accomplished by composing a song, advising them to go away, telling them where to go, and what road to take, the danger awaiting them where they are, and the plenty awaiting them in their new quarters. This song is called the Rat (or Mouse) Satire, and if well composed the vermin forthwith take their departure.

When the islet of Calv (*an Calbh*, the inner door), which lies across the mouth of Tobermory harbour, was let in small holdings, the rats at one time became so numerous that the tenants subscribed sixpence a-piece, and sent for *Iain Pholchrain** to Morven, to come and satirize the rats away. He came and made a long ode, in which he told the rats to go away peaceably, and take care not to lose themselves in the wood. He told them what houses to call at, and what houses (those of the bard's own friends) to avoid, and the plenty and welcome stores – butter and cheese, and meal – to be got at their destination. It is said that after this there was an observable decrease in the number of rats in the island!

J. G. Campbell, *Superstitions of the Highlands and Islands*, 1900

*Iain Polchrain was a resident of Polluchairn on the Drimnin Estate. Information from Iain Thornber, Morvern, 2001.

THE RAT SATIRE

A belief in the effectiveness of this method seems to have been very common in the past. The earliest mention I know of comes from Ireland and is to be found in a romantic historical tale called 'The Adventures of the Great Company' set in the 6th century. Further references are to be found scattered throughout Gaelic literature of all ages . . . [This] was composed in Morvern over a hundred years ago by John MacDougall (1820–1891) of Inversanda, Ardgour. It is curious that in such rhyming and satire the absolute destruction of the rats was never wished for; the spell if it was to be successful must distinctly assign them some other place of residence generally separated from the point of origin by a loch, burn, an arm of the sea or a ridge of hills . . .

You will be ferried from Bunavullin
Across the Sound of Mull in bondage,
And let the schoolmaster count you
In case any of you are left behind.
If you do not go in Martin's boat
Get the fair lads of the 'Phoenix'
And if none of them are about the place
You will swim if necessary.

If you make it to Salen
Leave David alone since he is poor.
Spend a night at the Inn
And do not hesitate to take everything you can get hold of.
In spite of your eating and drinking there

They will have plenty after you have left.
Many people are adding to their wealth
It was from liquor that they made it.

You will reach 'Greenhill' at Gruiline –
Would that the country was at peace with him:
And even if you stay there for some time
He will not notice it very much.
When you climb Mam Clachaig
See that you do not become separated from one another,
And descend to Kinloch Sgridain
And you will get everything you need there.

Spend one night in Pennyghael
In the house of the old man with the spectacles,
And leave nothing in the house
Except limpets and fishbones for him.
Eat all his butter and cheese
And all the white-meal and fat there.
Eat all oats and potatoes
And leave not one grain on an ear of corn.

You will arrive across at the Laird of Carsaig*
And be at peace with your fellow brothers there,
And see that you leave nothing there
Just as the plagues of Egypt did
Let one of you, with his paw, write for him
The sentence of Belshasar of the Chaldees.
And since I sent you to Carsaig
Let Carsaig send you away himself.

Iain Thornber, 'Rats', *TGSI*, vol. 55, 1986–88

* The Laird of Carsaig at this time was a Maclean who, like Lady Gordon of
Drimnin, was also involved in clearing people off the land, thereby incurring the
bard's wrath. The verse is part of a translation by Calum Campbell of 'Eachdraidh
agus Imrich Radan' ('The History and Journey of Rats').

THE CUCKOO: OMENS

I heard the cuckoo, with no food in my stomach,
I heard the stock dove on the top of the tree . . .
I saw the wheatear on a dike of holes,
I saw the snipe while sitting bent.

And I foresaw that the year
Would not go well with me.

David Ross, The Pocket Book of Scottish Quotations, 2000

Chuala mi 'chubhag gun bhiadh 'am bhroinn,
Chunnaic mi 'n searrach 's a chùlaobh rium,
Chunnaic mi 'n t-seilcheag air an lic luim,
'S dh' aithnich mi nach rachadh a' bhliadhn' ud leam.

I heard the cuckoo while fasting,
I saw the foal with his back to me,
I saw the snail on the flag-stone bare,
And I knew the year would be bad for me.

Attributed to the 'Cailleach Bhéurra', a distinguished Sybil.

Alexander Nicolson, Gaelic Proverbs, 1882

Chunnaic mi seilcheag air leac lom,
Chunnaic mi uan 's a chulthaobh rium,
Chuala mi 'chuthag 's gun bhiadh 'nam bhroinn,
'S gun d'aithnich mi nach rachadh a' bhliadhna leam.

I saw a snail on a bare flagstone,
I saw a lamb with his back to me,
I heard a cuckoo on an empty stomach,
And I knew that the year would go against me.

Peter: Tha cuimhne 'am air mo sheanair, bhiodh daonnan pìos de dh'aran na briosgaid na rudeigin ri taobh a leabaidh. Nuair a dhùisgeadh e anns a' mhadainn bha e 'g ithe sin, eagal gun cluinneadh e cuthag gun bhiadh 'na bhroinn.

Translation: I remember my grandfather, he would always have a piece of bread or a biscuit or something beside his bed. When he wakened in the morning he would eat that, for fear that he would hear the cuckoo on an empty stomach.

Peter MacLean, Dervaig, 2000

Note: Dwelly's Gaelic Dictionary, under *Cubhag*: '*greim cubhaige*, a piece of food to be eaten early, in order not to hear the cuckoo's call on an empty stomach; *chuala mi a' chubhag gun bhiadh 'nam bhroinn*, "I heard the cuckoo before tasting food" – considered a sign of an unlucky year to follow.'

LORE ABOUT THE CUCKOO

The cuckoo is an *eun sìth*, a 'Fairy bird', because, as is said, its winter dwelling is underground . . . Any one finding a cuckoo's nest will live to be widowed . . . If the cuckoo calls on the house-top, or on the chimney (*luidheir*), death will occur in the house that year.

J. G. Campbell, *Superstitions of the Highlands and Islands*, 1900

Because of the distinctive cry of the cuckoo, the bird has been considered one which showed the gift of prophecy, especially as it announces the coming of Spring with such enthusiasm. In Scotland's islands though, it was considered unlucky to hear the cuckoo before breakfast because it brought bad luck for the rest of the day. The bird is also known as the messenger of Thor, the Scandinavian god in whose gift were happy marriages, but some looked upon the cuckoo as a rain-bird and a bringer of warm weather after showers. In the northern counties of Scotland, where the cuckoo is known as the *Gowk*, a 'gowk-storm' is the rough weather foretold by its song.

Raymond Lamont-Brown, *Scottish Superstitions*, 1990

Note: All Fools' Day is variously known as Cuckoo Day (*Latha na Cuthaig*). See Chapter 2.

WEATHER AND SEASONS

Seo mar a bha seann chunntas na Bliadhna a' dol.

> Mìos a dh'Fhaoilteach,
> Trì làithean Gobaig,
> Trì làithean Feadaig,
> Seachdain a' Ghearrain,
> Sgarrthaichean na Feill-Connain,
> Doirionn Feill-Pàdraig,
> Seachdain na Caillich,
> Siud suas an t-Earrach.

This is how the passing of the seasons of the year was reckoned of old.

> A month of the wolf month,
> Three days of the dog-fish (biting wind),
> Three days of the plover (whistling wind),
> A week of the horse or gelding,
> The blasts of foul weather of Connan's feast,
> The inclement weather of St Patrick's feast,
> The week of the old woman,
> That is how the spring goes.

Faoilteach or *Faoilleach* (now Gaelic for January) – last fortnight of winter and first fortnight of spring.

Gobag – dog-fish, 'little mouth' – biting wind.

Feadag – plover (*fead* 'whistle') – whistling wind.

Gearran – horse or gelding (now Gaelic for February).

Connan – no saint of that name. Conan 'a rash quarrelsome, meddlesome character of Fenian tales' (Alexander Nicolson's *Gaelic Proverbs*).

Doirionn (or *doinionn*) – inclement weather.

St Patrick's feast – 17th March; 30th March (O.S.).

Se 25eamh de'n Mhàrt Latha na Bliadhn' Ùire a nuas gu mìos na Dùdlachd 1599 an Albainn. Se sin an latha air am bheil an solus a' buadhachadh thairis air an dorchadas, am blàths thairis air an fhuachd agas fàs thairis air marbhantachd a' gheamhraidh.

Translation: The 25th of March was New Year's Day down to December 1599 in Scotland. That is the day light overcomes the darkness, warmth overcomes cold and growth overcomes the deadness of winter.

Rhyme from Peter MacLean, Dervaig, 2000 (he was given this by the late Ronald MacDonald of Soay and Craignure).

Notes and translation by Donald W. MacKenzie

WEATHER: THE SPRING SCHEME

In the Hebrides what might be called the 'Spring Scheme' ran much as follows:

Faoilleach (The Stormy), which corresponds more or less to February. During this month, stormy weather was not only expected but welcomed:

> February cold and keen,
> Welcome has it ever been

and the old people said that the furrows should be filled three times in this month, 'once with water, once with snow and once with the thatch from the house roofs'. In Skye it was said that, 'the Faoilleach should come in with a serpent's head and go out with a peacock's tail but that if it should come in with the feather of a peacock and go out like the serpent, then the Gearran will give seven leaps of madness: that means these nine days will be a veritable cataclysm'.

Feadag (The Plover), first week of March (also called 'The Whistle'), a week of whistling winds.

> I am the bare, swift, leggy plover,
> I can kill both sheep and lambs.

Gobag (The Dog-fish), second week of March, a week of heavy rains.

> Gobag! Gobag! Mother of the month of cold,
> Thou didst kill the sheep and the lean lamb,
> Thou didst kill the grey goat in two watches
> And the speckled stirk in one.

Gearran (The Gelding), till the end of March. For some reason unknown to me he was white and lame.

> I am the white, lame gelding;
> I'll put the cow in the hole
> Till the wave comes over her head,

The word 'hole' meaning a bog. The Gearran usually lasted until the false spring came, 'the cuckoo's greening', which, on 12th April is followed by,

Cailleach (Old Woman, 'Hag of the Ridges'), 12th to 18th April. In Mull and Skye the Cailleach (Winter) held sway for many months. She was terribly ugly, with only one eye, a blue face and tusk-like teeth, but she was a most important person and the Stormy, Plover, Dog-fish and Gelding were her servants. Whenever the Cailleach leaves the Isles to see if Corryvreckan (her wash-tub) is boiling fast enough, Spring comes up behind her with mild days. This annoys her intensely and she returns hurriedly to drive him off. After several such short visits to her washing pot, during each one of which Spring gets busy in the Hebrides and has to be driven out, she usually ends by staying too long testing the temperature of the water, and the grass really begins to grow. When the Cailleach notices this she rushes back to Skye and begins to hammer down the grass with her mallet. (For 'March grass won't see summer'.) She works very hard for some days and finally, despairing of controlling the young growth, attacks Spring in person: for three days they fight in the Cuillin Hills and the air is full of her cold rage, storms sweep the land, then Spring conquers, the Hag throws down her mallet (frost) under a holly tree and flounces angrily off to Mull. While she hammers at the grass she can sometimes be heard singing and the sound of her song is like the sough of the wind:

> It escapes me up and down,
> Twixt my very ears has flown.
> It escapes me here and there,
> Twixt my feet and everywhere;
> This 'neath holly tree I'll throw,
> Where no grass nor leaf shall grow.

The Cailleach dies of rage after reaching Mull, and her husband, a great sea-beast, comes to lament for her. His tears are the bitter showers of early Spring. After her comes

Sguabag (The Brushlet), drying winds from 18th April for a week, then

Ceitein (First of Summer), sometimes called 'The False Summer', till 12th May, when *Budhe Bealtain* (May Day) comes and the cuckoos' call ushers in the Spring.

Besides all these there were the borrowings (and repayments) with their reasons. 'Stormy' began it by borrowing three warm days from July: 'Three Dog days in February, three days of cold in the dog days.' Why Stormy did it is not clear; it was most unpopular. 'Better foray coming to the land than mild morning in the cold month of storms.' Then March, not to be outdone, borrowed three days from April, or, as some say, April it was who borrowed from March. It comes to the same thing as all the months (except May) always returned what they had borrowed. These three warm April days in March were sometimes called 'The Days of the Ewes' because, according to tradition, Christ, the Good Shepherd, always sent three mild days in pity for the ewes at the lambing. (One has to remember that all these dates belong to the Old Calendar and so are eleven days out. March would last till what is now 11th April, so the lambing might well be 'on'.) Another tradition makes the Lord send three good days to the Israelites to go out into the desert to eat the Passover, and these days should be followed by the dark clouds of Easter, for was not the sun darkened on Good Friday? Meanwhile, April gets in return three cold days from March. There is a mainland rhyme which runs:

> To March said Averill,
> I see three hogs on yonder hill,
> And if you'll lend me dayis three,
> I'll find a way to gat them dee.
>
> The first o' them was wind and weet,
> The second o' them was snaw and sleet,

The third o' them was such a freeze
It froze the birds' feet to the trees.

When the three days were past and gane,
The silly poor hogs cam' hirplin' hame,

the word 'hogs' of course meaning sheep, not pigs. So much for April's efforts!

'A false appearance' of each month is reputed to appear in the previous one – as the False Spring or Cuckoo's Greening in April, in preparation for Yellow May Day, a foretaste of June's blossom time. But then on the 12th, 13th and 14th, May produces the three days of the Ice Saints, cold as their name implies. No one now seems to remember who the Saints were, nor why they gave or lent May three days.

Otta F. Swire, *The Inner Hebrides and their Legends*, 1964

DAYS OF THE YEAR

Uair a' Cheum Coilich: January 5th. Hour or time of the lengthening of the cockerel's step, meaning extra time to the day.

Uair a' Ghille Chonnaidh: January 12th. Time of the stickman, meaning also that there is extra daylight in which to take in firewood.

Peter MacLean, Dervaig, 2000

Note: Uair a' ghille-chonnaidh air an latha, Là Fhéill Brìghde. 'The woodgather's hour is added to the day on St Bridget's Day.' This proverb, from *The Campbell Collection*, offers St Bridget's Day (1st February) as a variation.

FISHING SUPERSTITIONS

'Se fasan a bh' ann aig Oidhche na Collainn dar a bhuail e meadhon-oidhche rachadh daoine mach a dh'fhaicinn . . . a dh'fhaireachdainn dé ghaoth a ghabhadh a' Chollainn againn. Bha rud mar sin a' dol, 'fhios agad. Anns a' mhadainn dar a bha thu falbh a dh'iasgachd dh'fheumadh tu am bàta thionndadh leis a' ghrian. 'S cha robh e gu diofar dé cho duilich 's a bha e, dh'fheumadh tu dhol mu'n cuairt mar sin agus chan e dòigh a bha furasda idir dol mu'n cuairt leis a' ghrian. Bha, bha am fasan ann an sin agus tha mi 'smaointinn gu bheil am fasan sin a' dol fhathast.

Duine seo a Tobair Mhoire agus 'se iasgair a bh' ann, iasgair sgadain. Anns a' mhadainn dar a bha e 'cur air a bhrògan, nan tachradh gun togadh e a' bhròg cheàrr – a' bhròg dheas – cha rachadh e a dh'iasgachd idir. 'Se 'bhotainn chlì a dh'fheumadh e thogail agus nan taghadh e 'bhotainn deas cha rachadh e dh'iasgachd idir.

O ai, ai, bha sin ann cuideachd. Cha robh math dhuit sgian-phòcaid gheal a thoirt do'n bhàta idir. Nan robh sgian gheal agad thilgeadh iad far na cliathaich i.

Droch chomharradh, droch chomharradh.

Note: *Dar* – a dialectical form of *nuair* 'when', common in Mull Gaelic.

Translation:

Ann: Can you tell me a bit about fishing superstitions and the winds at New Year?

Peter: Yes, yes. It was a custom at Hogmanay when it struck midnight for people to go out to see . . . to feel . . . which wind Hogmanay would take. A thing like that was going, you know.

Ann: And any customs about taking the boat out?

Peter: O ay, o ay, och ay. In the morning when you were going to fish you had to turn the boat sunwise. And it didn't matter how difficult it was you had to put about in a sunwise direction and it was not at all easy to put about sunwise. Yes, that was the custom then and I think that custom is still going.

Ann: Did you ever hear any other superstitions in Mull at all?

Peter: Well, yes, I know, I didn't *know* but I know *of* him – a man from Tobermory – he was a fisherman, a herring fisherman. In the morning when he was putting on his boots, if it happened that he would lift the wrong boot – the right boot – he wouldn't go fishing at all. It was the left sea-boot he had to lift and if he chose the right sea-boot he wouldn't go to fish at all.

Ann: Did you ever hear of words you would not say? You told me something about a penknife you couldn't take . . .

Peter: O ay, ay, that was in it, too. You needn't take a white pocket knife to the boat at all. If you would have a white knife they would throw it over the side.

Ann: Why?

Peter: A bad omen. A bad omen.

Peter MacLean, Dervaig, 2000

Chapter 9

PROVERBS

MULL – GENERAL

Cho leòmach ris an aon fhaoileig a bh'air taobh Chaoil Muile.
As conceited as the one seagull along the Sound of Mull.

Long ago the Mull people were supposed to be unable to support more than one seagull, but that one seagull, petted and spoilt to its heart's content, was as full of conceit as all the other Hebridean seagulls put together. [Another interpretation given in *The Campbell Collection* is that it is an allusion to the scarcity of shellfish etc. on the Sound of Mull. The usual food of the seagull is so scarce that only one can survive, and it has consequently little of which to be proud.]

Kenneth Macleod, *The Celtic Monthly*, vol. 17, 1908–09

Cha bhi 'n àirde na 'n ìsle nach fhaic sùil an Ilich; cha bhith 'n cùil na cùilibh nach fhaic suil a' Mhuilich.
Nought in either height or depth escapes the eye of the Islayman; nought in a nook or in corners escapes the eye of the Mullman.

Fionn, *The Celtic Monthly*, vol. 17, 1908–09

Muileach is Ileach is donas.
A Mull man, and Islay man and a devil. (A proverb of comparison)

The Campbell Collection of Gaelic Proverbs, 1978

Cha bhi an àrd no ìosal nach sanntaich sùil an Ilich; cha bhi an cùil no cuilbh nach iarr sùil a' Mhuilich; na dh'fhàgas am Muileach, goididh an Collach; is mairg a dh'earbas a chuid ris a' chealgair Bharrach; ach bheir an Tirisdeach rudhadh-gruaidhe air muinntir Iutharna.
There is nothing high or low which is not coveted by an Islay man's eye; there is nothing in a corner or a store which is not sought by a

Mull man's eye; a Coll man will steal what a Mull man leaves behind; pity the poor person who entrusts his goods to a deceitful Barra man; but the Tiree man gives the inhabitants of Hell a red face.

The Campbell Collection of Gaelic Proverbs, 1978

Ma bheir thu Muile dhiom, cha toir thu muir is tìr dhiom.
You may take Mull from one, but you can't take sea and land from one.

Fionn, *The Celtic Monthly*, vol. 18, 1910

Cha'n 'eil 'an cùil na'n cuilidh
Nach fhaic sùil a' Mhuilich,
'S cha'n 'eil 'an àird na 'n ìosal
Nach fhaic sùil an Ilich.
Na dh' fhàgadh am Muileach
Ghoideadh an Collach,
Ach 's mairg a dh' earbadh a chuid no anam
Ris a chealgaire Bharrach.

There is not in nook or corner
What the Mullman's eye won't see;
There's not in height or hollow
What the Islayman won't see.
What the Mullman would leave
The Collman would seize,
But woe to him, his goods or life
Who trusts to treacherous Barra man.

Fionn, *The Celtic Monthly*, vol. 18, 1910

Muileach is Ileach is deamhan,
Triùir a's miosa san domhan,
'S miosa am Muileach na'n t-Ileach
'S miosa an t-Ileach na'n deamhan.

A Mullman, an Islayman, and a devil,
The three worst in creation,
The Mullman is worse than the Islayman,
And the Islayman worse than the devil.

Fionn, *The Celtic Monthly*, vol. 18, 1910

Cha'n fhaic am Muileach nach sanntaich am Muileach; na shanntaicheas am Muileach goididh an Collach; 's na ghoideas an Collach cuiridh an Tirisdeach am folach.

What the Mullman sees, he covets; what the Mullman covets, the Collman steals; and what the Collman steals, the Tiree man hides.

Fionn, *The Celtic Monthly*, vol. 18, 1910

Slìob am Muileach is sgrobaidh e thu;
Sgròb am Muileach is slìobaidh e thu.
Stroke the Mullman and he'll scratch you;
Scratch the Mullman and he'll stroke you.

Fionn, *The Celtic Monthly*, vol. 18, 1910

Ged a bhiodh tu cho carach ris a' Mhuileach, gheabhar a mach thu.
Were you as tricky as the Mull man, you'll be found out.

Alexander Nicolson, *Gaelic Proverbs*, 1881

SPECIFIC PLACES

Ged is mór Creag-a'-Choth, is beag a math.
Though Creag-a'-Choth is big, it is of little use.

The reply of a Mull man when he was complimented on the size of his wife.

The Campbell Collection of Gaelic Proverbs, 1978

Note: *Creag-a'-Choth* is a hill called Craigiehowe in the Black Isle, under which is a cave containing a dropping well much frequented in the past by those seeking a cure for deafness. The existence of this proverb in Mull demonstrates the distance people were willing to travel in hopes of a cure – and the disappointment they experienced when it did not work.

Uisge Spinne 's duileasg Leac-fraon.
Speinn water, and dulse from Lec-fraon.

Both places are in Mull, and Speinn water, and dulse from Lec-fraon were cures for all ills, but especially stomatic diseases.

Fionn, *The Celtic Monthly*, vol. 18, 1910

Ma théid thu do Shorn bheir do lòn leat.
'If you go to Sorne take your food with you.' Sorne is in Glengorm
and this could well be a reference to the evictions.

Calum MacDonald, Tobermory, 2001

Seisreach Dhoire-chuilinn. Seisreach gun each gun duine – Dà
chapull agus tàillear.
['The team of Doire-chuilinn. A team lacking horses or men – it
consisted of two mares and a tailor.']
Dhoire-chuilinn is in Mull.

Fionn, *The Celtic Monthly*, vol. 19, 1911

Ceithir busacha fichead 'an Ile, 's ceithir ardacha, fichead am Muile.
Twenty-four 'buses' in Islay, and twenty-four 'Airds' in Mull.

Fionn, *The Celtic Monthly*, vol. 21, 1913

Rathad Mhoirinis a dhol do Chillfhinicheinn.
The Mornish road to go to Kilfinichen.
A very probable way of showing that a man is taking a round-about
way, in dealing with whatever matter he may have in hand.

Fionn, *The Celtic Monthly*, vol. 17, 1908–09

Dùn Bhuirg 'na theine!
Dun Bhuirg is on fire! (Uist)

Used when a person shows excitement or great persistence in
attending to work. Originally the reply given by a Uist woman to
fairies who requested work. Their fortress was known as Dùn
Bhuirg and on hearing this they immediately retreated in
confusion. (See TGSI, xlv, p. 18. Tiree tradition states that the fairies
once invaded the island from Mull where they had their fortress,
Dùn Bhuirg. When the above cry war raised, they returned to Mull
as quickly as possible . . .)

The Campbell Collection of Gaelic Proverbs, 1978

Bàrr òir a' cuartachadh Eilean Ulbhaidh.
A golden crop surrounds the Isle of Ulva.

[A reference to the profits accruing to the landowners from the

kelp industry e.g. the MacDonald lairds of Ulva.] Up to the middle
of last century, over a hundred tons of kelp were exported annually
from this island.

The Campbell Collection of Gaelic Proverbs, 1978

Facal ann, a Mhaighstir Iain, 's am Brugh a' lionadh.
Get on, Mr. John, the channel is filling.

The Rev. John McLean was minister of Kilninian . . . in Mull,
including Ulva and Gometra. These islands are separated by a
narrow channel called the 'Brugh', which is passable on foot except
at high water. Mr. M. was preaching at Gometra, and the beadle
reminded him in the above words, proverbial in Mull, that it was
time to be winding up.

Alexander Nicolson, *Gaelic Proverbs*, 1882

Nuair bhios an Gilmein Muileach a bleid,
Bidh an Losgunn Lathurnach ri sgeig.

Gilmean is a knoll, and the 'Gilmein Muileach' is in Mull, opposite
the Toad of Lorn.

Fionn, *The Celtic Monthly*, vol. 18, 1910

MISCELLANEOUS

Muc, madadh is maraiche.
A pig, a dog and a sailor. [A Mull proverb of comparison]

The Campbell Collection of Gaelic Proverbs, 1978

An latha mharbhas tu fiadh, 's an latha 'n diabhal gin.
[To] the day you kill a deer, and the day you kill none. [A toast.]

The Campbell Collection of Gaelic Proverbs, 1978

Crann geàrr, glagach,
Eich gun rian 'ga tharruing,
Bean gun chiall 'nan ceann,
'S an talamh tana, teann.

A short, ramshackle plough, with uncontrollable horses pulling it, a senseless woman leading them, and the soil tough and shallow.

The reply of a Mull man to the question, 'Ciod an t-euradh as miosa 'san robh thu riamh?' ('What was the hardest difficulty you ever experienced?').

The Campbell Collection of Gaelic Proverbs, 1978

A' cur leannan air sgeilp.
'Putting a lover on a shelf.'

Revd D. W. MacKenzie

The proverb 'Putting a lover on the shelf', owes its origin to Allan na Sop having been thrown on a shelving rock, on the isle of Cairnburg, and held there until promises were extorted from him.

J. P. MacLean, *History of the Island of Mull,* vol. 2, 1925

Is mairg a loisgeadh a thiompan dut!
Pity him who would burn his harp for you!

Alexander Nicolson, *Gaelic Proverbs,* 1882

Note: In J. P. MacLean, *History of the Island of Mull,* vol. 2, 1925, this is said to refer to the Harper of Mull.

Another of Garnett's interests was in proverbs and folklore, and he recounts the origin of the local proverb: 'What a fool I was to burn my harp for her (him)', which indicates ingratitude from someone who has benefited from your generosity. In former times a celebrated harpist was married to an exquisite beauty; next to his wife, the harp was his pride and joy. On a visit to a sick relation, she fainted because of the cold and storm. In order to warm her he kindled a fire and burnt his harp to feed the flames. A young gentleman passing was distressed to see her condition and offered food and spirits. She revived and joined in 'animated' conversation with the gentleman, whom, it transpired, she had known in her early life, while being brought up by her grandmother on a nearby island. On her grandmother's death she had left the island and returned to Mull, and they had never met since. Now, however, their romance was reawakened, and by means of a ruse, they gave the husband the slip and eloped together. Hence his exclamation, 'Fool that I was to burn my harp for thee'.

Eve Eckstein, *Historic Visitors to Mull, Iona and Staffa*, 1992

Ubh air tòir eireig.
An egg seeking a pullet.

An inversion of natural order.

The Campbell Collection of Gaelic Proverbs, 1978

Ubh gun ìm, gun luath, gun salann,
'N ceann seachd bliadhna gun tig galar.

An egg without butter, without ash, without salt, at the end of seven years, disease will come.
There is nothing as dangerous as an egg.

A Gaelic proverb told to Donald W. Mackenzie by Seonaidh Russell, Salen

Note: The white of an egg is an ingredient of many traditional cures. There is a similar phrase in Nicolson's *Gaelic Proverbs*. This refers to one of the Highland notions about certain foods, which are often fanciful.

Uisge nan uibhean. The water in which an egg was boiled was also considered to bring bad luck, if spilled.

Calum MacDonald, Tobermory, 2001

Ge b'e chì no 'chluinneas tu, cùm an cat mu'n cuairt.
Whatever you see or hear, keep the cat turning.

This was said on the last occasion that a horrid species of sorcery, called the *Taghairm*, was performed by two men in Mull.

Alexander Nicolson, *Gaelic Proverbs*, 1882

Note: See Tales section.

Air Oidhche Shamhna theirear gamhna ris na laoigh,
Oidhch' Fheill Eòin theirear aighean ris na gamhna.
On Hallowe'en the calf is called a stirk,
On St John's Eve the stirk is called a heifer.

Roddy MacNeill, Salen, 1992

Note: This relates to seasonal changes.

CLANS

Mac 'Illeathain làmh-fhadach, Mac Shimidh ball-dubh 's Mac 'Ille Chalum cama-chas.
Long-handed Maclean, black-spotted Fraser, and bandy-legged Macleods (of Raasay).

Fionn, *The Celtic Monthly*, vol. 19, 1911

Tha 'fhortan fhéin air Mac-Cuaradh, biodh e cruaidh no biodh e bog.
MacQuarrie has his own luck, whether it be hard or soft.

This refers to the ancient chiefs of Ulva's isle.

Alexander Nicolson, *Gaelic Proverbs*, 1882

Is treasa Dia na Doideag; is treasa Doideag na MacIlleathain.
God is stronger than Doideag; Doideag is stronger than MacLean.

Doideag was a witch, at one time much feared in the island of Mull. She was peculiarly dreaded for her power in raising storms. MacLean of Duart, the Chief of that great Clan, was of course paramount in Mull.

Alexander Nicolson, *Gaelic Proverbs*, 1882

Ghabhadh Mac-a-Phì 'n a rabhadh e.
Mac Phie would take it for warning.

A Mull saying. Mac Phie, chief of Colonsay, went to a feast at Duart Castle, Mull, where his hospitable friend MacLean intended to kill him. The door-keeper, being of friendly mind, asked him if he had come down Glen Connal? He said he had. ''S am faca tu m' eich-sa, 's d' eich fhéin?' – '*Did you see my horses and your own there?*' Mac Phie took the hint, and escaped with all speed.

Alexander Nicolson, *Gaelic Proverbs*, 1882

A' Chlach Bhreac. ('The Inscribed Stone') – a stone with a Gaelic inscription uncovered by men working on a drain near Mingary. Peter did not see it although he searched for it.

Caith mar a gheibh	Spend as you receive
Agus gheibh mar a dh'fhóghnas	And get what will suffice
Agus caomhain – ach co-dha?	And save – but for whom?

Note: An adage that advocates living within one's income, getting only what one needs; but saving up? Who is going to benefit? A homely way of expressing the biblical 'Take no thought for the morrow . . . Sufficient for the day . . .'

But why should anyone want to engrave the adage on stone? Could it be the work of an apprentice monumental stone-mason practising his skill in engraving lettering on tombstones, etc., and using proverbs for practice? (When we were learning to write with pen and ink we had copybooks with proverbs printed in copperplate writing which we tried to copy.) Or perhaps it was the actual test piece that an apprentice mason had to submit to serve his apprenticeship. Peter's father served his apprenticeship as a blacksmith and the final test piece was to make a full set (four) of horseshoes before breakfast.

Peter MacLean, Dervaig, 2000: translation and notes from
Donald W. MacKenzie

Appendix

BARDS AND SONG

Eachann Bacach, Hector Maclean: Although little is known of his life he is said to have come from the Ross of Mull and his life is given as *c*.1600–post 1650 (Ó Baoill). He was a survivor of the Battle of Inverkeithing (1651) and wrote several poems in praise of the MacLean chiefs. He composed an elegy to Sir Lachlan MacLean on his death.

Revd John Beaton, Minister of Kilninian (1689) and the last Episcopal minister of Kilninian and Kilmore. He composed a poem on the 1688 Revolution and on the silencing of the Episcopalians in Mull. He was deposed in 1700. He was the last learned member of the famous medical family. He was also involved in the collection of folklore of Edward Lhuyd (see extracts from this in Chapter 8). He was succeeded by Maighstir Seathan.

Archibald Currie, Gilleasbuig MacMhuirich: He was probably from the Craignure area and worked for Allan Maclaine, tacksman of Scallasdale. He composed, as if for his master, 'Òran Fear Sgalasdail' and a lament for the MacLaines of Scallasdale who fought in the Napoleonic Wars.

Donald MacKinnon, Dòmhnall Ruadh am Bàrd: A native of Penmore, he lived in Tobermory and Morvern and was possibly a joiner.

John MacKinnon: Nicknamed 'Keeks' (from local pronunciation for the English poet Keats). He was a native of Tobermory and was a ship's carpenter on the Clipper Tea ships. In 1866 his ship the *Taeping* won the race from Foo-Chow-Foo to London. (The Captain was Donald MacKinnon from Tiree.) John MacKinnon composed the song 'Deoch Slàinte nan Gillean' which is given below.

Captain Andrew MacLean of Knock (Morvern), Anndra Mac an Easbuig, b. 1635: He was the son of the Bishop of Argyll and moved from Morvern to Mull and possibly Tiree. He was married to a daughter of MacLean of Ardnacross, formerly the wife of John MacQuarrie of Ulva. He may have lived at Lagganulva. It is also reported that he was a captain in Dundee's army at Killiecrankie.

John MacLean, Iain mac Ailein 1665–1760. He was said to have come from Quinish and lived latterly in the Calgary area. He composed many lampoons and his best known work is a poem on the Battle of Killiecrankie and 'An am dol sìos bu deònach'.

Revd John MacLean, Maighstir Seathan, was born *c.* 1680 and died 1756. He was the fourth and eldest son of Ewan, the ninth MacLean of Treshnish. Before becoming a minister in 1702 and being ordained at Kilninian and Kilmore in the same year, he had been a soldier in Flanders. He was also involved in Edward Lhuyd's researches and may have been an informant for some of the folklore material, see Campbell and Thomson's *Edward Lluyd in the Scottish Highlands*. He composed a poem in praise of Lhuyd.

Margaret MacLean, Mairearad nighean Lachlainn, *c.*1660–1751: One of a group of women poets who flourished between the 1640s and 1750s. A panegyrist of the MacLeans, she was a MacDonald married to a MacLean. She composed 'Gaoir nam Ban Muileach' ('The Mull Women's Cry of Woe') on the death of Sir John Mac-Lean of Duart in 1715. He was the last of the powerful Duart Lords and fought on the Royalist side at Killiecrankie and again at Sheriffmuir in 1715, after which he became ill in Perth and died at Gordon Castle on 12th March 1716. He is buried at Raffin church-yard, Banffshire, in the family vaults of the Gordons of Buckie. Donald W. MacKenzie, who was taken to the site of the grave, was told that Mairearad nighean Lachlainn was buried face downwards (*beul-sìos*) in Kilninian churchyard. (As was Màiri nighean Alasdair Ruaidh, a poet from Harris, in Rodel, possibly at her own request.)

Neil MacLean, Niall Ruairidh Channaich: He was a native of Tobermory, but his people were from the Island of Canna. As he worked in Govan, Clydeside, he was also known as 'the Govan Bard'. He wrote modern Gaelic songs about Mull.

Catherine Munn, Ceit Mhunn. Born 1789. Her family were from Antuim, Dervaig, and she lived in Tobermory. 'Tha mo Rùn air a' Ghille', her most popular song, was composed in 1820. It is printed, without attribution, in *A' Chòisir-Chiùil: St Columba Collection of Gaelic Songs*.

OTHER BARDS

Angus Beaton, Dervaig
Lachlan MacLean, fl. 1882
An t-Aireach Muileach. (1) Pen name of Maighstir Seathan. (2) 'The Aireach Muileach was a MacLean. He was, as his name imports, a herdsman, and lived in Mull. It is said that he was in the employ of Maclaine of Lochbui [*sic*]. He had a clear head and a sharp tongue, and was a bitter satirist.' (Revd A. MacLean Sinclair, *Na Baird Leathanach: The MacLean Bards*, vol. 1, 1898)
Hector MacLean, Tobermory. Eachainn Ruadh, a porter on Tobermory quay. He composed 'Litir gu Caraid an Canada'.

HARPERS

MacLean of Torloisk had a family of harpers from Cailleach who lived at Fanmore (*Fan Mór nan Clàrsairean*), confirmed by 1662 and 1674 rentals.

MacLean of Coll had a harper called Murdoch MacDonald for the island of Coll; he was the last professional harper of Scottish birth. He retired to Quinish in 1734.

PIPING

The last piper of the MacLeans was Neil Rankin of the famous Rankins of Kilbrennan (see chapter on Tales, and the stories of the Rankin family). The school at Kilbrennan was disbanded in 1760 with only seventeen pupils, and the last piper there was Eoghan mac Eachainn mhic Chon-Duiligh.

Sources: Calum MacDonald, Tobermory; Donald W. MacKenzie; J. P. MacLean, *History of the Island of Mull*, vol. 2, 1925; C. Ó Baoill, *Eachann Bacach and other Maclean Poets*, 1979; Revd A. MacLean Sinclair, *Na Baird Leathanach: The MacLean Bards*, vol. 1, 1898.

'DEOCH SLÀINTE NAN GILLEAN'

This song was composed by the carpenter on board the China Tea Clipper *Taeping* of which Captain Donald MacKinnon (*Dòmhnall mac Nèill 'ic Dhòmhnaill Ruaidh*), Heanish, Isle of Tiree, was in command on three notable voyages. The first of these was in 1864, when he set up the record for the fastest voyage between Foo-chow-foo and London. This was achieved in eighty-eight days. That record, we believe, still stands. His ship, however, was not the first home that year, as he had the misfortune to meet with a typhoon in the China seas that nearly sent ship and crew to the bottom, and he had to have extensive repairs done to the gallant ship at Hong Kong. The following year, 1865, Captain MacKinnon again beat all comers. This voyage occupied 102 days.

The year 1866 witnessed what might be called a national event in the memorable race between the China Tea Clippers for a prize of £100. A remarkable coincidence saw seven of the tea vessels crossing the bar of Foo-chow practically together, but it soon developed into a close contest between the two Clyde-built ships, the *Ariel* and the *Taeping*, commanded by two Scotsmen, Captains Keay and MacKinnon.

For weeks and weeks they had lost sight of one another, until, as the song tells us, the *Taeping* outsailed them in a group when crossing 'the Line'. Once more they lost sight of each other and not till they were sailing up the English Channel did Keay espy a sail on the horizon that instinct told him was the *Taeping*. So close were the two ships together at Gravesend that it was touch and go that Keay, having the weather of MacKinnon, got the first pilot and the first tug. MacKinnon, according to Lubbock (whom we cannot exculpate from his partiality for Keay) got the faster tug. Or, was it not that the *Taeping*, being of shallower draft, was a lighter tow than her rival?

The tide was making, but the *Ariel* could not get into her dock, though lower down the river than that of her rival. The result was that the *Taeping* was moored twenty minutes before the *Ariel* and the prize went to worthy MacKinnon. His was a gentlemanly act, and characteristic of him, when he handed over half of his reward to Captain Keay.

It is generally agreed among mariners of the time that while the better ship lost, the better skipper won. On the very next voyage out Captain MacKinnon succumbed to the effects of the privations he had suffered during the great and memorable race.

Calum MacDonald, Tobermory, 2001

Deoch Slàinte nan Gillean

Deoch slàinte nan gillean a b' àill leam a thilleadh,
Mo chàileachd air mhire 'ga sireadh 'san am.
Cha b'e rùn a bhith 'pòit a dh'fhàg sunndach 'ga h-òl mi
Ach cliù nam fear òga nach sòradh an dram.

Gu'n gabh sinn an t-òran a rinneadh do Dhòmhnall,
Bho'n tha e cho foghlaimt' air seòladh nan long;
Bho'n fhuair e an t-urram eadar China is Lunnainn,
Gur feàrr leam na Muile gu'm buidhinn e 'n geall.

Bha 'n *Ariel* bhòidheach 'gar fiachainn aig seòladh,
Gur h-i a bu chòir a bhith còmhl' ruinn 's an am.
'S le mheud 's fhuair thu dh'fhoghlam an toiseach do thòisich
Gu'n bheat thu iad còmhla 'n am crosadh na Line.

'S i 'ghearradh an fhairge mar shiosar air caimrig,
Is Chinaman mailgheach 'na dhealbh air a sròin.
'S i thàirngeadh an t-sùrdag air bhàrr nan tonn dùbhghorm
Mar fhiadh anns a' bhùireadh air chùl nam beann mór.

Nuair thogadh tu 'h-aodach am bàrr a cruinn chaola
'S i 'shnàmhadh gu h-aotrom mar fhaoileag nan tonn,
Gaoth-tuath 's i 'na frasan mar luaidhe 'ga sadadh –
Is fuaim aig a darach 'n am sgapadh nan tonn.

Tha na Sasannaich tùrsach, 's na Goill chan eil sunnd orr'
O'n choisinn thu 'n cliù seo do dhùthaich nam beann
Le d' sgoilearachd Bheurla 's tu 'd sheòladair gleusda
Gheibh a' ghaoth fo 'cuid bhréidean 'n am reubadh nan tonn.

Gur mis' th' air mo léireadh 's a mhadainn 's mi 'g éirigh,
An driùchd air mo léine 's mi éisleanach fann
An China na dunach 'gam lot leis a' chuileig –
Gu'm b' fheàrr a bhith 'm Muile fo dhubhar nam beann.

TRANSLATION: A TOAST TO THE LADS

A toast to the lads I would welcome returning,
Now would I seek it with relish and glee.
Not for love of the dram do I joyfully drink it
But to honour the lads who would share it with me.

A song we shall sing to the honour of Donald,
A skipper so skilled in the ways of the sea;
Since he won the honour from China to London,
I'd prefer to all Mull that the prize should be his.

The beautiful *Ariel*, our rival in sailing,
Took her place rightly along by our side.
It was your early schooling from the very beginning
That beat all the rest of them crossing the Line.

She would cut through the waves like scissors through cambric,
A beetle-browed Chinaman carved on her stem.
She would cut a caper on the crests of the blue waves
Like deer in the rut at the back of the bens.

When you hoisted her sail to the top of her mast-tip
As light as a gull she would glide on the waves,
Tossed by a north wind with showers like lead-shot –
Her timbers would sing as her stem cleaves the waves.

The English were sad and the Lowlanders joyless
When you won this renown for the land of the bens:
With your study and learning and skill as a seaman
You enabled her sails to get hold of the wind.

I am sorely distressed in the morning when rising
With dew on my shirt, I am feeble and ill
In woebegone China, attacked by mosquitos –
Far better in Mull neath the shade of the hills.

By John MacKinnon, a native of Tobermory, known locally as 'Keeks' (a corruption of Keats), the carpenter of the *Taeping*, the China Tea Clipper (Captain Donald MacKinnon, Heanish, Tiree), which won the race between Foo-chow-foo, China, and Gravesend, London, in 1866, with the *Ariel* a close second.

ÒRAN FEAR SGALASDAIL

Hè hòrann ò robha hó
Mo nighean donn bhòidheach
Hè hòrann ò robha hó

Mi so an Sgalasdail chreagach
Gun bheadradh gun mhórchuis,

Mi air cuallach na spréidhe
Is cha léir dhomh le deòir iad.

Mo chuideachd ri caillich
'S cha tig caraid dham fheòraich.

Chan iarr iad a sìos mi:
Chan fhiach leo mun bhòrd mi.

Gur i buidseach Chloinn Ghriogair
Dh'fhàg gun mhisneach ri m' bheò mi,

(B: Hug òrann ò robha hó)
My bonnie brown-haired lass
(Hug òrann ò robha hó)

I am here in rocky Scallasdale
Without joy or pride,

I am herding cattle
And cannot see them for tears.

No company but an old woman
And no friend comes to ask after me

They won't ask me along:
They don't care to have me at their table.

It is the witch of Clan Gregor
Who has robbed me of spirit for life,

Dol gam phòsadh air daoraich
'S gun mo ghaol a bhith òg oirr'.

By getting me married while I was drunk
Though I never loved her in my youth.

Bho'n a chuir mi 'n t-snaim rithe
'S toll am chridhe rim bheò e.

Since I tied the knot with her
It has pierced my heart while I live.

Ciamar sheinneas mi fidheall?
Tha mo chridhe ro-bhrònach,

How can I play the fiddle?
My heart is too heavy,

Na pìob uallach nam feadan –
'S tric a spreig mi i'm sheòmar.

Nor the proud barrelled bagpipes –
I have often blown them in my room.

Neo-bhuidheach mi dh'Eachann
Rinn mo leannan a phòsadh:

I give no thanks to Hector
Who did marry my love:

'S e a fhuair a' bhean mhaiseach,
Té nam meallshuilean bhòidheach,

He has got a handsome wife,
The lass of the bonny alluring eyes,

Bean mhór an deagh nàduir
Thug mi gràdh dhi 'n tùs m'òige,

The tall even-tempered woman
I fell in love with in my early youth,

Nighean bàillidh na dùthcha –
'S e bhith cliùiteach bu chòir dhuit.

The daughter of the local factor –
You have a right to be well spoken of.

Miar is grinne air piàno,
Beul is àille bho'n tig òran.

The nimblest finger on the piano,
The fairest mouth to utter a song.

Gur tu thigeadh ri m'inntinn
'N am a' ridhle bhith 's t-seòmbar:

It is you who would suit me well
When a reel was danced in the room:

Bu leat urram ban Mhuile
'Nuair a chruinnicheadh iad còmhla.

You were the flower of the women of Mull
When they were gathered together.

Tunes: A, from *SA 1963/35/A3*, recorded by Morag MacLeod, and a tape loaned by Mrs Mary Morrison: from the late Alec MacDougall, Treshnish, and Colin Morrison, Mornish, Mull. B, from

SA 1974/172/B3, recorded from the Rev. William Matheson, N. Uist/Edinburgh, by Iain Paterson. Mr. Matheson learned the song from the Rev. D. W. MacKenzie (born in Ulva, now minister of Auchterarder), the late Duncan MacGillivray, Salen, Mull, and others. Text selected from A (verses 4, 5, 6, 10, 12), B (verses 2, 8, 9, 11) and the Morison MSS . . . verses 1, 13, 15, 16 from a nineteenth-century copy written by Hector (?) Morison, verses 3, 7, and 14 added by Conn Morison 'from James Stewart, New Year 1908'.

This song, once very popular in Mull, was composed according to the Morison MSS. by Alasdair MacMhuirich (the poet from whom Dugald MacPhail borrowed the refrain of 'An t-Eilean Muileach') who was for many years in the service of Allan Maclaine, tacksman of Scallasdale, and composed the song as if expressing his feelings, to the tune of an existing song ('Gura mis tha fo mhulad / Air an tulaich 's mi m'ònar') from which traditional versions may have borrowed some verses. According to tradition Allan Maclaine was married to the daughter of Gregorson of Ardtornish when he was too drunk to know what was happening. We have not identified the Hector who married the daughter of the factor (Campbell of Ardnacross).

Tocher, no. 17, 1975

GLOSSARY OF GAELIC TERMS

SPECIAL OCCASIONS, FESTIVALS, CELEBRATIONS

A' Bhliadhn' Ùr	New Year
A' Chàisg	Easter
A' Challainn	Hogmanay
An Nollaig	Christmas
Baisteadh (Baistidhean)	Baptism(s)
Caisean Callaig, caisean a' bhuilg	Hogmanay hide
Comanachadh, na h-Òrdaighean	Communion
Coronach	A lament
Duan Challainn	Hogmanay poem
Gillean Callaig	Hogmanay lads
Gillean Nollaig	Christmas lads, guisers
Là na Cubhaige	April Fool's Day
Oidhche Shamhna	Hallowe'en
Seann Bhliadhn' Ùr	Old New Year
Tòrradh, pl. *torraidhean*	Funeral

CLEARANCES

A' bhliadhna a dh'fhalbh am buntàta	Potato famine
Fuadach, fuadaichean	Eviction(s)
Gaiseadh a' bhuntàta	Potato blight
Obair na ceilpe	Kelp industry

SUPERNATURAL, SUPERSTITION

Buidseach, buidseachan	Witch(es), wizard(s)
Buidseachd	Witchcraft
Dà shealladh, dàrna sealladh	Second sight
Deiseil	Sunwise
Droch shùil	Evil eye
Frìth, frìthear	Augury, augerer
Manadh	Omen, apparition

Rathadach	Lucky
Rosadach	Unlucky
Seanachaidh; sgeulachd	Tale teller; tale
Seanfhocal	Proverb
Sian	Charm against war
Taghairm	A method of divination
Taibhs	Object seen in a vision
Taibhse	Ghost
Taisg	A cry foretelling death
Tein-éigin	Fire against plague
Tuathail	Antisunwise, widdershins

BIBLIOGRAPHY

Am Muileach (community newspaper) 1981–

Anon., 'Aig an Fhaidhir Mhuileach', *The Celtic Monthly*, vol. 19 (1911), pp. 164–66.

Anon., 'Gaelic Superstitions connected with Funerals', *The Celtic Monthly*, vol. 18 (1910), p. 180.

Anon., 'Puzzle for the Mull People', *The Celtic Monthly*, vol. 15 (1906–07), p. 24.

Archibald, Malcolm, *Scottish Animal and Bird Folklore*. Saint Andrew Press, Edinburgh, 1996.

Beaton, C. (Mackay, Queensland), 'A Curious Old Gaelic Play', sent by Donald Beaton, *The Celtic Monthly*, vol. 14 (1905–06), pp. 94–95.

Beaton, Donald (Mackay, Queensland), 'Famous Cailleachs', *The Celtic Monthly*, vol. 13 (1904–05), p. 239.

Beith, Mary, *Healing Threads: Traditional Medicines of the Highlands and Islands*. Polygon, Edinburgh, 1998.

Bennett, Margaret, *Scottish Customs from the Cradle to the Grave*. Polygon, Edinburgh, 1992.

Black, Ronald I. M., 'Scottish Fairs and Fair-Names', *Scottish Studies*, vol. 33, 2000, pp. 1–75.

Boswell, James, *Journal of a Tour to the Hebrides*. London, 1785.

Bristol, Nicholas Maclean, *Hebridean Decade: Mull, Coll and Tiree, 1761–1771*. Society of West Highland and Island Historical Research, Coll, 1982.

Brown, Olive, and Whittaker, Jean, *A Walk around Tobermory*. Oban Times, 1988.

Bruford, A. J., and MacDonald, D. A., *Scottish Traditional Tales*. Polygon, Edinburgh, 1994.

Cameron, A. D., *Go Listen to the Crofters*. Acair, Stornoway, 1986.

Cameron, John, *The Gaelic Names of Plants*. 2nd edn, John Mackay, Celtic Monthly Office, Glasgow, 1900.

Campbell, Duncan M., *The Campbell Collection of Gaelic Proverbs*, ed. Donald E. Meek. Gaelic Society of Inverness, 1978.

Campbell, John Gregorson, *Clan Traditions and Popular Tales*. London, 1895.

——, *Superstitions of the Highlands and Islands of Scotland*. Glasgow, 1900.

——, *Witchcraft and Second Sight in the Highlands and Islands of Scotland*. Glasgow, 1902.

Campbell, John Lorne, *A Very Civil People*, ed. Hugh Cheape. Birlinn, Edinburgh, 2000.

——, and Thomson, Derick, *Edward Lhuyd in the Scottish Highlands, 1699–1700*. Clarendon Press, Oxford, 1963.

Carmichael, Alexander, *Carmina Gadelica*, 6 vols. Edinburgh, 1900, 1928, 1940, 1941, 1954, 1971.

Cheape, Hugh. See Campbell, John Lorne.

Craig, David, *On the Crofters' Trail: In Search of the Clearance Highlanders*. Jonathan Cape, London, 1990.

Currie, Jo, *Mull Family Names*. Brown and Whittaker, Tobermory, 1998.

——, *Mull: The Island and its People*. Birlinn, Edinburgh, 2000.

Davidson, Thomas, 'Animal Treatment in Eighteenth-Century Scotland', *Scottish Studies*, vol. 4 (1960), pp. 134–149.

Devine, T. M., *The Great Highland Famine*. John Donald, Edinburgh, 1988.

Dieckhoff, Cyril H., 'Mythological Beings in Gaelic Folklore', *Transactions of the Gaelic Society of Inverness*, vol. 29 (1914–19), pp. 235–58.

Duckworth, C. L. D., and Langmuir, G. E., *West Highland Steamers*. T. Stephenson, Prescot, Lancashire, 1967.

Dwelly, Edward, *The Illustrated Gaelic–English Dictionary*. 1994 edn, Gairm Publications, Glasgow.

Eckstein, Eve, *Historic Visitors to Mull, Iona and Staffa*. Excalibur Press, London, 1992.

Ferguson, Malcolm (Callander), 'The Spanish Princess (A Legend of Mull)', *The Celtic Monthly*, vol. 3 (1894–95), pp. 91–93.

Fionn [Henry Whyte], 'Gaelic Proverbs and Maxims', *The Celtic Monthly*, vol. 17 (1908–09), pp. 127–29, 155–56, 167–68, 188–89, 216–18, 234–35.

——, 'Gaelic Proverbs', *The Celtic Monthly*, vol. 19 (1911), pp. 67–68, 154; vol. 20 (1912), pp. 45, 65, 85, 120, 124, 149, 178–79, 194, 217, 236–37; vol. 21 (1913), pp. 7, 28, 60, 69, 94, 109, 136–37, 148–49.

——, 'Gaelic Rhymes and Expressions on Place-Names', *The Celtic Monthly*, vol. 18 (1910), pp. 6–7, 33–34.

——, 'Oidhche Shamhna: Halloween from a Celtic Point of View', *The Celtic Monthly*, vol. 4 (1895–96), pp. 39–40.

——, 'The Grizzly Lad's Leap (Leum a' Ghille Riabhaich)', *The Celtic Monthly*, vol. 8 (1899–1900), pp. 174–75.

Galbraith, Dr J. J., 'Medicine among the Gaelic Celts', *Transactions of the Gaelic Society of Inverness*, vol. 39/40 (1942–50), pp. 63–78.

Garnett, Dr Thomas, *Observations on a Tour through the Highlands and Part of the Western Isles of Scotland*, 2 vols, London, 1811.

Gaskell, Philip, *Morvern Transformed*. Cambridge University Press, 1968.

Gillies, H. Cameron, *The Place-Names of Argyll*. D. Nutt, London, 1906.

Grant, I. F., *Highland Folk Ways*. Routledge and Kegan Paul, 1961.

Green, Miranda, *Dictionary of Celtic Myth and Legend*. Thames and Hudson, London, 1992.

Hannan, Thomas, *The Beautiful Isle of Mull, with Iona and the Isle of Saints*. Grant and Murray, Edinburgh, 1926.

Howard, J., and Jones, A., *The Isle of Ulva: A Visitors Guide*. Harlequin Press, Oban, 1995.

Hunter, James, *The Making of the Crofting Community*. John Donald, Edinburgh, 2000.

Lamont-Brown, Raymond, *Scottish Folklore*. Birlinn, Edinburgh, 1996.

——, *Scottish Superstitions*. Chambers, Edinburgh, 1990.

LeMay, J., and Gardner, J. (eds), *Glen More: A Drive through History*. Brown and Whittaker, Tobermory, 2001.

Livingstone, Sheila, *Scottish Customs*. Birlinn, Edinburgh, 2000.

——, *Scottish Festivals*. Birlinn, Edinburgh, 2000.

Low, Margaret, *Highland Memories*. Published privately, 1990.

Mac a Phi, Eoghan (ed.), *Am Measg nam Bodach* (a collection of stories and oral traditions broadcast on Gaelic radio between November 1936 and February 1937). Glasgow, 1938.

MacBain, Alexander, 'Highland Superstitions', *Transactions of the Gaelic Society of Inverness*, vol. 14 (1887–88), pp. 232–72.

——, *Celtic Mythology and Religion*. Eneas MacKay, Stirling, 1917.

MacCormick, John, 'History of Mull . . . : Chapter XVII. – Continued. Social Condition of the People', *The Celtic Monthly*, vol. 25 (1917), pp. 151–55.

——, *The Island of Mull*. A. MacLaren and Sons, Glasgow, 1923.

MacCulloch, Donald B., *The Island of Staffa*. A. MacLaren and Sons, Glasgow, 1927.

MacDonald, Alexander, 'Social Customs of the Gaels', *Transactions of the Gaelic Society of Inverness*, vol. 32 (1924–25), pp. 273–300, and vol. 33 (1925–27), pp. 122–46.

Macdonald, Donald, *Tales and Traditions of the Lews*. Birlinn edn, Edinburgh, n.d. [2000].

MacDougall, Betty, *Folklore from Coll*. Privately published, with assistance from HIDB, 1978.

MacDougall, H., *Island of Kerrera: Mirror of History*. Published by the author, 1979.

MacDougall, Revd J., *Waifs and Strays of Celtic Tradition: Folk and Hero Tales*, 3 vols. D. Nutt, 1891.

McGowan, Iain, *Hebridean Images*. Creative Monochrome, Surrey, 1993.

MacInnes, John, 'Looking at Legends of the Supernatural', *Transactions of the Gaelic Society of Inverness*, vol. 59 (1994–96), pp. 1–20.

MacKay, John, 'Oidhche Shamhna', *Transactions of the Gaelic Society of Inverness*, vol. 9 (1879–80), pp. 136–42.

Mackenzie, A., *A History of the Highland Clearances*. Inverness, 1883.

MacKenzie, Donald W., *As it Was, Sin Mar a Bha: An Ulva Boyhood*. Birlinn, Edinburgh, 2000.

MacKenzie, W., 'Gaelic Incantations, Charms, and Blessings of the Hebrides', *Transactions of the Gaelic Society of Inverness*, vol. 18 (1891–92), pp. 97–182.

MacKinnon, Marjory Mary (Tobermory), *1874: A Talk to the S.W.R.I.* Privately published.

Maclean, Allan, *Telford's Highland Churches*. Society of West Highland and Island Historical Research, Coll, 1989.

MacLean, Calum I., 'Death Divination in Scottish Folk Tradition', *Transactions of the Gaelic Society of Inverness*, vol. 42 (1953–59), pp. 56–67.

Maclean, Charles, *The Isle of Mull: Placenames, Meanings and Stories*. Maclean Publications, Dumfries, 1997.

MacLean, J. P., *A History of the Clan MacLean*. Robt. Clark, Cincinnati, 1889.

——, *History of the Island of Mull*. Vol. 1, Greenville, Ohio, 1923; vol. 2, Eugene MacLean, publisher, San Mateo, California, 1925.

Macleod, Kenneth, 'Gaelic Proverbs and Maxims', *The Celtic Monthly*, vol. 16 (1907–08), pp. 233–35; vol. 17 (1908–09), pp. 16–18, 38–40, 56–57, 67–69, 87–89, 111–13.

MacNab, P., *Tall Tales from an Island*. Luath Press, Edinburgh, 1998.

McNeill, F. Marian, *The Silver Bough: Scottish Folklore and Folk Belief*, 4 vols. Wm MacLellan, Glasgow, 1957.

MacPhail, I. M. M., *The Crofters' War*. Acair, Stornoway, 1989.

MacQuarrie, Duncan M., *The Placenames of Mull*. Inverness, 1982.

Martin, Martin, *A Description of the Western Islands of Scotland c. 1695*. London, 2nd edn, 1716, repr. Mercat Press, Edinburgh, 1981.

Meek, Donald E. See Campbell, Duncan M.

Monro, Sir Donald, *Description of the Western Isles (1549)*. Edinburgh, 1774.

Morrison, Neil Rankin, 'Clann Duiligh: Pìobairean Chloinn Ghill-Eathain', *Transactions of the Gaelic Society of Inverness*, vol. 37 (1934–36), pp. 59–79.

Munro, Jean, *The Founding of Tobermory*. Society of West Highland and Island Historical Research, Coll, 1976.

Murray, W. H., *The Islands of Western Scotland: The Inner and Outer Hebrides*. Eyre Methuen, London, 1973.

Napier, James, *Folk Lore or Superstitious Beliefs in the West of Scotland within this Century*. A. Gardner, Paisley, 1879.

Neat, Timothy, *When I was Young: Voices from Lost Communities in Scotland*. Birlinn, Edinburgh, 2000.

New Statistical Account of Scotland, 15 vols. Wm Blackwood and Sons, Edinburgh.

Nicolson, Alexander. *A Collection of Gaelic Proverbs and Familiar Phrases*. 2nd edn, Edinburgh, 1882.

Ó Baoill, Colm (ed.), *Eachann Bacach and other Maclean Poets*. Scottish Gaelic Texts Society, Edinburgh, 1979.

Pennant, Thomas, *A Tour of Scotland in 1769*. Melven Press, Perth, 1979.

Ross, Alexander, *Scottish Home Industries*. 1st edn 1895, repr. Molendinar Press, Glasgow, 1974.

Ross, Anne, *The Folklore of the Scottish Highlands*. Batsford, London, 1976.

Ross, David, *The Pocket Book of Scottish Quotations*. Birlinn, Edinburgh, 2000.

Ross, W. A., *A Little Book of Celtic Verse*. Appletree Press, Belfast, 1996.

Royal Commission on the Ancient and Historical Monuments of Scotland, *Argyll, Vol. 3: Mull, Tiree and Northern Argyll*. 1980.

Sacheverell, William, *An Account of the Isle of Man . . . with a Voyage to I-Columb-Kill*. London, 1702.

Scottish Vernacular Buildings Working Group, *Highland Vernacular Building*. Edinburgh, 1989.

Sinclair, Marion (ed.), *Hebridean Odyssey*. Polygon, Edinburgh, 1996.

Somers, Robert, *Letters from the Highlands on the Famine of 1846*. 1st edn 1848, repr. Melven Press, Perth, 1985.

Statistical Account of Scotland 1791–1799, 2nd edn, 20 vols. EP Publishing, Wakefield, 1983.

Sutherland, Elizabeth, *Ravens and Black Rain: The Story of Highland Second Sight*. Corgi, London, 1987.

Swire, Otta F., *The Inner Hebrides and their Legends*. Collins, London, 1964.

Thompson, Francis G., 'The Folklore Elements in "Carmina Gadelica"', *Transactions of the Gaelic Society of Inverness*, vol. 44 (1970), pp. 226–55.

——, *Crofting Years*. Luath Press, Edinburgh, 1984.

Thomson, Derick S., 'The McLagan MSS in Glasgow University Library', *Transactions of the Gaelic Society of Inverness*, vol. 58 (1992–94), pp. 406–24.

—— (ed.), *The Companion to Gaelic Scotland*. Blackwell, Oxford, 1987.

Thornber, Iain, 'Rats', *Transactions of the Gaelic Society of Inverness*, vol. 55, 1986–88, pp. 128–47.

Titley, Alan, *A Pocket History of Gaelic Culture*. O'Brien Press, Dublin, 2000.

Tocher (quarterly magazine of the School of Scottish Studies, Edinburgh) 1957–

Walker, Revd Dr John, *Report on the Hebrides of 1764 and 1771*, ed. Margaret M. McKay. John Donald, Edinburgh, 1980.

Whittaker, Jean, *Mull: Monuments and History*. Brown and Whittaker, Tobermory, 1999.

Whittet, Martin, 'Gaeldom's Remedies', *Transactions of the Gaelic Society of Inverness*, vol. 55 (1986–88), pp. 346–449.

SOURCES

PUBLICATIONS

Anon., 'Aig an Fhaidhir Mhuileach': *The Celtic Monthly*, vol. 19 (1911), p. 166.

Anon., 'Gaelic Superstitions connected with Funerals': *The Celtic Monthly*, vol. 18 (1910), p. 180.

Anon., 'Puzzle for the Mull People': *The Celtic Monthly*, vol. 15 (1906–07), p. 24.

Beaton, C., 'A Curious Old Gaelic Play': *The Celtic Monthly*, vol. 14 (1905–06), pp. 94–95.

Beaton, Donald, 'Famous Cailleachs': *The Celtic Monthly*, vol. 13 (1904–05), p. 239.

Beith, Mary, *Healing Threads*: pp. 168, 179, 180–81.

Bennett, Margaret, *Scottish Customs from the Cradle to the Grave*: p. 158.

Black, Ronald I. M., 'Scottish Fairs and Fair-Names': p. 27.

Bristol, Nicholas Maclean, *Hebridean Decade*: pp. 5, 9–11, 12, 15–29, 21, 25–26.

Cameron, A. D., *Go Listen to the Crofters*: pp. 61–63.

Campbell, Duncan (ed. Meek, Donald), *The Campbell Collection of Gaelic Proverbs*: pp. 15, 26, 66, 74, 83, 98, 137, 171.

Campbell, J. G., *Superstitions of the Highlands and Islands*: pp. 5, 15, 27–29, 47, 59–60, 80, 88–89, 105–07, 144, 145, 152, 178, 180–81, 183, 221–22, 225–26, 237, 242, 244, 256, 270–71, 307–08.

——, *Witchcraft and Second Sight in the Highlands and Islands*: pp. 9, 18, 19, 42, 45–46, 46–47, 50–51, 99–100, 113, 118, 118–19, 133, 134–35, 135, 147–48, 230–33, 233, 266–67.

Campbell, J. L., and Thomson, Derick, *Edward Lhuyd in the Scottish Highlands*: pp. 35, 52–72.

Carmichael, Alexander, *Carmina Gadelica*: vol. 2 (2nd edn, 1928), p. 306.

Davidson, Thomas, 'Animal Treatment in Eighteenth-Century Scotland': pp. 134–45.

Devine, T. M., *The Great Highland Famine*: p. 156.

Duckworth, C. L. D., and Langmuir, G. E., *West Highland Steamers*: p. 5.

Eckstein, Eve, *Historic Visitors to Mull, Iona and Staffa*: pp. 20, 81.

Ferguson, Malcolm, 'The Spanish Princess': *The Celtic Monthly*, vol. 3 (1894–95), pp. 91–93.

Fionn [Henry Whyte], 'Gaelic Proverbs and Maxims': *The Celtic Monthly*, vol. 17 (1908–09), pp. 216, 235.

——, 'Gaelic Proverbs': *The Celtic Monthly*, vol. 19 (1911), p. 67; vol. 21 (1913), p. 137.

——, 'Gaelic Rhymes and Expressions on Place-Names': *The Celtic Monthly*, vol. 18 (1910), pp. 6, 7, 33.

——, 'Oidhche Shamhna': *The Celtic Monthly*, vol. 4 (1895–96), pp. 39–40.

——, 'The Grizzly Lad's Leap': *The Celtic Monthly*, vol. 8 (1899–1900), pp. 174–75.

Garnett, Thomas, *Tour through the Highlands and Part of the Western Isles*: vol. 1, pp. 159–61, 162–63, 167–88, 191.

Grant, I. F., *Highland Folk Ways*: p. 151.

Hannan, Thomas, *The Beautiful Isle of Mull*: pp. 21–22, 68–69, 71–73, 81–82.

Lamont-Brown, Raymond, *Scottish Superstitions*: p. 31.

Livingstone, Sheila, *Scottish Customs*: pp. 3, 31, 42.

MacCormick, John, 'History of Mull . . . : Chapter XVII': *The Celtic Monthly*, vol. 25 (1917), pp. 152–53.

——, *The Island of Mull*: pp. 30–31, 52, 60–61, 191.

MacCulloch, Donald B., *The Island of Staffa*: pp. 51–56.

Macdonald, Donald, *Tales and Traditions of the Lews*: pp. 166–67.

MacDougall, Betty, *Folklore from Coll*: p. 25.

MacDougall, H., *Island of Kerrera: Mirror of History*: pp. 52, 105–06.

Mackenzie, Alexander, *A History of the Highland Clearances*: pp. 350–51.

MacKenzie, Donald W., *As it Was, Sin Mar a Bha: An Ulva Boyhood*: pp. 82–83, 85, 97–98, 101–02, 127–28, 128, 128–29, 129, 132–35.

Maclean, Charles, *The Isle of Mull: Placenames, Meanings and Stories*: pp. 152–53, 155.

MacLean, J. P., *A History of the Clan MacLean*: pp. 40, 371–72.

——, *History of the Island of Mull*: vol. 1, pp. 145–48, 150, 150–51, 158–60, 161–63, 165, 166, 166–67, 219–20, 220–21, 229; vol. 2, pp. 103, 104, 109, 119–20, 121, 136–37, 158, 159, 159–66, 231–33, 242.

Macleod, Kenneth, 'Gaelic Proverbs and Maxims': *The Celtic Monthly*, vol. 17 (1908–09), p. 40.

Martin, Martin, *A Description of the Western Islands of Scotland*: pp. 38–39, 76, 250, 254.

Meek, Donald: see Campbell, Duncan.

Morison, Neil Rankin, 'Clann Duiligh: Pìobairean Chloinn Ghill-Eathain': pp. 59–69.

New Statistical Account of Scotland: vol. 7, part 2, p. 346.

Nicolson, Alexander, *Gaelic Proverbs*: pp. 111, 144, 192–93, 202, 267, 289, 357, 385.

RCAHMS, *Argyll, Vol. 3*: pp. 186, 188–89, 240–42.

Ross, Anne, *The Folklore of the Scottish Highlands*: p. 119.

Ross, David, *The Pocket Book of Scottish Quotations*: p. 154.

Sacheverell, William, *An Account of the Isle of Man . . . with a Voyage to I-Columb-Kill*: pp. 128–30.

Somers, Robert, *Letters from the Highlands on the Famine of 1846*: pp. 158–59.

Statistical Account of Scotland: vol. 20, p. 336.

Sutherland, Elizabeth, *Ravens and Black Rain*: p. 35.

Swire, Otta F., *The Inner Hebrides and their Legends*: pp. 27–30, 120–21, 125–26, 146–47, 147–48, 213–14.

Third Statistical Account of Scotland: The County of Argyll: p. 103.

Thornber, Iain, 'Rats': pp. 130, 143–44.

Tocher: no. 5, pp. 156–59; no. 17, pp. 14–15; no. 23, pp. 283–84; no. 52, p. 156.

Walker, Revd Dr John, *Report on the Hebrides of 1764 and 1771*: pp. 152, 160–61.

RECORDINGS AND NOTES

Beaton, Alan, Tobermory. Recorded by Ann MacKenzie 1992.

Cameron, Alexander, Tobermory. Recorded for School of Scottish Studies 1968.

Campbell, Donnie, and MacCuish, Archie, Cailleach. Notes taken 2001.

Fletcher, Colin, formerly Ulva and Torloisk. Recorded by Ann MacKenzie 1992.

Lloyd, Ishbel, and MacKeracher, Janet, Tobermory. Recorded for An Tobar by Margaret Bennett and Sheena Walker 1996.

MacAllister, Willie. See MacLean, Iain.

MacCuaig, Effie, Dervaig. Notes and photograph 2001.

MacCuish, Archie. See Campbell, Donnie.

MacDonald, Calum, Tobermory. Articles written by, and notes from, 2001.

MacDonald, Morag. See MacLean, Iain.

MacFarlane, Jane Ann, Gometra and Ulva. Notes taken 1992.

MacGillivray, Kirsty, Dervaig. Notes from conversations with 1999–2001.

MacKenzie, Donald W., formerly of Ulva. Recorded by Ann MacKenzie
    1992–
MacKeracher, Janet. See Lloyd, Ishbel.
MacLean, Betty, Dervaig. Notes and photographs 2001.
MacLean, Iain, MacDonald, Morag, and MacAllister, Willie, Tobermory.
    Recorded for An Tobar by Margaret Bennett and Sheena Walker
    1996.
MacLean, Lachie, Knock. Recorded by Ann MacKenzie 2001.
MacLean, Peter, Dervaig. Recorded by Ann MacKenzie 2000 and 2001,
    Gaelic translated by Donald W. MacKenzie 2000–01; recorded for
    An Tobar by Margaret Bennett and Sheena Walker 1996.
MacNeill, Lachie, Ulva Ferry. Notes taken 1992.
MacNeill, Roddy, Salen. Recorded by Ann MacKenzie 1992.
MacNeillage, Duncan, Dervaig. Notes taken 1992.
Morrison, Donald, Ardtun. Recorded by Donald MacLean and Roddy
    MacNeill 1977. Tape kindly loaned by Mrs D. MacLean,
    Tobermory, translated from Gaelic by Donald W. MacKenzie.
Morrison, Mary, Penmore. Recorded by Ann MacKenzie 1992.
Robertson, Iain, Tobermory. Recorded by Ann MacKenzie 1992.
Simpson, Johnnie, Fanmore. Recorded by Ann MacKenzie 1992.

OTHER SOURCES

'Archive List', Isle of Mull Museum, Tobermory.
Archives, Isle of Mull Museum, Tobermory.
Garvie, Alistair, notes on 'Ferries', Isle of Mull Museum, Tobermory.
Morison, Counnduille Rankin. 'Mull Traditions and Songs', manuscript
    in School of Scottish Studies, Edinburgh.
Muile air Mheamhair, Mull Oral History Project, 1992–
SWRI History of Tobermory Folder, Isle of Mull Museum, Tobermory.

ABBREVIATIONS

Dwelly	Edward Dwelly, *The Illustrated Gaelic–English Dictionary*. 1994 edn, Gairm Publications, Glasgow
edn	edition
HIDB	The Highlands and Islands Development Board
NSA	*The New Statistical Account of Scotland*, 15 vols. Edinburgh
OSA	*The Statistical Account of Scotland 1791–1799*, 2nd edn, 20 vols. Wakefield
RCAHMS	The Royal Commission on the Ancient and Historical Monuments of Scotland
repr.	reprinted
SWRI	The Scottish Women's Rural Institute
TGSI	*The Transactions of the Gaelic Society of Inverness*

DETAILED CONTENTS